ENGLISH RECUSANT LITERATURE
1558–1640

Selected and Edited by
D. M. ROGERS

Volume 257

RICHARD BROUGHTON
*The Second Part of the
Protestants Plea*
1625

RICHARD BROUGHTON

The Second Part of the
Protestants Plea
1625

The Scolar Press

1975

ISBN o 85967 253 o

Published and printed in Great Britain by
The Scolar Press Limited, 59-61 East Parade,
Ilkley, Yorkshire and
39 Great Russell Street,
London WC1

NOTE

Reproduced (original size) from a copy in the library of St. Edmund's College, Ware, by permission of the President.

References: Allison and Rogers 169; STC 20445.

THE
SECOND PART
OF THE PROTES-
TANTS PLEA, AND PE-
TITION FOR PREISTS AND

Papiſts . Beeing an hiſtorie of the holy
preiſthood , and ſacrifice of the true
Church of Chriſt.

Inuincibly prouing them to be, the preſent ſacrificing preiſthood : prouing alſo the ſacrifice of the Maſſe, vſed in the Catholike Roman church: and that theſe were promiſed,
and foretold by the Prophets, inſtituted by
Chriſt, and exerciſed by all his Apoſtles.

Moreouer that they haue euer from the firſt plan-
tinge of Chriſtianitie in this our Britanye, in
the dayes of the Apoſtles, in euery age,
and hundred of yeares, beene conti-
nued and preſerued here.

All for the moſt part, warranted by the writinges, and
teſtimonies of the beſt learned Proteſtant
Doctors, and antiquaries of England,
and others.

The preiſthood beeing chaunged , there is made of neceſſi-
tie a chaunge alſo of the lawe . Hebr. cap. 7. ver. 12.

WITH LICENCE, Anno 1625.

AN ADMONITION OF THE
Author, to all Readers of this his historie: comprehending the Argument and contents thereof.

Nowinge well by longe and daiely purchased experience, the great and greeuous persecutions, which formerly haue beene rayfed, and persecuted in England against consecrated Preists of the Romane Church, and professors of that Religion; and for nothing more, then holy priesthood, and the sacred functions thereof. And yet often hearinge all sorts of people, euen persecutors themselues, contestinge and crying out, they would willingly stand to the Iudgement of, and bee arbitrated by diuine Authoritie, and reuerend antiquitie: I an vnworthie member of that holy order, a longe student in diuinitie, to which these are either parts, or haue a subordination, for my discharge of dutie to God, and his holy Church, comfort and strengtheninge those that bee in truth, and satisfying, or confounding such, as bee in error, haue taken in hand to write a briefe history of this subiect, beginning at the first originall of Christianitie, especially in this Kingdome of great Britaine, to which onely after my more generall Introduction,

A 2 *and*

and preface ended, to preuent tediousnes both in Writer, and Readers, I will confine my selfe.

And to winne the loue and likinge of all, and auoide the dislike of any, I meane to follow that most frendly, and to all protestants, fauourable maner, and methode in writinge, insinuated in the Title of this Worke, alwaies, or moste commonly to carry with mee, the allowance, and warrant of the best learned Doctors, and Antiquaries of their Religion. And yet for Catholicks, I trust none of them shall finde the least occasion of feare, that though I shal walke vpon so vnl. uell ground, I will betray their moste iust, and holy cause: but rather adde a greater luster, and splendor of glory, then bringe any the least diminution of honor vnto it. And make this matter so palpably manifest, by all Authorities, diuine, and humane, the scriptures both of the old and new testament, and all kinde of expositors of them, friends or eunemies, that they which shall not acknowledge the vndoubted, and onely truth of the doctrine of the holy Catholike Church in these misteries, must needes bee said wilfully with malice to close their eyes against it.

And though the lawe of Moises wherein the Prophets liued, and God spake by them, was but a figure of thinges to come, and gaue but a darke shadowe, or glimeringe of the gratious brightnes, and shininge, which our blessed Sauiour, the true light of the world, reuealed vnto it in the lawe of the ghospell: yet I shall in the very beginning as a preface to this holy historie, so inuincibly proue, by the

scrip-

ſcriptures of the old teſtament, by all originall texts, hebrue or greeke, all Authors, the Rabines before Chriſt, the beſt learned Doctors of the primatiue Church of Chriſt, and proteſtants themſelues, that the Meſsias promiſed and foretold by the Prophets, was to ordeine a new ſacrificing prieſthood, and that bleſſed ſacrifice of his bodie, and blood which wee comonly name the ſacrifice of the Maſſe, and this was one of the moſt apparant diſtinctiue ſignes to know him by; ſo that whoſoeuer denieth this, conſequently denieth Chriſt to bee the true Meſsias.

And the more plainely to demonſtrate this, when I come to the firſt plantinge of the faith of Chriſt, in this kingdome in the Apoſtles time, I will make manifeſt, by all teſtimonies, and antiquities, that Chriſt our bleſſed Sauiour and Meſsias accordingly to the propheſies of him did inſtitute this ſacrificing prieſthood, and both celebrated, and ordeined the ſacrifice of Maſſe, for his Church for euer. That all his Apoſtles were ſacrificing maſsing preiſts, and offered that bleſſed ſacrifice And that in this kingdome of Britanie in particular, as in the whole Chriſtian world beſides, in euery age, and hundred of yeares, from the firſt preachinge, and receiuing of Chriſtian Religion here, in the Apoſtles time, in the firſt, ſecond, third, fourthe, fift, and ſix hundred yeares, of Chriſt, and ſo longe as the beſt learned proteſtants affirme, that holy primatiue Church remained vnſpotted, in the firſt receiued truthe, and integritie thereof.

The ſame holy ſacrificinge prieſthood, a continual

A 3

succession of sacrificinge massinge preists, and Bishops, and sacrifice of Masse euer continued here, in
the same maner as they are now vsed and obserued
in the present Romane Church, without any the least
essentiall change, or difference. By reason whereof
many cheise Articles in Religion now questioned, as
the supernaturall change or transubstantiation of
bread and wine into the blessed body, and blood of
Christ, there offered a propitiatorie sacrifice for sinne; prayer to the blessed Virgin, S. Mary, & other
Saints, and Angels, prayer for the faithfull departed, merit of sacrifice, and good workes, with in-
sufficiencie of sole faith, and other principall things
which protestants commonly disallow in Catholicke
Religion, will bee thus proued, and deduced in euerie age, in this our Britanie, euen with the allowance of our best learned protestants, and such antiquities, as they approue, and cannot disallow. One
most materiall point of the Popes power and spirituall prerogatiue in this nation, from the first embracinge of Christian Religion in all ages, which I
promised in my first parte, I vnderstand to bee effec-
tually performed already. Therefore I shall sparing-
lie make mention thereof, in this history, except in
somethings, and places, where it shall bee needfull
for the more perfect handlinge of the present subiect
of this worke.

   And hereby it will sufficiently appeare, vnto all
protestants, and persecutors of the holy Catholike
Romane Church, that seeing the controuersie is,
whether the Catholike, or protestant church is the

true church of Christ, that by no possibilitie the protestant congregation can bee this true and holie
church. For by their owne Articles of their Religion,
to which all protestant Bishops and ministers haue
sworne and subscribed. (Articl. of Engl. protest. Relig. articul. 19.) The visible Church of Christ is
a congregation of faithfull men, in which the
pure worde of God is preached, and the Sacraments bee duly ministred, according to Christs
ordinance, in all those things that are requisite
to the same. Which bee the verie wordes of their
owne subscribed, and sworne Article of Religion.

Therefore when they require three things to the
true Church, true and lawfulle consecrated preists,
and preachers, the pure word of God preached, and
Sacraments duely ministred, and all these shall be
found in the Roman Church in all ages from the first
preaching of Christ, and not any one of them in the
protestant parlamentary Church of England, or any
such other, but a manifest opposition and persecution
of those sacred preachers of the word, and ministers
of the Sacraments, as of the word, and Sacraments
themselues, so preached, and ministred, none of these
can possibly bee the true Church of Christ, but a
company of professed aduersaries and enemies vnto it:
and that the onely true Church which they haue so
vnchristianly persecuted, the Catholike Romā church
is that true and most holy church of Christ.

THE

THE PREFACE PROVING
THE CONTENTS OVT OF THE
Prophets.

Wherin sacrificing and Massinge Preisthood,
Preists, and the sacrifice of Masse, are pro-
ued by learned Protestants, and other testi-
monies, from the history of Melchisedech.
Gen. 14.

THE I. CHAPTER.

SO vndoubted a veritie, and necessary
a thinge it was, for our blessed Sauiour
cominge into the worlde, to perfect the
Lawe of Moyses, and euacuate the externall, vnperfect preisthood, sacrifices, and
ceremonials thereof, and to institute and
ordeine a sacrifice, and preisthood more
perfect and independant, to continue for
euer, as his lawe and Religion is to doe,
and to geue a most sure, and timely war-
ning and notice of this to the world, that
when God had made the first promise of
the Messias vnto Abraham, in the 12. and
13. chapter of Genesis, in the very next the

14. chapter following, hee reuealed by the preiſthood and ſacrifice of Melchiſedech longe before either the lawe, preiſthood, or the ſacrifices thereof were deliuered to Moiſes, what the euerduringe preiſthood, and ſacrifice of the Meſſias, and his lawe ſhould bee.For ſo both the Prophet Dauid, S. Paule to the Hebrues, S. Peter in the canon of the holy Maſſe, being Author therof, as ſhall bee proued hereafter, the auncient-Rabines before Chriſt,as proteſtants them ſelues acknowledge, ſo likewiſe by their warrant, the moſt auncient and holy Fathers of the Church of Chriſt, doe proue their preiſthood,and ſacrifice of Chriſt, and his ſacrificinge preiſts, in the lawe of the Ghoſpell, from the wordes of Moiſes: theſe be our engliſh proteſtants tráſlation.

2. *Melchiſedech Kinge of Salem,brought forth bread and wine : and hee was the preiſt of the moſt high God.* The greeke readinge, is : *For hee was the preiſt of the moſt high God :* ſignifying thereby, that hee did the preiſtly ſacrificall office, with that breade and wine : and although in the hebrue the verbe *Hotzi,* which our proteſtants tranſlate, *brought forth,* ordinarily where it is

not

not otherwise limited and reftricted, hath
that fignification, yet beeing confined as
here it is, to the office of a facrificing preift,
fuch as Melchifedech was, it muft bee ap-
propriated to his office of facrificinge, o-
therwife the reasó which the fcripture maketh. *becaufe hee was a preift*, is fuperfluous.
And the rather in this cafe, becaufe in the
hebrue text, this bringinge forth of breade
and wine by this extraordinary preift, hath
relation vnto God; and fo muft needes bee
a facrificall action: for the bringinge forth
of bread and wine, or matter of any facrifice to God, by a preift that is a facrificer,
muft needes bee a facrifice. The hebrue is
thus: *Melchifedech Kinge of Salem brought
forth breade and wine, hee beeing a preift, to
God the moft highe.* The name God here in
Hebrue *Leeb*, beeing the datiue cafe, and
anfweringe the production of the breade
and wine, and not the word preift, for o-
therwife it would not bee true conftructió
in that language, the particle *le* there fer-
uinge to the datiue, and not genitiue cafe.
And therfore, as *Francifcus Stancarus* that
great proteftant profeffor of hebrue, and
others tell vs, Rabbi Samuel vppon this
place

place of Genesis, doth thus expound it: *ac-*
tus Sacerdotij tradidit: erat enim ipse sacrifi-
cans panem & vinum Deo sancto & benedic-
to . Hee deliuered the acts of preisthood, for
hee was sacrificing bread and wine to God ho-
lie and blessed. Where hee plainely expoundeth it, as I did before, referring the brin-
ging forth of the bread and wine by Melchisedech the preist, *to God holy and blessed.*
Which is more plaine by the words immediatlie following in the hebrue : *veiebare-*
chehu- and *hee blessed him :* That is to say,
hee blessed or praysed God , of whome the
immediate laste speach was . *Rabb. Samul.*
in cap. 14. Geness. Francisc. Stancar. in l. 10.
de art. fid. Petr. Galat. ibid. c. 6. & alij.

3. So that a preist that vsed to sacrifice,
beeing proued by the original text of scripture to haue offered or brought forth bread
and wine to God the most high and blessed, and praised him, must needes bee said
as the Rabbine expoundeth it , to haue sacrificed bread and wine vnto him. So doe
the holy fathers : *panem & vinum obtulit:*
Melchisedech offered bread and wine : saith S.
Cyprian, the old Roman Masse and S. Ambrose: *Quod tibi obtulit summus Sacerdos*
Mel-

Melchiſedech: The high preiſt *Melchiſedech* offered ſacrifice to God. S. Hierome ſaith: *In Typo Chriſti panem & vinum obtulit, & myſterium Chriſtianum in Saluatoris corpore & ſanguine dedicauit.* In figure of *Chriſt*, hee offered bread and wine, and dedicated the Chriſtian myſtery, in the body and blood of our *Sauiour.* So S. Auguſtine, S. Leo, Arnobius, Eucherius, Primaſius, Euſebius Cæſarienſis, Theodoretus and others of the primatiue church, both greeke and latine. *Cyprian. epiſt.* 63. *Miſſ. Rom in can. Ambroſ. l.* 4. *de Sacram. c.* 6. *l.* 5. *c.* 1. *ad cap.* 5. *ad Hebr. Hierom. epiſtol.* 17. *ad Marcell. c.* 2. *in quæſt. in Gen. in pſal.* 75. 109. *ad cap* 26. *Math. Auguſt. in pſal.* 33. *de ciuitat Dei. l.* 6. *c.* 22. *epiſt.* 95. *Arnob. Rom. in pſal.* 109. *Leo ſerm.* 2. *anni verſ. Aſſumpt. Eucherius Lugd. homil.* 5. *de Paſch. Primaſ. in c.* 5. *ad Hebr. Theodoret. quæſt.* 63. *in Geneſ. & ad pſalm.* 109. *Proteſt. Articl. of Relig. articul.* 7. *ſcriptures.*

4. And except wee will ſay there was a tradition of ſo great a miſtery and neceſſarie to ſaluation (which the Religion of our engliſh proteſtãts denieth) or that the Prophet Dauid had ſome new particular reuelation

lation of this thing, which though it should bee gratis spoken by protestants, doth inuincible confirme what hath bene said of this matter; wee must needes graunt that this holy prophet, did expound and vnderstand that action of Melchisedech, as so many authorities remembred did, for hee maketh it a thinge so certaine, that hee bringeth in God him selfe testifyinge by oath, that it was so: Thus by protestantes translation hee speaketh of Christs preisthood and consequently sacrifice, from this place: *The Lord hath sworne and will not repent, thou art a preist for euer: after the order of Melchisedech.* (*psal.* 109. *or* 110. *vers.* 4.) For wee doe not reade in any other passage of scripture, before Dauids time but in that place of Genesis, what the order, preisthood, or sacrifice of Melchisedech was. The same is testified by S. Paule the Apostle to the Hebrues. (*Hebr.* 5. 6. *&* 7. 17.) And all learned texts Hebrue, Chaldy, Greeke and Latine agree; onely the Hebrue maketh it plaine, that God had made such a promise to Melchisedech, that Christ should bee a preist after his order for euer.

5. For where our English protestantes
takinge

takinge vppon them to tranſlate and followe the Hebrue , and as before tranſlate:
Thou art a preiſt for euer after the order of
Melchiſedech: The Hebrue is: *Our Lord*
hath ſworne , and will according to my word,
or, *as I promiſed to Melchiſedech. Hal dibrati*
Malchiſedech . Where wee cannot without
corrupting the Hebrue *dibrati,* takinge the
laſt letter away reade otherwiſe. Therefore
ſeing S. Paul plainely ſaith, *that Chriſt was*
a preiſt after the order or maner of Melchiſe-
dech : κατὰ τηὺ ταζιυ μελχισεδεκ repeating it
in diuers places : And the Prophet Dauid
ſaith, that God ſwore it , and ſo promiſed
to Melchiſedech: wee muſt needes beleeue
that Chriſts preiſthood and ſacrifice, after
this order to continue for euer is vndeniably teſtified and expreſſed in that place of
Geneſis, and act of Melchiſedech. Which,
to leaue S. Paul vntill I come to the new
teſtament , is proued by the greateſt proteſtants that euer were.

  6. Luther vppon that place alleaged by
Dauid. (*in pſalm.* 110. *Tom.* 8.) ſaith: *Mel-*
chiſedech Rex erat, & Sacerdos , obtulit pa-
nem & vinum, pro Patriarcha Abraham & e-
ius familia. Quid eſt vero oblatio panis & vi-
                                                              ni

ui pro Abrahamo? Hoc exprimit Sacerdotium Christi ab hoc tempore vsque ad finem mundi, quo mysterium altaris Sacramentum pretiosi corporis & sanguinis sui offert Ecclesia. Melchisedech was a Kinge and Preist, hee offered bread and wine for *Abraham* , and his family. What doth the offeringe of bread and wine for *Abrahã* meane? This doth expresse the preisthood of Christ from this time to the end of the world, in which the church doth offer the mistical Sacrament of his pretious body and blood. Philip Melancthon *in concil. Theolog. part. 2. pag. 373.* saith : *Excipit Melchisedech redeuntem ex prælio Abraham, & eum ad sacrificium admittit, eique benedicit.* Melchisedech receaueth Abraham returninge from battaile, and admitteth him to sacrifice , and blesseth him. Caluine diuers times confesseth. *in c. 7. ad Hebr. vers. 9. pag. 924.* That this was the opinion of the old Fathers , and hee plainely saith . *Veteres Ecclesiæ Doctores in hac opinione fuerent, vt in oblationem panis & vini insisterunt, sic autem loquuntur · Christus Sacerdos est secundum ordinem Melchisedech, atqui panem & vinum Melchisedech obtulit , ergo panis & vini sacrificium Sacerdotio Christi conuenit.* The auncient Fathers

were

were in this opinion, that they insisted in the oblation of bread and wine, for so they speake, Christ is a preist after the order of Melchisedech, but Melchisedech did offer breade and wine, therefore the sacrifice of bread and wine agreeth to the preisthood of Christ.

7. The godly and learned man, as Maſter *Doctor Sutcliffe* calleth *Andreas Craſtouius* the Caluiniſt. (*l. 5. de Miſſ. papiſt. c. 26. Andr. Craſtouius l. de opific. miſſ. 1. ſect. 66.*) ſaith : wee may not reiect the conſent and harmony of the auncient Fathers, both for their nearenes to the Apoſtles age, and the ſingular agreemēt of them al together: yet he addeth : *hic omnium veluti conſpiratione oblatio Melchiſedechi ſacra proponitur, vt non tantum Abrahæ militibusque, ſed etiā Deo incruentum ſacrificium ſimbolicè oblatum videatur. Here as it were with conſent of all, the holy oblation of Melchiſedech is propoſed, that it was not onely to Abraham and his ſouldiers, but that it ſeemeth to haue beene an vnbloody ſacrifice ſimbolically offered alſo to God.* Theodor Bibliāder a learned proteſtant. (*L. 2. de Trinit. pag. 89.*) writeth: *erat apud veteres Hebræos dogma receptiſsimum, in aduentu Miſsiæ benedicti ceſſatura eſſe omnia legalia*

galia sacrificia, tantumque celebrandum sacri-
ficium Thoda gratiarum actionis, laudis &
confessionis: & illud peragendum pane & vi-
no, sicut Melchisedech Rex Salem & Sacerdos
Dei altissimi, temporibus Abrahami panem &
vinum protulit . It was among the old Hebrues a most receaued Maxime, that at the
coming of the blessed Messias, all legall sacrifices should cease , and onely the sacrifice Thoda of thankes geuing , praise and
confession, should bee celebrated, and that
to bee done with bread and wine, as Melchisedech King of Salem and preist of God
most high in the time of Abraham brought
forth breade and wine . Thus this learned
protestant.

8. But where hee saith, onely that the
Rabbines wrote thus ; Melchisedech did
bringe forth bread and wine, that is his
glosse; for Fraciscus S tancarus. (*Apud Petr.*
Gallat. l. 10. de arcan.) The best learned protestant of his time in the Hebrue antiquities, doth assure vs from the most auntient
Rabbines (of which I haue cited Rabbi
Samuel before) the like , or more plaine,
for the sacrificing of Melchisedechs bread
and wine; and that onely neuer to cease,

B   but

but to continue in the time of the Meſſias
So haue R. Moſes Hadarſan, R. Pinhas, and
R. Ioai, as the ſame proteſtant with others
teſtifieth. So that wee plainely ſee, by all
authoritie, the holy ſcriptures, the auncient Rabbines, and the generall conſent
of the holy primatiue Fathers of Chriſts
church, as they are warranted by the beſt
learned proteſtants of forrein natiós, whether Lutherans, or Caluiniſts, that both
Melchiſedech (the plaine figure of Chriſt
in this) did offer ſacrifice in bread & wine:
and this kinde of ſacrifice though after a
more excellent maner, as the lawe of the
Meſſias ſo requireth, was to bee offered by
him, and his holy preiſts in that lawe. Now
let vs come to our Engliſh proteſtants: to
make all ſure from any contradiction, and
learne of them that the beſt learned of thē
doe ſo write, and all of them ought ſoe to
acknowledge by their owne Religion.

9. For euidence whereof, it is a common maxime and ground of Religion a-
mong them, that the ſcriptures eſpecially
as they tranſlate them, and logically deduced concluſions from them, are the word
of God. (*Feild· pag.* 226. *wotton def. of Par-*
kins

kins pag. 467.) To speake in their wordes: *all matters concluded logically out of the scriptures ar the word of God, aswel as if they were expressely set downe in it word by word*. And so of necessitie must they all say, if they will maintaine any externall shew of Religion, for reiecting traditions, and the authoritie of the church, as they doe, and claiminge onely by scriptures in all matters of faith, they must needes allowe soe ample authoritie to deductions from scriptures: for euident it is, and they willingly confesse, that all things which they hold euen as matters of faith, are not expressely sett downe in scriptures. And this is an expresse article of faith with them, sett downe in the 6. article of their Religion, confirmed by parlaments, and subscribed and sworne vnto, by all protestant Bishops, and ministers of England. The wordes of this their sworne and subscribed vnto Religion in this point are these. *Articles of Engl. protest. Religion ratified by the parlaments and canons of Q. Eliz. and King Iames articul.* 6.

10. *Holy scripture conteyneth all thinges necessary for saluation: so that whatsoeuer is not read therin, nor may bee proued thereby,*

is not to bee required of any mā, that it should bee beleeued as an article of the faith. Therfore things so reade in scripture and therby proued, must needes bee articles of faith, otherwise Religion should bee without articles of faith, which is vnpossible, for by this protestant Religion, there is no other meanes to make or proue them such. Being thus directed by these protestants and by their direction, I make this Argument and proofe from scriptures as they translate thē: Euery high preist is ordeined to offer sacrifice for sinnes. (*Hebr.* 5. 1. 8. 3.) But Melchisedech was an high preist: Therefore ordeyned to offer sacrifice for sinnes. The first or maior proposition, is the very wordes of S. Paule, as our protestants translate him. The minor or second proposition, is theire translation of the Prophet Moises: *Melchisedech was the preist of the most high God.* (*Gen.* 14. 18.) Where hee is called, *the preist*, by excellency and blessing Abraham, and called by S. Paule, better or greater then Abraham. (*Hebr.* 7. 6. 7. 9.) Who also was a great preist and patriarke, and as a superiour receauing tithes of him: and so eminent and cheife, that the order of
which

which hee was, is not onely called the order of Melchisedech, but Christ himselfe often termed high preist after the order of Melchisedech: and as our protestants also translate, after the similitude of Melchisedech, as both the Greeke and Latine texts also are: Therefore Melchisedech of necessitie was an high preist . Therefore againe the conclusion, which in a true Argument and Sillogisme, as this is , cannot bee denied , that Melchisedech offered sacrifice, beeing therto ordeyned , is most certaine and an article of faith by these protestants Religion before.

11. And because by the rule of their Religion, wee may not seeke but in scripture to knowe what sacrifice it was, which hee offered, it must needes bee that sacrifice of bread and wine, which the scripture Rabbins , Fathers , and forreine protestants haue told vs of before: for wee do not find any other sacrifice, or matter like a sacrifice in scripture attributed to Melchisedech. If any man shall say, that S. Paule speaking of all high preists offering sacrifice , meaneth sacrifice vnproperly , as prayers and such deuotions: I answere this is not onely

B 3   vn-

vnproperly, but by true confequence blaf-
phemoufly fpoken, vtterly denyinge that
either the preifts of the Lawe of Nature, or
Moifes, or Chrift did offer any facrifice,
and fo no facrifice for finne beeinge offered by Chrift, mans redemption was not
wrought by Chrift, but man is vnredee-
med, and Chrift was not the Sauiour of the
world; for in that place as S. Paul fpeaketh
of euery high preift and preiftly orders, he
alfo fpeaketh of the externall facrifices of
of them, in their order and time. And fo
doth the proteftant publicke gloffe vppon
thofe wordes of S. Paule: *Euery high preift
is ordeyned to offer facrifice* : expound them
in thefe termes: *Hee bringeth a reafon, why
it muft needes bee, that Chrift should haue a
body that hee might haue what to offer, for
otherwife hee could not bee an highe preift.*
(*Proteft. Annotat. in cap.* 8. *Hebr. v.* 3)
Therfore by thefe proteftants S. Paul fpeaketh of an externall and properly named
facrifice, and that therefore Melchifedech,
as well as other high preifts, did offer an
external facrifice, otherwife by their owne
reafon the fame which S. Paul alleageth,
bee could not bee an high preift, as the holy
                                                    fcrip-

scripture proueth hee was, not offering any externall sacrifice, which both by S. Paule so many testimonies before , and the publicke and authoritatiue exposition of English Protestants, is essentially and vnseparably belonging to al true preists & preisthood.

12. The Protestant Bishop D. Morton. (*Appeale l. 3. c. 13. pag. 394.*) plainely graunteth that Melchisedech offered an externall sacrifice, *wherein there was really bread and wine*. Hee further proueth from the Rabbins and Bibliander. (*supr. cent. 1.*) That at the cominge of the Messias, *all legall sacrifices should cease , and a sacrifice in bread and wine should onely stil continue.* And constantly auoucheth for the common doctrine of English Protestants in these wordes: *The protestants acknowledge in the Eucharist a sacrifice Euchaaristicall.* (*Mort. sup. l. 3. c. 13.*) The present protestant Archbishop of Canterbury director of Master Mason , and hee directed by him directly graunt , that the words of Christ concerning his body and blood to bee giuen, *argue a sacrifice to God*. (*Franc. Mason. lib. 5. pag. 233.*) And cite and graunt further in

this

this maner. (*pag.* 243.) *Chriſt hauinge offe-red himſelfe for a ſoueraigne ſacrifice vnto his Father*, *ordeyned that wee ſhould offer a re-membrance thereof, vnto God, in ſtead of a ſa-crifice.* An other ſaith. (*Middle.papiſtom·pag. 92.113.*) *The ſacrifice of the Altare, and vn-bloodye ſacrifice*, *were vſed in the primatiue church*: *and the auncient Fathers called the ſacrifice of the body and blood of Chriſt*, *a ſa-crifice.* And againe. (*pag.* 49. 137. 138. 47. 45.) *The primatiue church did offer ſacrifice at the Altar*, *for the dead. Sacrifice for the dead, was a tradition of the Apoſtles, and the auncient Fathers.* And Iſaac Caſaubon the knowne french ſtipendary champion for the Proteſtants of England, writeth thus of our Kinge in this matter. (*Reſpons. ad Card. Peron.pag.* 51.) *The Kinge is neither ignorant of, nor denieth, that the Fathers of the primatiue church did acknowledge one ſa-crifice in Chriſtian Religion*, *that ſucceeded in place of all the ſacrifices in the lawe of Mo-ſes.* And leaſt any man ſhould doubt, what ſacrifice hee ment, by ſo ſpeaking, hee tel-leth vs, it is. *The body of Chriſt in the Eucha-riſt*, as Catholicks hold: and addeth there: *Hæc eſt fides Regis*, *hæc eſt fides Eccleſiæ Angli-*

Anglicana. This is the faith of the Kinge, this is the faith of the English church. And writeth to Cardinall Perron in these wordes: *The Kinge said in the hearing of manie, and wished him so to signifie to Cardinal Perron, that hee agreed with the Cardinal in his opiniõ, de duplici sacrificio, expiationis nempe, & commemorationis, siue Religionis. Concerning two kinds of sacrifice, the one of expiation for the world, the other commemoratiue, or of Religiõ.* Which last Cardinall Perron with all Catholicks take to bee the sacrifice of Masse: Therefore if the English Protestant church and his maiestie, agree so far with Catholicks, the attonement wil sooner bee made in this matter.

13. Neither did Casaubon here assume for his maiestie, and English Protestants, any new thinge, but the same, which they had professed and graunted in their most solemne and publicke decrees and proceedings, from the first beginning of their parlamentary Religion in the time of Queene Elizabeth, or sooner. For wee are taught by these protestants, that in the first parlamẽt of that Queene, when Catholick Religion was suppressed, yet both shee, her nobles,

new

new Bishops, and the rest continued in this
opinion, that there was an externall sacrifice in the church, and the Masse was this
externall sacrifice: for appointing a kinde
of disputation in questions they most disli-
ked in Catholike Religion, or wherin they
thought themselues to haue most aduanta-
ge, they set downe but three conclusions:
The first of a straunge tongue, in common prayer: the second concerninge ceremonies: And the third and laste is thus: *It*
cannot bee proued by the worde of God , that
there is in the Masse offered vp a sacrifice pro-
pitiatory for the quicke and the dead.Ih.Stow
and Howes histor. an. 1. Elizab. Theater of
Brit. an.1. Eliz.) Where they do not deny
an externall sacrifice, in the churche of
Christ, nhether that the Masse is this externall sacrifice, but so farre agree with Catholicks; but they only deny, that by scripture , which they onely vnderstand by *the*
worde of God, the sacrifice of Masse can bee
proued a sacrifice propitiatory for the quick
and dead . Neuer denying it to bee a commemoratiue and Eucharistical sacrifice, or
of Religion as his maiesty before calleth it,
by the mouth of Casaubon . Neither doe
they

they abfolutly deny it to bee a propitiatory
facrifice for the quicke and dead , but that
it cannot bee fo proued by fcripture: neuer
denying but by traditiō it may fo bee proued, as fome proteftants haue confeffed
before, and fhal manifeftly be proued hereafter by all teftimonies.

14. And to make euident demonftra-
tion by thefe proteftants of England , that
they all doe, or fhould, both allowe an external facrifice, and facrificing preifts, and
preifthood, which they haue fo longe and
greeuoufly perfecuted, there was yet neuer
any proteftant Prince , Kinge, or Queene
in England, but by publick authoritie and
lawe of Parlament allowed , and receaued
the holy facrifice of Maffe, & confequent-
lie facrificinge and maffinge preifts and
preifthood, beeing as al learning teacheth,
indiuifible and vnfeparable correlatiues ,
maturally and mutually dependinge one of
the other . It is euident that Kinge Henry
8. (*Stat. Hen. 8. teftament. vlt.*) Both by
Parlament, and his lafte wil allowed Maffe
both for the quick and dead. King Edward
the fixt . (*Theat. of great Brit. in Henr. 8.*
Statut. an. 1. Edward. 6. cap. 1.) Enacted a
a par-

a particular ſtatute thereof confirming the doctrine of reall preſence, and it was in force, al his life: & was repealed by Queene Mary in reſpect it did allow to communicants to receaue in both kindes. (*Stat.an.1. Mar. parlam. 1. ſeſſ. 2. cap. 2.*) Queene Elizabeth in her firſt parlament, reuiued this ſtatute againe and it continued in force all her life. *Parlam. an. 1. Elizab.* And his maieſtie that now is, in his firſt parlament receaued and confirmed this very ſtatute of the holy ſacrifice of Maſſe, & the reall preſence, and is ſtill in force neuer by him repealed. *Parlament an. 1. Iacobi cap. 5.* The ſtatute it ſelfe is ſo cleare in this point, as it cannot bee contradicted. And beſides this, the iniunctions of Kinge Edward the ſixt, the beſt interpretors of his lawe doe ſo aſſure vs, where in the 3. 21. 22. Iniunction of his time wee finde then by his Regall Authoritie *Maſſe, high Maſſe, altare, high altare, lights vppon the altare before the Sacrament, Chriſts reall preſence therein, and tranſubſtantiation*, vſed commonly in England after this ſtatute was enacted. (*Iniunct. of Kinge Edw. 6. iniunct. 1. 21. 22.*) And both for the time of Queene Elizabeth

beth

beth, as alſo his maieſtie that now is receauinge that ſtatüte.

15. The publicke collection of our ſta-
tutes. (*Collectiō of Engl.ſtatutes an.D.* 1611.
Titul . ſeruice and Sacraments cap. 1.) Printed *cum prixilegio* , by his maieſties allowance and commonly vſed by our proteſtant
lawyers & others, hath this note and theſe
words vppon this ſtatute: Anno 1. Eduardi ſexti cap. 1. This act was repealed by 1.
Mar. parl. 1. ſeſſ. 2. cap. 2. and is reuiued by
1. Iacobi cap. 25. *But note the time of the*
firſt making of this ſtatute, which was before
that the Maſſe was taken away, when the
opinion of the reall preſence was not remoued
from vs. Whereby it is manifeſt, that both
Queene Elizabeth, and Kinge Iames re-
uiuing and giuing full life, and validitie te
this ſtatute, of the doctrine of Maſſe, and
reall preſence , muſt needes giue the ſame
allowance to thoſe holy doctrines confirmed by that ſtatute, and ſoe ought all Engliſh Proteſtants cōforming themſelues in
matters of Religion, to the lawes and parlaments of Proteſtant Princes, the cheifeſt
rules and ſquares by them in ſuch proceedings . And ſo neither any Catholicke or
Pro-

Proteſtant of England , except they will
bee ſingular againſt the lawe of their owne
Religion , can or may take exception a-
gainſt that is ſaid before, or profeſſe himſelf an aduerſary or perſecutor of holy conſecrated ſacrificinge Catholicke preiſts, or
ſacrifice of holy Maſſe, but rather reuerẽ-
ce & embrace them. And thus much from
the booke of Geneſis, that the true Meſſias
was to bee a ſacrificinge preiſt, according
vnto the order of Melchiſedech , to inſtitute a new ſacrificinge preiſthood, and the
externall holy ſacrifice of Maſſe, to bee cõtinued in his church for euer.

The ſame proued with like allowance, and ap-
probation of Proteſtants, out of the booke
of Exodus.

THE II. CHAPTER.

NOw let vs come to Exodus the next
booke of Moyſes. Where the proteſtants ſhall informe vs , that both the auncient Rabbines before Chriſt, the Fathers
of the primatiue church, and the ſcripture
it ſelfe expounded by the grounds of proteſtant

teſtant Religion doe warrant vs, not onely
that there was an externall ſacrifice to bee
continued in the time , and Religion of
Chriſt, but that this ſacrifice in particular
was the bleſſed body and blood of Chriſt,
vnder the formes of bread and wine , as it
is offered in the holy Maſſe , by maſſinge
and ſacrificinge Catholicke preiſts; wee
are told aſſuredly not onely from Catholicks ſome of them liuing and writing before theſe controuerſies began, and which
had beene eye witneſſes of theire relation,
but from proteſtants alſo, and thoſe Sacramentary Caluiniſts , the greateſt enemies
to the holy ſacrifice of Maſſe , and tranſ-
ſubſtantiation, that vppon theſe wordes of
Exodus in the 25. chapter where the vulgare latine readeth: *Et pones ſuper menſam
panes propoſitionis in conſpectu meo ſemper:*
and our Engliſh Proteſtants tranſlate: *and
thou shalt ſet vppon the table shew bread before mee alwaies.* Petr. Gallatin. de Arcan Cathol. veritat. l. 10. cap. 6 Ioh. Vitus epiſt.
Wintonicus l. durcoſiomartyrion. Franciſcus
Stancar. in correct. Petri Gallatini l. 10. c. 6.
Præfat Proteſtant.ad lectorem ante Petr. Gallatin. edit. Francofurti an. 1612.

12. That

2. That the auncient Rabbines longe before Chriſt, expounded this place of the holy ſacrifice of Chriſtians, inferinge alſo from thence, as the text will giue warrant vnto (as I ſhall proue hereafter by proteſtant Religion) that this bread did ſignifie the ſacrifice of the Meſſias, and that in his time, & in this ſacrifice bread ſhould be miraculouſly chaunged into his body : Stancarus the great Sacramentary linguiſt, citeth and approueth Rabbi Iudas, liuing as hee ſaith many yeares before Chriſt , to write in theſe wordes : *Erit hic panis duarum facierum , de quo ſcriptum eſt Exodi* 25. *capite. Lehem Phanim Æphanai tamid. panis facierum coram me ſemper. Quare autem dicatur panis facierum, ratio eſt, quia ait R. Iudas, tranſmutabitur ex ſubſtantia panis, cum ſacrificabitur, in ſubſtantiam corporis Meſſiæ, qui deſcendet de cælis. Et ipſe idem erit ſacrificium. Eritque inuiſibilis atque impalpabilis, cuius rei fidem facit ſedes Eliæ . Et Magiſtri aiunt, eam ob rem dictum eſſe panem facierum, quia in ipſo ſacrificio erunt duæ ſubſtantia, diuinitas & humanitas .* This bread ſhall bee of two faces, of which it is written in the 25. chapter of Exodus, Bread of faces before

fore mee continually. And why it is called bread of faces, the reason is as Rabbi Iudas saith, because it shall bee chaunged when it is sacrificed out of the substance of bread into the substance of the body of the Messias which shal come from heauen, and hee himselfe shall bee the sacrifice, and shal bee inuisibly and vnpalpable. To which the state of Elias giueth credit, and the Masters say, that for that cause, it is called bread of faces, because in that sacrifice, there shal bee two substances, diuinitie and humanitie.

3. Neither doe the auncient Fathers of the Law of Christ expound it otherwise, but not finding how the things there spoken can bee rightly applied to the figuratiue sacrifices of the Lawe of Moises, doe glosse it, as the old Rabbins did, expounding it, of the holy sacrifice of Masse, in the Law of Christ: among whome, Theodoret that auncient learned greeke Father, (*Quæst. in Exod. quæst. 60.*) expoundinge that scipture, and not finding how it could bee ment or intended for the things of that Law of Moses, saith in respect of that: *perspicuum est ista fuisse superflua, Deoque minime*

C

me grata. Nos autem sacrificium interiora pe-
netrans celebramus , offerentes Deo incensum
cum lumine lucernarum,& mystica sacramen-
sæ consecratione. It is euidēt that these thinges were superfluous and not acceptable to
God . But wee (Christians) doe celebrate
the sacrifice that penetrateth the internall
thinges , offering vnto God incense with
light of candels , and the mysticall confecration of the holy table. Which in other
places. (*In Philotheo c.* 20. *Dialog.* 2. *& ad*
cap. 6. epistol. ad Hebr.) Hee calleth , *mysti-*
cum diuinum & salutare sacrificium,corpus &
sanguinem Christi: The mysticall, diuine,
and sauing sacrifice, the body, and blood
of Christ. *Which he commannded the preists*
of the new lawe to offer when hee said to his
Apostles, doe this in my commemoration.

4. Neither can this place of scripture,if
wee will bee directed by protestants,carry
any other so proper interpretation: for first
by their rule of the originall Hebrue tongue, in this place to bee followed, it is as I
haue shewed before *Lehem, Phanim, bread*
of faces , Aquila readeth as the Hebrue, αρ-
τος Προϛωπῶν. The common Greeke, αρτο ϛ
ϛυωπιος *bread before* God, as Sebastian Castalio,

ftalio *panis appofitiuus*, bread fet before God, and our proteftants feeme to meane no other, when they tranflate it, fhew bread: for by their owne tranflation God thus commaundeth : *Thou shalt fet vppon the table shew bread before mee alway .* (*Exod.* 25. *v.* 30.) The table on which this bread was thus to bee placed , was of *Shittim* incorruptible wood , the table to bee couered with pure gold, *with a crowne of gold rounde about it. And foure rings of gold , and ftaues of Shittim incorruptible wood couered with gold to beare it by . All the veffels belonginge to this holy table were of pure gold, and feuen golden lamps of gold befides cādlefticks of gold to burne before this holy facrifice ,* and a table continually , and all this in the moft holy place the propitiatory , where God fpake vnto that people : which beeing fo ftrictly commaunded by God, of this, and noe other facrifice, argueth, that which was figured herin fhould bee the moft honorable, and continuinge facrifice , not to end with the propitiatory, and Gods appearing there, but to continue in the holy Religion of the Meffias, therin prefigured . Which muft needes bee of that excellency there

def-

described with so great glory , to bee euer
in the sight of God.

5. What superstition and idolatrie by
Protestant Religiō allowing(no such Reuerence but to Christ himselfe) was this,
except some great supernatural mistery and
worthie that reuerence, had beene figured
therin? and nothing there is by their Religion, that can haue so much , but the blessed body of Christ . Therefore they must
needes graunt this moste holy, continuall,
and most pleasing sacrifice to God , to bee
there prefigured . And if wee follow their
rule of concordance of places , they para-
lell with this, the 24 chapter of Leuiticus,
where this sacrifice is made of pure flower,
baked into cakes, set vppon the pure table be-
fore the Lord, it is a memoriall , an offeringe
made to the Lord, an euerlasting couenant, to
be eaten in the holy place, most holy of all offe-
rings, by a perpetuall statute. Thus our protestants. Which as it cannot bee verified of
any sacrifice of Moises Lawe , vnperfect,
figuratiue , and ended by Christ so longe
since , neuer to bee reuiued againe , neuer
holy in themselues, and protestants pretend
no such sacrifice for them , beeing in all
                                        things

thinges most euidently confonant, and a-
greeinge with that, which Catholickes
maintaine, and proue of the most blessed
sacrifice, of Chrifts most sacred body, and
blood, offered vpon an euer duringe altar,
and most acceptable in the fight of God,
it muft needes be vnderstood of this, and
nothing els.

6. Alfo in the fame Booke of Exodus
written by Mofes, the sacrifice of the Paf-
chall Lambe (a figure of this most holy facrifice) was inftituted : for although this
may be faid to forfhew the death of Chrift,
yet it cannot bee denied denied, but it alfo
& properly reprefented this our holy commemoratiue sacrifice, and that this Pafchal
lambe was alfo a sacrifice, for fo the scriptures witneffe. (*Exod. c. 12. v. 6.*) *Ve sha-
hatu otho*: and they fhal facrifice him: Thus
the Hebrue, fo the Greeke, fo the Latine,
immolabitque eum: and our proteftants tranflatinge : *shall kill it* : make it a new text,
the fcripture beeingotherwife, and fo they
themfelues tranflate in the fame chapter.
(*Exod. c. 12. v. 27.*) *It is the facrifice of the
Lords paffouer*, as the Hebrue, *Sebac*, Greek
Cobia, Latine *victima* is. And in the booke
C 3 of

of members. (*c. 9. v. 13.*) Our proteſtants
tranſlate it, offerringe equiualent with ſacrifice, ſo it is in the new teſtament in diuers places, (*Marc. cap. 14. Luc. c. 22. v 7.*)
And that it more properly ſignifieth Chriſtes holy oblation in the Euchariſt, then
vpon the Croſſe, the reaſons ar many and
manifeſt. His oblation vpon the Croſſe did
not fall vppon the fourteenth day, neither
at eueninge, as the commaundement of
this was. (*Exod. 12. Num. 9.*) but vpon the
fifteenth day at none time and not the eueninge. Neither was Chriſt crucified in memory of any paſſouer or deliuery, neither
crucified ſo to bee eaten, neither did or
might any eate or drinke his body or blood
ſo ſacrificed. Neither was hee ſo ſacrificed
in any houſe as the commaundement was,
or in Hieruſalem, but without the towne
in the open feild. And not onely the baptized and cleane, but all others ought to eate
and receaue by faith Chriſt ſacrificed vppon the Croſſe: which was forbidden in
the Paſchall Lambe and that which was
figured in it as an euerlaſting memoriall.
(*Exod. 12. v. 14. Leuit. 23. Num. 28. Exod. c.*
12. v. 45. 46. 47. 48. Num. c. 9, 22.)

7. And

7. And this sacrifice of the Lambe was instituted before Aarons preisthood , as that of Melchisedech was, and so as Philo writeth. (*l. 1. de vita Moisis.*) The old custome therein continued, that the cheife of families should exercise the preistly function , and so that sacrifice of the Lambe as wel as that of Melchisedech, figures of our most holy sacrifice and Sacrament , were eaten and receaued by all: whereas the sacrifices of Moises Law offered by the preistes of Aarons order, were onely receaued by the preists, & those of the tribe of Leui. (*1.Corinth.9.13. Deuter.*18. 1.*Num.*10. 9 & 18. 20.) And of all men our protestantes that would haue the Eucharist celebrated only with a communion for others besides the preist to receaue , and communicate should bee of this opinion , if they would speake consequently, as learned and truely religious men must doe : and except they can proue a bit of Bakers breade to bee a more excellent and honorable signe , and more perfectly to figure and represent the oblation and death of Christ, then an Innocent Lambe so ceremoniously, and religiously sacrificed and receiued as that was,

C 4   and

and say with the blasphemous Iewes, that the lawe of Christ is not more perfect then the lawe of Moises, and still offer vp a Paschall Lambe, they must needes acknowledge, that wee Christians haue a farre more excellent sacrifice, figured by that Lambe, then Caluins communion is.

And this is plainely proued by our blessed Sauiour himselfe, who so soone as hee had celebrated the sacrifice of the Paschall Lambe, and imposed an end vnto those sacrifices of the law, there presently at the same time, and in the same sacrificing wordes wherewith hee ended that which was to ceafe, hee founded and instituted the most holy sacrifice of the law of the ghospell to continue for euer, and neuer to bee altered or taken away. (*Matth. c. 26. v. 18. Luc. c. 22. v. 19.*) And the Hebrue worde, *Gasha,* in which language Christ spake at that time, is an vsuall sacrificinge word, in holy scriptures, and must needes bee the same, wherwith hee spake in S. Luke, and S. Paul thus repeateth. *Doe this in my commemoration.* (*1. Corinth. cap. 11. v. 25.*) For although wee haue not any Hebrue text of those places, yet that sacrificinge Hebrue word,

word , beeing the Hebrue to that Greeke
and Latine which wee haue, seing Christ
spake in Hebrue, wee must needes affirme,
they were both alike, and is a sacrificinge
word, so vsed seuen or eight times, in one
(the 29.)chapter of Exodus, and so many
other scriptures, as I haue here quoted : as
likewise the greeke which wee haue , and
protestants should as they protest to doe,
follow in the new testament . *Leuit.c.* 16.
v. 9. *Exod.c.* 10.*v.*25.*Numer.c.* 6.*v.*10.11.
Leuit.c. 9. *v.* 7. *c.* 16. 22. *Leuit.* 14. *v.* 18.
19. 29. 30. 31. *cap.* 15. *v.* 14. 15. 29.30.*c.*16.
v. 9. 24. *c.* 17. 9. *c.* 22. *v.* 23. 24. *c.* 23.*v.*11.
12. 18. 19. *Numer. c.*6.*v.* 10. 11. 16.17. *c.*8.
*v.*12. *cap.* 9. *v.*1. 2. 3. 4. 5. 6. 7. 10. 11. 12.
13. 14.*cap.* 15. *v.* 3. 4. 5. 6. 7.8. 9. 10. 11.
12. 13. 14. 15. 24. *cap.* 15. *v.* 29. 30. *Fr. Mas.*
l. 5. *cap.* 6. *pag.* 235-243.

9. And our protestants of England freelie acknowledge , that both the primatiue
Fathers and councels doe so testifie : The
present protestant Archbishop of Canterbury, director to Master Mason, together
with his directed scribe confesse:*This is the*
iudgement of the Fathers:Irenæus saith,that
Christ did then teach, the oblation of the new
testa-

*testament , which the church throughout all
the world doth vse.* Chrisostom *saith, the wordes of the Lord , giue strength to the sacrifice vntill the end of the world.* So they and
others write of S. Cyprian, S. Ambrose, S.
Augustine, S. Cyrill, S. Leo Fulgentius, and
others, (*Park. problom. pag.* 153. 154. *Morton. appeal l.* 2. *cap.* 6. *Mason. l.* 5. *pag.* 243.)
And for councels say: *The Nicen* (first) *councell in that Canon which Caluine and all
others receaue, saith plainely, that the Lambe
of God offered vnbloodely , is laide vppon the
holy table.* And for their owne opinion are
forced to confesse , that Christ did in that
place offer his body and blood in sacrifice:
for beeinge vrged with this Argument.
Christ *said: This is my body which is giuẽ for
you,* or as it is in *S. Paul, which is broken for
you:* and againe. *This is my blood of the new
testament, which is shedd for you, is shedd, is
broken, is giuen not to you, but to God for you,
doe not these wordes argue a reall, actuall and
proper sacrifice?* They aunswere and graunt
in these words: *They argue a sacrifice to God.*
(*Prot. Archb. Abb. and Franc. Mason supr. l.*
5. *pag.* 233.) Therefore of necessitie must
also graunt, that it is the most holy sacrifice

fice of Chrifts body , and blood figured in
that Paſchall Lambe, as ſo many authorities haue told vs : and except the ſacrifice
of Chrifts body and blood be not a propitiatory ſacrifice for ſinnes (which they may
not ſay) they muſt needes confeſſe , that
in holy Maſſe preiſts doe offer, not onely a
commemoratiue, but a propitiatorie ſacrifice.

*The ſame proued with allowance and conſent
of Proteſtants out of the booke of
Leuiticus.*

THE III. CHAPTER.

THe Proteſtant correctors of Petrus
Gallatinus doe aſſure vs . (*Franciſcus
Stancar. in l. 10. c. 7. Petr. Gallatin. de Ar-
can. Leuit. cap. 21. v. 8.*) That where our
Engliſh Proteſtants tráſlate in the 21. chap-
ter of Leuiticus: *Thou ſhalt ſanctify him ther-
fore , for he offereth the breade of thy God:*
They ſhould reade: & *ſanctificabis eum, quia
carnem Dei tui ipſe eſt, vel erit ſacrificans.
Thou ſhalt ſanctifie him* (the preiſt) *becauſe
hee is, or ſhall bee ſacrificinge the fleſh of thy
God*

God. There teaching, that the preifts of the
new law are vnderftood, as alfo their holy
facrifice of Maffe, wherein they offer the
bleffed body and blood of Chrift our God:
and therefore great fanctification and fan-
ctitie is required to their callinge. And they
proue by the Iewes themfelues. (*Leuit.c.* 21.
v. 6. 8. 17. 21.) That the worde *Lehem*,
which our Englifh Proteftantes tranflate
bread, doth in that place fignifie flefh and
not bread, as it often doth, and except thofe
proteftants deceaue vs, it fo fignifieth foure
times in that chapter. Accordinge to that
faying of Chrift by Englifh Proteftants:
*My flesh is meate in deed, and my blood is
drinke in deede.* (*Ioh. cap.* 6. *v.* 55.) And
their fréd Frofterus with other Hebritians
acknowledgeth, that it is taken for flefh e-
uen in facrifices, and citeth: Gen. 3. Exod.
18. 1. Samuel. 14. 2. Samuel. 9. pfal. 136.
Prouerb. 30. and concludeth with Malachias c. 1. v. 6. In which places the word
is *Lehem*, the fame which in this place of
Leuiticus. And the cited proteftants correctors of Gallatinus bringe Rabbi Dauid
Kimhi. (*in Serafsim apud proteft. fup.*) al-
leaging for this reading of *Lehem*, not onlie

lie this place of Leuiticus) but cap. 8. Deuter. Numer. 2 8. Ioh. cap. 6. Where they proue this to bee ſenſe of that place, and of the Hebrue word, ſignifying there the moſt holie ſacrifice of Catholick Chriſtians.

2. They further proue it, by the auncient Rabbins R. Simeon & others. (*Franciſc. Stanc. ſup. l. 10. c. 7. in Gallatin.*) That when this ſacrifice ſhould bee offered, all others were to ceaſe, and this to be celebrated, *in bread and wine, and by the great power of words from the mouth of the preiſt, this ſacrifice on euery altare ſhall bee chaunged into the body of the Meſſias. Virtute ingenti verborum Sanctorum quæ ab ore Sacerdotum manabit, illud omne ſacrificium quoad in vnaquaque ara celebrabitur, in corpus Meſſiæ conuertetur.* And this is no more then our Engliſh Proteſtants doe by publicke allowance publiſh and print, both of the doctrine of the primatiue church of Chriſt, and themſelues alſo in this: ſome of them aſſure vs the holy Fathers taught, *that breade is made the body of Chriſt. It is chaunged, not in ſhape but nature. Chriſtes body is made of breade, and his blood of wine. The preiſt by ſecret power doth chaunge the viſible creatures*

into

into the substance of Christs body and blood.
The bread doth passe into the nature of our
Lords body. The primatiue church thought
the sanctified and consecrated elements, to bee
the body of Christ. (*Mason.pag.243. Parkins:*
pag. 153. 154. *Morton. appeale l. 2. c. 6. Sut-*
cliff. Subuers. pag. 32. *Feild. pag.* 150.

3. And to shew that diuers of the best
learned of them for themselues are wholly
of this opinion, besides diuers cited in o-
ther places, one of their most iudicious writers writeth with publick priuilege. (*Couel.*
def. of Hooker pag. 116. 117. 276.) *The om-*
nipotency of God maketh it his bodie . And a-
gaine: *To these persons* (preists) *God impar-*
teth power ouer his misticalbodie, which is the
societie of soules, and ouer that naturall, which
is himselfe, a worke which antiquitie calleth
the making of Christs bodie. And confesseth it for a reasonable satisfaction, to say,
it is done by transubstantiation. And in an
other worke speakinge of this preistlye
power, hee addeth. (*Couel.examin.pag.* 105)
By blessing visible elements, it maketh them
inuisible grace, it hath to dispose of that flesh,
which was giuen for the life of the world, and
that blood which was powred out, to redeeme
                                    soules.

soules. And yet if wee neither had the auncient Rabbins, nor Fathers thus allowed vnto vs by proteſtants, neither the conſent of forreine and domeſticall proteſtants in this matter, but ſtand onely vpon the text of holy ſcripture it ſelfe in that one chapter of Leuiticus, and let it bee graunted that the word *Lehem*, may ſignifie in that place *Breade*, as probably as fleſh, or more probably, if any man would ſo deſire; yet ſeing wee finde it ſo often as foure times in one chapter, (*Leuit. cap.* 21. *per totum.*) *The bread of God*, with an excellency aboue other bread, and offered in ſacrifice to God by preiſts, that are appointed and commaunded to bee ſo extraordinarily holy by annointing with oile bleſſings and ſanctifications, and to bee ſo chaſte, continent, and holy as is there commanded, & knowing it was there but a figuratiue ſacrifice, a figure of a more excellent to come, and preiſthood alſo, when we ſee no ſuch thing either for preiſtly dignitie, or holy ſacrifice in the Sacramentary Religion, but all reallie and truely verified in the Catholicke Romane Church, wee muſt needes interpret it of the holy preiſthood and ſacrifice
thereof

4. Wee reade in the fame booke of Leuiticus often mention of the facrifice Thodah: in one (the feuenth) chapter: (*v.*11.12.
13. 14. *Leuitic. cap.* 22. *v.* 28.) there is diuers times fett downe this *Sebac Thodah, facrifice Thodah*. And it is defcribed to bee
Caloth Matzoth. Our proteftants tranflate
it : *Sacrifice of thãks giuing, vnleuened cakes,*
and, *Caloth Beluloth, vnleuened wafers,* by
our proteftants tranflation. Who there call
it alfo. (*v.*13.15.) *Sacrifice of thankfgiuing,
of peace offerings.* And againe : *Sacrifice of
peace offerings, for thankfgiuing* : Such was
the dignitie of this facrifice, at leaft in that
which it prefigured, for of it felf but meane
as we fee, that as many learned proteftants
Theodor Bibliāder, Francifcus Stancarus,
the Englifh Proteftant Bifhop D. Morton,
and others affure vs : *erat apud veteres Hebræos dogma receptifsimum :* It was a mofte
commonly receaued opinion amonge the
olde Hebrues, that at the cominge of the
bleffed Meffias, all other legall facrifices
fhould ceafe, and onely the facrifice Thodah, of thankfgiuing praife & confeffion,
fhould bee celebrated : and that to bee celebrated

lebrated with bread & wine. *Theod. Bibliäd.*
2. de Trinit. pag. 89. Francis. Stancar: in emēd.
lib. Petr. Gallatin. l. 10. Morton appeale Hie-
ronym, à Sancta fide l. 1. contr. Iud. cap. 9. Tal-
muld. apud. eund. 16. Froster. Lexic. v. Thoda.

5. And to make all sure from exception,
the Prophet Dauid testifieth as much. (*psal.*
50. v. 7. 8. 9. 10. 11. 12. 13.) For making rela-
tiō in the 49. (by the Hebrues 50.) psalme,
how God would reiect the sacrifice of the
Iewes, and haue a new more pleasinge
sacrifice offered vnto him: when hee had
reiected the former, hee addeth for the new
that was to continue : *Sebac Leholim Tho-*
dah . Sacrifice to God Thodah . Where both
by the sacrificing Verb *Sebac*, and *Thodah*
to bee offered in sacrifice vnto him, he addeth of them that shall offer it : *and thou*
shalt glorifie mee : as our protestants translate it. And wheras in Leuiticus is onely
mention made of cakes or wafers in this
sacrifice, the same Prophet Dauid in the
116. psalme as the Rabbines before, maketh also mention of the cup or challice in
this sacrifice. For saying there. (*psal. 116. v.*
17.) I will sacrifice the sacrifice Thodah
Sebac Thodah; hee saith also, as our Pro-

testants

teſtants tranſlate. (*v.* 12. 13.) *What shall
I render vnto the Lord for all his benefites
towardes mee? I will take the cup of ſaluation,
and call vppon the name of the Lord.* Where
the Hebrue readeth: *I will lift vp or offer, Eſe
the cup of ſaluation* : for that which in the
Greeke Latine and Proteſtant Engliſh is: *I
will take the cup or chalice, calicem ſalutaris
accipiam, of ſaluation.* So that if wee will
iuſtifie both readings, it is euident that an
holy chalice, was both to bee offered and
receiued in this: and to take which text we
will (as one wee muſt) becauſe thinges offered in ſacrifices were receiued, and thinges alſo in them receiued, were before offered, it is manifeſt by the Prophet, that the
holy conſecrated challice, was to bee offered and receiued in this ſacrifice Thodah,
as it is with Catholicks at this time.

6. And this was ſo knowne a veritie a-
monge the Iewes, that as Hieronymus, *à
ſancta fide,* proueth againſt the Iewes. (*l.*
1. *contr. Iudæos cap.* 9.) hee himſelfe a Iew,
it is often reiterated in theire Thalmud it
ſelfe, *eſt quædam locutio ſæpe in Thalmud rei-
terata, quæ dicit ſic: in tempore futuro vni-
uerſa ſacrificia, excepto ſacrificio confeſsionis
anni-*

annihilata erunt. And wee doe not finde in any Religion Chriſtians or others, any cup or chalice, which truely or putatiuely, is termed the cup or chalice of ſaluation, but that which is conſecrated and offered in holy Maſſe : of which Chriſt ſaid as our proteſtants tranſlate it. (*Luc. cap.* 22. *v.* 20. 1. *Corinth. cap.* 11. *v.* 24.) *This cup is the new teſtament in my blood, which is ſhed for you.* *Marc.* 14. 24. *This is my blood of the new teſtament, which is ſhed for many. Matth.* 26. 28. *This is my blood of the new teſtament which is ſhed for many, for the remiſsion of ſinnes.* So that except wee will bee Antichriſtians, and deny the truth of the words of Chriſt, that which hee then gaue and offered, and is lawfully conſecrated , preiſts doe ſtil offer in holy Maſſe , was and is this cup or chalice of ſaluation, fortold by the Prophet Dauid in this place.

7. And howeſoeuer wee will interpret this word Thoda with proteſtant Hebritians, to ſignifie *gloria gloriatio, laus laudatio, celebratio confeſsio,* glory, glorification praiſe, commendation, celebration, confeſsion. (*Froſter. in Lexic. in v. Thoda pag.* 355.) it cannot poſſibly bee better expreſſed and

verified in any thinge then the holy sacrifice of the blessed body & blood of Christ, which therfore the old canon of the Masse calleth *sacrificium laudis*, sacrifice of praise. For as S. Augustine saith. (*l. 1. contr. aduersar. leg. & Prophetar. cap. 18.*) *Quid est sacratius laudis sacrificium, quàm in actione gratiarum? Et vnde maiores agendæ sunt Deo gratiæ, quam pro ipsius gratia per Iesum Christum Dominum nostrum? quod totum fideles in Ecclesiæ sacrificio sciunt, cuius vmbra fuerunt omnia priorum generum sacrificia.* What sacrifice of praise is more holy, then in thankfgiuing? and wherefore are more or greater thankes to bee giuen to God, then for his grace by Iesus Christ our Lord? All which the faithfull doe know in the sacrifice of the church, of which all sacrifices of the former kindes were shadowes· And our protestants of England haue graunted as much before, acknowledginge the Eucharist to be a sacrifice of Religion, a sacrifice of thankfgiuing, a commemoratiue sacrifice, and a remembrance and memoriall of Christ offered and sacrificed for the sinnes of the worlde, and mans redemption: which deserue and binde all Christians to

giue

giue the greatest glory, praise, commendation, thankes and confeſſion to God for ſo
an ineſtimable grace and benefite they poſſibly are able.

7. Therefore moſt truely and properly
this holy ſacrifice of Maſſe, which Catholicks vſe, was by the holy Scriptures, Rabines, Fathers, Catholicks and proteſtants
before termed Thoda. For beſides all thoſe
Etimologies, and ſignifications thereof,
before alleaged from proteſtant Hebritiās,
they further add. (*Iob. Froſter. Lexic. Hebraic. in Thoda pag. 355.*) *Vocat ſcriptura hoc
nomine ſpeciem ſacrificy, quo offerentes confite-
bantur accepiſſe ſe beneficium à Deo, celebrant-
que & prædicabant gloriam clementiæ, & be-
nignitatis, de græci tranſtulerunt Θυσίαν
αινέσεως ſacrificium laudis, Germani Liboſſer.
(Leuit. cap. 7. verſ. 11.) Ac conſtabat vt eius
deſcriptione Leuitici 7. habetur, ex placenta
Azima, offerebanturque ab illis, qui cum à periculo aliquo liberati, gratos ſe Deo declarare
volebāt.* The ſcripture calleth by this name
Thoda the kinde of ſacrifice, by which they
that offered it, did confeſſe, that they had
receiued benefits from God, and they celebrated, & declared the glory of the mercy,

and

and bountifulnes of God, the Greeks translated it, sacrifice of praise, the Germans
Libopffer, and it consisted, as appeareth
by the description of it, in the 7. chapter
of Leuiticus, of an vnleuened Cake, and
it was offered of them, that beeing deliuered from any daunger would shew themselues thankfull to God. All which properties in a most excellent manner, are found
and proued to belonge to the holy sacrifice
of Masse, for more then any other rite or
ceremonie vsed by any Christians.

THE IIII. CHAPTER.

Prouing the same, by the same warrant from
the Prophet Dauid.

Now let vs come to the Prophet Dauid: who in the 21. 22. psalme by the
Hebrues speaking of the conuersion of the
gentiles and all nations to Christ, and setting downe many particulars of his holy
life and passion, amonge the rest, when by
protestants transtation hee had said: *all the*
ends of the world shall remember and turne to
the Lord: and all the kindreds of the nations
shall

shall worship before thee. *For the kingdome is
the Lords, and hee is the gouernor among the
natiōs*, which we see performed by Christ,
hee immediatlie addeth : *all they that bee
fat vppon the earth* (the potent and mightie) *shall eate and worship* . The Hebrue
which our protestants should follow there,
is *Istachahu* haue bowed downe themselues in worship. So is the Greek Προσεκυνσαυ
So the vulgare Latine : *manducauerunt &
adorauerunt*, so Sebastian Castalio the protestant, *comedent & adorabunt* : so readeth
S. Augustine, (*Augustin.in psal. 21.*) *Manducauerunt & adorabunt omnes diuites terræ.*
Euen all the rich vppon earth haue eaten,
and shall worship . And examining what
holy food this should bee, which euen the
ritchest and most potent should worship,
when they did eate it, not findinge any o-
ther food, worthie such worship, hee concludeth : *manducauerunt corpus humilitatis
Domini sui etiam diuites terræ* . Euen the
ritch of the earth haue eaten the body of
the humilitie of their Lord. Whereuppon a
very learned writer & linguist before these
times of controuersies. (*Iacob. Perez de Valentia quæst. 5. contra Iudæos.*) Writing a-

against

gainst the Iewes saith: *although this Sacra-*
ment was figured by many signes and figures
in the Lawe , yet Dauid in manifest wordes
hath expressed it in the 21. *psalme.* And citing the wordes before alleaged , thus hee
writeth: *vbi manifestè ostenditur, quòd fide-*
les debebant māducare & adorare Deum suum.
Where it is manifestly shewed , that the
faithful ought to eate and adore their God.

2. And whereas the same holy Prophet
in his 98. psalme saith: *adorate scabellum pe-*
dum eius , quoniam sanctum est . Adore the
footestoole of his feete , because it is holy:
The same S Augustine hauing related those
wordes of God in the Prophet Isay, as our
protestants trāslate them (*Isay cap.66.v.1.*)
The heauen is my Throne , and the earth my
*footestoole:*thus speaketh: *Fluctuans conuer-*
te me ad Christum, quia ipsum quæro hic , &
inuenio quomodo sine impietate adoretur ter-
ra . Sine impietate adoretur scabellum pedum
eius. Suscepit enim de terra terram, quia caro
de terra est, & de carne Mariæ carnem acce-
pit, & quia in ipsa carne hic ambulauit, & ip-
sam carnem nobis manducandam ad salutem
dedit: nemo autem illam carnem manducat, nisi
prius adorauerit : Inuentum est quemadmo-
                                          dum

dum adoretur tale scabellum pedum Domini, &
non solum non peccemus adorando , sed pecce-
mus non adorando. Doubtfull I conuert mee
to Christ, because I seeke him here , and I
finde, how without impiety earth may be
adored. For from earth hee receaued earth,
because flesh is from the earth , and from
the flesh of Mary he receaued flesh, and because he walked here in the same flesh, and
gaue the same flesh to bee eaten of vs , to
saluation: and no man eateth that flesh, but
first he adoreth it: we haue found how such
a footestoole of the feete of our Lord may
bee adored, and wee doe not onely not sinne in adoringe it, but wee should sinne, if
wee did not adore it. Thus this holy and
learned Doctor.

3. And of all men our English Protestants, which vtterly deny all worship or a-
doration to relicks, and holy material thinges , and singularly at their communion,
differently from all other protestantes by
strict and very penall commaundement vse
the ordinary act and gesture of adoration,
kneeling to their communion , must needes bee of this opinion : for in their Religion there is nothinge vnder God but the
blessed

bleſſed body, blood & humanitie of Chriſt which may haue that externall religious and adoring geſture vſed vnto it. The wordes of their article Religion to which they are all bound. (*Articul. 22.*) are theſe: *worshipping and adoration aswell of Images as of relicks, and also inuocation of Saints is a fond thinge, vainely inuented, and grounded vppon no warrant of ſcripture, but rather repugnant to the word of God.* Where wee ſee all other thinges prohibited to haue any worſhip or adoration, or acts thereof done vnto them. And the Prophet here is plaine euen in the originall tongue, Hebrue, which theſe men appriſe ſo much, that it is Gods commaundement, that wee ſhould worſhip this body of Chriſt, Gods footeſtoole, *incuruate vos ſcabello, Laharum, pedum eius ſanctum ipſum, Chadosh hu.* It is holy. And our proteſtants profeſſinge to allowe and follow the Hebrue do falſely tranſlate: *worship at his footeſtoole, for hee is holy.* For the Hebrue is plaine : *worship or adore his footeſtoole.* And ſo the proteſtant Sebaſtian Caſtalio tranſlateth, *eius pedum ſubſellium veneramini:* worſhip the footeeſtoole of his feete. So the Greeke Προσκυνειτε τω ὑποπcδiω

τῶν

τῶν ποδῶν αὐτȣ. *Adore his footestoole* . **And**
our proteſtants cannot excuſe themſelues,
becauſe it is in the Hebrue *La harom, to the*
footestoole, and the particle la , is an adiect
to Harom , but by this more condemneth
them, for the word *Haſtitachu, incuruate*
vos, bowe downe your ſelues in worship, to the
footestoole , or his footestoole, doth demonſtrate the worſhip was done to the footeſtoole . And theſe men condemne themſelues in this matter: for in the 20. chapter of
Exodus. (v. 5.) Where they would haue a-
doration to creatures forbidden, they tranſlate the very ſame worde : Thou ſhalt not
bowe downe thy ſelfe to them: *La hem:* and
yet here the expreſſe commaundement is:
bowe downe yourſelues to his footestoole.

    4. Againe, where the Prophet Dauid
ſpeaketh as our proteſtants tranſlate him.
(*pſal. 39. alias 40. ver. 7.*) *Sacrifice and offe-*
ring thou didst not deſire &c ſpeaking of
the old ſacrifices to ceaſe , and the lawe of
Chriſt to bee receaued: S. Paul. (*Hebr. 10.*
5. 6. 7. thus expoundeth it of Chriſt: *when*
hee cometh into the world hee ſaith , ſacrifice
and offeringe thou wouldest not , but a body
thou hast prepared mee in burnt offerings and
                      ſacri-

sacrifices for sinne thou hast had no pleasure,
then said I, loe I come to do thy Wil o God &c.
And in that place of the psalme the Greeke
reading is as S. Paule readeth , *a body thou*
hast prepared mee: ρωμα δε κατκρτισω μοι. So
readeth S. Augustine, S. Basile, and others.
And S. Augustine thus concludeth from
that place. (*Augustin. in psal. 39. l. 17. ciui-*
tat. cap. 20. Basil. inpsal. 72.) *vocem illam in*
psal. 39. Mediatoris per prophetiam loquentis
agnoscimus: sacrificium & oblationem noluisti,
corpus autem perfecisti mihi . Wee acknowledge that voice of the Mediator speaking
by prophesy in the 39. psalme: Thou wouldest not haue sacrifice and oblation , but
thou hast perfected a body for mee . And
then thus hee declareth how this the body
of Christ our Mediator was made our sacrifice, in place of those that were abrogated. (*Augustin l. 17. ciuitat. cap. 20.*) *Quia*
pro illis omnibus sacrificijs & oblationibus cor-
pus eius offertur, & participantibus ministra-
tur . Because for all those sacrifices and o-
blations his body is offered, and ministred
to the participants.

5. And vppon those words of that psalme thus hee writeth. (*Augustin. in psal. 39.*
v. 7.)

v. 7.) *Sacrificia ergo illa, tanquam verba pro-*
missiua, oblata sunt. Quid est, quod datum est
completiuum? corpus quod nostis. Videte quan-
do dictum est, Christus enim ille est Dominus
noster, modo loquens ex persona sua, sacrifi-
cium inquit. & oblationem noluisti. Quid er-
go? Nos iam hoc tempore sine sacrificio dimis-
si sumus? absit, corpus autem perfecisti mihi:
Ideo illa noluisti, vt hoc perficeres: illa voluisti
antequam hoc perficeres, perfectio abstulit
verba promittentia. Nam si adhuc sunt pro-
mittentia, nondum impletum est, quod promis-
sum est. Hoc promittebatur quibusdam signis,
ablata sunt promittentia, quia exhibita est ve-
ritas promissa. Therefore those sacrifices,
beeing as promising wordes, are taken a-
way, what is that which is giuen fulfilling
them? The bodie which you know consider when it was spoken, for that Christ is
our Lord now speaking in his owne parson, sacrifice saith hee, and oblation thou
wouldest not haue. What therfore? are we
in this time left without a sacrifice? God
forbid. But thou hast perfected a body to
mee: Therefore thou wouldest not haue
those sacrifices, that thou mightest perfect
this: Thou wouldst haue them before thou
diddest

diddeſt perfect this. Perfection tooke away the promiſing wordes, for if ſtill they are promiſinge, that is not yet fulfilled, which was promiſed. This was promiſed by certaine ſignes, the promiſing ſignes are taken away, becauſe the truth which was promiſed, is giuen.

6. Neither may this place bee otherwiſe expounded of any, ſeing S. Paul himſelfe. (*Hebr.* 10.*v.* 1. 2.3. 4.5. 6.7. 8. 9. 10.) doth ſo expound it, being beſt acquainted with the meaning of the holy Ghoſt: and therfore at large proueth from hence, the ceaſing of the ſacrifices of the Lawe of Moiſes, for their vnperfectnes, and a new and perfect ſacrifice of Chriſts body to ſucceed in place of them: and thus concludeth by our proteſtants tranſlation: *hee taketh away the firſt, that hee may eſtabliſh the ſecond.* So it is in Greeke: ſo in the Latine readinge. αναιρεῖ τὸ πρῶτου, ἵνα τὸ δεύτερου ϛήρε. *Aufert primum, vt ſequens ſtatuat.* Therefore our proteſtants makinge this concordance of theſe ſcriptures, and graunting before an external ſacrifice of Religion among Chriſtians, cannot poſſibly make other conſtruction of this place of the Prophet, then

S.

S. Paule, and S. Augustine after him hath
done before, and to endeuour the contrary,
would be to recal the sacrifices of the Iewes
to bee still in force, and euacuate the Law
of Christ . S. Chrisostome writing vppon
the 95. psalme saith plainely , *that the Pro-*
phet there plainely interpreteth the misticall
table, the vnbloody sacrifice, the heauenly and
exceeding venerable sacrifice of Christians.
Luculenter, & dilucidè mysticam interpreta-
tus est mensam, quæ est incruenta hostia, cæ-
leste summeque venerandum sacrificium. And
in the 72. psalme by the Hebrues speaking
at large of the cominge of Christ, our Messias, as our protestants. (*protest. argum. in*
psal. 72.) and all agree, about many misteries of him, and many excellencies which
hee should haue, as that he should *rule from*
sea to sea , all Kings should fall downe before
him. *Hee shall bee a deliuerer, shall redeeme*
soules, hee shall daily bee praysed. (*Psal . 72.*
v. 11. 10.12. 13.14. 15.) and the like.

7. It immediatly in the next verse followeth of him in the Hebrue readinge ,
which by protestants wee must followe,
without any interruption, or interposition
of any one word : *Iehi Pissath Bar baaretz*

be

be *Rob Harim*. Hee shall bee *a little cake of bread*, *placentula panis*, as *Iacobus de Valentia* before thefe controuerfes, readeth. *in pfalm. 72. as an handfull of meale* , *fietque vt farris pugilli:* by the proteftant Sebaftian Caftalio. *Sebaft. Caftal. ibid. a cake of wheate*, *placenta frumenti*, *a facrifice of bread* . *Francifc. Stancar. in l. 10. Petr. Galletin. facrificium panis :* as an other proteftant linguift readeth, *a little cake of bread*, *a facrifice of bread: placentula panis & facrificium panis*, as Hieronimus a S. fide a Iew readeth, from the auncient Hebrues and Chaldeans in the fame maner . *Hieronymus à S. fide l. 1. contra Iud. cap. 9.* both Iewes, Catholicks, and proteftants as Sebaftian Munfter, Francifcus Stancarus , and others affure vs , that Rabbi Salomon reading vppon this place, *Iehi Pifath Bar, erit placenta frumenti: a cake of wheate:* confeffeth further : *Magiftri noftri expofuerunt hoc effe genus placentarum in diebus Meffiæ, & totum pfalmū de Rege Meffia explanauerunt.* Our Mafters or Rabbines expounded this to bee a kinde of cakes in the dayes of the Meffias , and interpreted the whole pfalme of the Kinge Meffias. The fame authors proue vnto vs , that the

Chaldy

Chaldy Paraphrases read on: *erit substanti-*
ficus panis: The Messias shall bee substanti-
ficall bread. *R. Salmon in psal. 72. Petr. Gal.*
l. 10. Petr. Burg. apud Genebr. in psal. 72. Ge-
nebr. ib. Sebast. Monster. in censura errorum
Iudæor. pag. 56. Francisc. Stancar. in l. 10.
Gallat. Hieronymus à sancta fide l. 1. contra
Iudæos.

8. The other Rabbi Ionathā Ben Vziel,
which wrote before the coming of Christ
as the Iewes themselues, besides both Catholick and Protestant witnesses, approue,
and cite him in their booke , *Besepher Bi-*
bakim, of collections: here readeth *: erit sacri-*
ficium panis in terra in capite montium Eccle-
siæ:he, the Messias shal bee a sacrifice of bread
on the head of the mountaines of the church.
Let him consider that hath eyes, that as it is
said, hee is the Messias of whome the whole
psalme speaketh , therefore when hee saith,
and hee shall bee a cake of wheate on earth, on
the head of mountaines , hee meaneth , and
would say, that a cake of bread shal bee the sa-
crifice ouer the heads of preists vvhich are in
the church. And *Iacobus de Valentia. (in psal.*
72.) longe before these times , proueth a-
gainst the Iewes, that theire Targum readeth:

deth: *erit placcutula tritici super capita Sacer-dotum.* Hee shall bee a little cake of wheate aboue the heads of preists . Neither doth either the Greeke, or any Latine reading contradict these most auncient and appro-ued readings : the Greeke sterigma signi-fieth, *fulcimentum flabilimentum or firma-mentum*, that which susteineth, beareth vp or strengtheneth some other: so is the La-tine, what exemplar soeuer wee follow, or readinge, *frumentum or firmamentum*, or as *Iacobus de Valentia* writeth. (*vt supra*) S. Ie-rome readinge, *memorabile triticum*, memo-rable wheate . For all these significations and properties , in an excellent maner are verified of Christ, and the holy sacrifice of his body . And the *Copula*, or *verbe* in all learned languages, Hebrue, Greeke, La-tine, *Iehi, estai, erit*, must needes haue re-lation, and connection with the Messias, onely there spoken of both immediatlie be-fore, and after: the next verse beeing, by our protestantes translation , the Hebrue Greeke and Latine agreeing. (*psal.* 7 2. *Hebr. vers.* 1 7.) *his name shall endure for euer: his name shall bee continued as longe as the sun-ne: and men shall bee blessed iu him, all nations*
shall

shall cal him blessed. And so to the end of the psalme: so the whole psalme before the 16. verse.

9. Therefore straunge it should be, that in a whole psalme, both by Iewes, Catholicks, and protestants, entreating onely of the Messias, there should bee one only verse, relatinge a matter quite extrauagant by protestants translation, beeing thus: *There shall bee an handful of corne in the earth vpon the toppe of the mountaines: the fruite therof shall shake like Lebanon, and they of the citie shall florish like grasse of the earth.* And then immediately followeth, of the Messias by these protestants translation: *His name shal endure for euer.* Which hath no connexion with the former, if we expound it of materiall corne, and for the prophet to say only, *there shall be an handful of corne in the earth vpon the top of mountaines*, neuer was, or can bee in that materiall sence, any signe or distinction to knowe the Messias by, which is the scope of that psalme. And yet in their psalmes in meeter printed . (*an.* 1614. *cum priuilegio Regis regali, conferred with the Hebrue,* as these men write) they make the matter worse: thus it is:

E 2　　　　*The*

The mightie mountaines of the land
　of corne shall bringe such thronge,
That it like Cedar trees shall stand
　in Libanus all alonge.
Their cities eke full well shall speed,
　the fruites thereof shall passe:
In plenty it shall far exceede,
　and springe as greene as grasse.

This is the Rithme, the reason I leaue to
others to finde, it passeth my skill: But this
I am certaine of, that neuer any such thing
chaunced in the time of Christ, since, or
before to my readinge: and for any protestant, or other, to say, that corne as high
as Cedar trees, with the rest described in
their Rithme, shall bee at the cominge of
the Messias, is to deny Christ, and with
the Iewes to expect an other, yet to come,
when such things may bee performed.

10. Therefore to let others passe, I will
conclude this matter with *Iacobus de Valen-*
tia, that learned Bishop of Cristopolis. (*in*
psal. 71. and Hieronymus *à S. fide* a Iew.)
both longe before this time of controuersies: The first saith: *per hoc quod additur, in*
summis montium: *by that which is added in*
the tops of mountaines, is expressed that this
　　　　　　　　　　　　　　aboun-

*aboundance is not to bee vnderstood of wheate,
or materiall corne, as the blind Iewes doe say,
that in the cominge of the Messias there shal
bee great aboundance of corne, and wine, and
oyle. Therefore here is recompted, and foretold, the sacrifice of the Eucharist , in which
Christ is daily offered in the forme of breade,
for Christ is daily lifted vp ouer the heads of
preists , as it is figured in the 29. chapter of
Exodus , where God commaunded a peece of
breade to bee lifted vp , ouer the heads of the
preists before the people. The same figure was
of the bread of proposition in the 25. chapter of
Exodus , and 24. of Leuiticus . Therefore in
an other translation which is called Targum, it
is: erit placentula tritici super capita Sacerdotum .* Hee shall bee a little cake of wheate
aboue the heads of preists . Therefore Dauid saith soe : *This Kinge the Messias shall
bee firmament, or corne, or memorable wheate
in earth vpon the tops of mountaines, that is,
he shall bee lifted vp ouer the heads of preists
in the forme of breade, for preists are often in
scriptures vnderstood by mountaines, for their
eminency of dignity, as is said before.* And a-
gaine : *after the Prophet had foretold, that
the Messias should bee God and man , and*

E 3   wor-

worshipped of all nations , and Kings of the world,after hee addeth,that this Kinge Mefsias shall bee corne and wheate , and a peece of of bread on the tops of mountaines , and ouer the heads of preifts , as hath beene declared there by many tranflations. And fo it is manifeft , how this Sacrament is not onely poffible, but alfo many wayes figured , and fore told in the lawe, and Prophets. And fo it plainely appeareth, that Chriftians doe not adore bread, as the blind Iewes doe lie , but we adore Chrift confecrated vnder thofe accidents.

11. The learned Iew. *Hieronym. à S. fide l. 1. contr. Iudæos .* hauing difputed in the like maner, thus concludeth: *we learne that the Iewes affirme that pfalme, Deus iudicium tuum Regi da: fpeaketh all thinges of the Meffias: now therfore vvhere it faith: hee shall bee firmament on earth on the tops of mountaines, and the Caldy trâflation faith, that hee (the Mefsias) shall bee a facrifice of bread on earth on the head of the mountaines of the Sinagogue: The mountaines of the Sinagogue are the preifts of the church , which de facto euery day doe eleuate or lift vp the Mefsias ouer their heads: and this is fo manifeft, that it cannot bee denied but by them, to*
whom

whom the malediction of Esay the Prophet is
come, that they should bee made blinde in eyes
and hart. *Is.* 42. And to this case and condition are all they brought, by these holy
and learned authorities, which deny the
truth of this holy sacrifice: for it is euident
that in the sence of protestant Sacramen-
taries, this prophesie to bee fulfilled at the
cominge of the Messias, was neuer performed: when in this Catholick constructió it
is iustified & effected in the whole world:
And if we should come to Libanus it selfe,
though now many hundred yeares vnder
the Mahumetans, yet wee are assured euen
by protestants themselues, that Christ in
the forme of bread is there most religiouf-
lie and aboue other places, eleuated dailie
by preifts ouer their heads in the holy sacrifice of Masse; there bee Catholicke Christians in greate number, with Patriarke,
Archbishop, Bishops and religious men o-
bedient to the Pope of Rome in all the dominions of the grád Segnior of the Turke,
there bee so many Christians frequenting
Masse, that a protestant telleth vs : They
make aboue two third parts of his Empire.
Cytraeus lib. de statu. Ecclesia pag. 20.21. *Mun-*
ster.

ster. in Cosmograph. Ed. Grimstom. booke of estates pag. 1053. *&* 1064. of that, which the Prophet speaketh of Christs beeing a preist after the order of Melchisedech, I haue spoken before: onely I add here from the learned Father (*Anastasius Abb.l.contra Iudæos*) disputing against the Iewes, who hauing proued from the history of Genesis, and S. Paule, the dignitie of the preisthood of Christians, aboue that of the old testament, and that of Melchisedech greater also then that was, inferred, that the sacrifice of Christians must needes be much more excellent: *Si Typus ille excelleñtior erat Iudaico Sacerdotum, profecto multo magis erit ipsa veritas.* If that Type or figure was more excellent then the Iewish preisthood, surelie the truth it selfe must needes bee much more excellent: which is no other by any Christiäs, but Christs most holy body and blood in the sacrifice of Masse.

THE V. CHAPTER.

Wherin the same holy doctrines are so also proued out of the Prouerbs of Salomon. cap. 9.

S. Ciprian. *ep.*63. *ad Cecil.* hauing cited the history of Melchisedech & how Christ institu-

inftitutinge the moft holy facrifice of his body and blood, to be offered by his preifts, in holy Maffe, therein fulfilled that figure of Melchifedech, he addeth: *Sed & per Sa-lomonem Spiritus Sanctus typum Dominici facrificij ante præmonstrat, immolatæ hostiæ & panis & vini, fed & altaris & Apostolo-rum faciens mentionem. Sapientia, inquit, ædificabit fibi domum, & fubdidit columnas feptem. Mactauit fuas hostias, mifcuit in cra-tera vinum fuum, & parauit menfam fuam & mifit feruos fuos, conuocans cum excelfa præ-dicatione ad crateram dicens: Quis est infi-piens declinet ad me: & egentibus fenfu dixit: venite, edite de meis panibus, & bibite vi-num quod mifcui vobis.* But by Salomon alfo the holy Ghoft doth fhew before the figure of our Lords facrifice, making mention of an offered hofte, and bread and wine, as alfo of an altare, and the Apoftles. Wife-dome, faith hee, did build for himfelfe an houfe, and put vnder it feuen pillers, kil-led his hoftes, mingled his wine in a boule, and prepared his table, & fent his feruants calling with a loude preachinge to his cup, fayinge: who is vnwife, let him decline to mee: and to needy in fence hee faid: come
you,

you, eate you of my breads, and drinke the wine which I haue mingled for you. This exposition of S. Cyprian is approued by the church of Christ. *Breuiar. Roman. in fest. corpor. Christ.* and S. Augustine in his 4. booke of Christian doctrine . *cap. 21. & l. 17. ciuitat. cap.* 20. And in his bookes, *de ciuitate Dei*, hee likewise so expoundeth it: and calleth the sacrifice there figured , *corpus , & sanguinem Christi ,* the body, and blood of Christ , *succeedinge the old sacrifices, id enim inquit sacrificium succesit omnibus illis sacrificijs veteris testamenti, quæ immolabantur in vmbra futuri .* For that sacrifice, saith hee, hath succeeded all those sacrifices of the old testament , which were offered in shadow of that was to come.

2. And Rabbi Samuel in his booke of the cominge of the Messias, which he sent to Rabbi Isaac Master of the Sinagogue, writeth thus, vppon that place, and of this holy sacrifice: *Rabbi Samuel l. de aduentu Messiæ cap.* 20. *hoc sacrificium pulcherrime & apte describit Salomon Propheta.* Salomon the Prophet doth moste excellently and aptly describe this sacrifice (*of Christians*) in the 9. chapter of his booke of Prouerbs : when
hee

hee faith, moſt high wiſedome hath com- „
municated his ſacrifice, mingled his wine, „
and prepared his table, then hee ſente his „
ſeruants, ſayinge, who is a little one, lett „
him come to me, and the vnwiſe ſhall eate „
my bread, and drinke my wine tempered „
with water, ô my Maſter what is this pre- „
pared table of the moſt high wiſedome but „
the altare, ô my Maſter? what is the breade „
& wine mingled, but the ſacrifice of bread „
and wine, and of water which is oſtered „
on the altare? who are the vnwiſe called „
by the ſeruants of wiſedome, but the gen- „
tiles, or nations which knew not God, cal- „
led by the Apoſtles? and it is to be noted, he „
faith, his bread and his wine, for by that „
hee doth inſinuate, that this ſacrifice is ac- „
ceptable to God, and that to this banquet „
ſo high, and ſo ſpirituall, hee did not call „
our Fathers which were wiſe in the lawe, „
who were occupied in the ſacrifice of the „
lawe, which carnall ſacrifice hee hath not „
left vnto vs. Whereuppon it cometh, that „
wee (the Iewes) deteſt in the gentiles the „
ſacrifice of bread & wine which God hath „
appointed, and in no reſpect reiecteth, as he „
doth reiect ſacrifices of fleſh. „

3. And

3. And Hieronymus *à S. fide. l. 1. contra Iudæos cap.* 1. by whofe booke diuers thou-fandes of Iewes (hee beeing alfo a Iewe) were conuerted, proueth againft them, that a principall reafon why they did not re-ceaue Chrift, was becaufe he taught a new law, preifthood, and facrifice, which can-not confift together with the lawe, preift-hood and facrifices of Moyfes. If we refort to the originall text of Hebrue, as our pro-teftants would feeme beft to allowe, wee haue a greater allowance there for thefe myfteries; for wheras S. Cyprian with the vulgare latine readeth, *wifedome builded to herfelfe an houfe*, *fapientia ædificauit fibi do-mum:* the Hebrue is Banetha Beithah, buil-ded his houfe : Chrift the wifedome of his father builded his houfe, his church, as it is commonly expounded : And where S. Cy-prian readeth, *mactauit fuas hoftias*, killed his facrifices, in the plurall number, as the latine vulgare, *immolauit victimas fuas*, fa-crificed his victims, the Hebrue in the fin-gular number, to defigne one fingular facri-fice, is, *Tabechah Tibchah, offered vp his fa-crifice*; and therefore our Englifh Protef-tants in their late priuiledged tranflation

rea-

readinge quite otherwife : *shee hath killed her beaftes* : haue prophaned that holy text in this point , foe the Hebrue readeth of Chrift in this place: *his table: his bread: his wine which hee mingled.* And this is fo euident and manifeft, that Sebaftian Caftalio the proteftant linguift tranflated: *victimam fuam immolauit, vinum libauit* : hee offered his facrifice· hee facrificed his wine: *Caftal. in hunc loc. Prou.* 9. So that the facrifice here mentioned, muft needs be that, which Chrifts eternal wifedome, offered, & therfore the altar wheron it is offered is called, *his table*, & when it is called *bread*, or *food*, or *flesh*, the Hebrue *Lehem* fignifying them all, or wine , it is not abfolutely fo called, but his bread, or his food, or his flesh, and his wine, *which hee mingled*, or facrificed, as this proteftant before hath taught vs. Therefore we muft needes conclude from hence, that the preifthood of Chriftians, is a true facrificinge preifthood, and neither proteftant or other, finding other facrifice then holy Maffe, it muft needes bee this.

Wherin

Wherin the same mysteries are proued by the same maner out of the Prophet Esay, and others.

THE VI. CHAPTER.

OVr Protestants of England in the Titles of the 56. 60. and 61. chapters of Esay the Prophet interpret them of Christ, and his holy Religion : so doe many scriptures, all readers may see cited and alleaged in the Margins there by them : and yet in these places the holy Prophet doth testify, that there shall bee a sacrificing preisthood an externall sacrifice, and altar whereupon it shal bee offered in this lawe of Christ, In the first place which Christ him selfe expoundeth of himselfe and his law, the Prophet speaking of the conuersion of the gentiles to Christ, writeth thus by protestants translation : *Euen them will I bringe to my holy mountaine* (his church*) and make them ioyfull in my house of prayer : their burnt offerings and sacrifices, shall bee acceptable vppon my altar: for my house shall be called an house of prayer for all people.* The Hebrue, Greeke,

and

and Latine readings doe all manifeftly expreffe facrifice and altar, whereon it was
to bee offered, and that facrifice to bee acceptable to God: therefore feeing an altar,
wheron facrifice is offered, a facrifice ther-
on offered, and a preift facrificinge or offeringe fuch facrifice, are in all learninge
mutuall correllatiues, and cannot poffibly
bee feparated, thefe muft needes bee found
among Chriftians by this place of the Prophet.

2. And in the 60. chapter v. 7. fpeaking
alfo of the conuerfion of the Gentiles, there
foretelleth, howe the preiftes, which hee
fhould choofe in them, whome hee vnder-
ftandeth by the Rammes of the flock, thefe
beeing cheife of naturall fheepe, as preifts
be in the fpiritual fold and fheep of Chrift,
fhall offer acceptable facrifice vpon the altar of God in the church of the Gentiles
conuerted. The Hebrue Greeke and Latine
texts all agree, propofing vnto vs, a facrifice offered on the altare in the lawe of the
Meffias: and can haue no other conftruc-
tion, except we will returne to Iudaifme:
for as a learned Father proueth. (*Anaftafius
Abb.l.contra Iudæos.*) *fignificat gentes facri-
ficaturos*

ficaturos esse Deo sacrificijs acceptis, quare non de sacrificijs legis intelligi potest, neque de altari terrestris Hierusalem, ergo spiritualis. The Prophet signifieth, that the Gentiles shall sacrifice to God with acceptable sacrifices, wherefore hee cannot bee vnderstood of the sacrifices of the lawe, nor of the altar of the material Hierusalem (being euacuated.*Is.c.61.v.5.*) *therfor of the sacrifice & altar of the spiritual Hierusalē* the church of Christ: as the whole chāp. sheweth of the glory of the house of God, among the gentiles, wanting among protestants. And in the next chapter, where our protestantes reade: *straungers shall stand and feede your flocks, and the sonnes of the Aliens, shall bee your plow-men, and your vine-dressers :.* The same Father together with S. Cyrill glosseth: *clarè hic vt annotauit Cyrillus, significat futuram esse translationem legis, & Sacerdotij: non enim amplius ex tribu Leui erant futuri Pastores & Sacerdotes. Quod si alia erit lex, & aliud Sacerdotium, ergo & alia hostia, & aliud Templum.* The Prophet doth here clearely signifie as S. Cyrill hath noted, that there should bee a translation or chaunge of the lawe and preisthood : for

pastors

paftors & preifts were not to be any more
of the tribe of Leui: But if there fhould bee
an other lawe, and preifthood, therefore
alfo an other facrifice and Temple muft
needes bee. So other holy and learned Fathers, all of them vnitinge to euery true
lawe,& Religion,a facrificinge preifthood
and facrifice: amonge whome Theodoret
vpon thofe words of S. Paul,by proteftants
tranflation, faith: *For the preifthood being
changed, there is made of necefsitie a change
alfo of the lawe: lex coniuncta est Sacerdotio,
neceffe eft enim, vt ceffante Sacerdotio, idip-
fum legi quoque accidat.* The lawe is ioyned to preifthood,for of neceffitie it is,that
the preifthood ceafing, the fame muft alfo
chaunce to the law. *Hebr.cap.7. v.12.Theo-
dor.in hunc locum.*This our proteftants haue
yeelded vnto before:Therfore,if now contrary to themfelues, & fo great reafon, and
authoritie, they would take a facrificinge
preifthood and facrifice from the lawe of
Chrift, they muft alfo take away the lawe
of Chrift, and Chrift himfelfe,except they
will leaue him without a lawe.

3. Againe in his 66. and lafte chapter,
the fame Prophet fpeakinge of the gentiles

F

to bee conuerted to Chriſt, and his church
of them, as our proteſtants expound him
by publicke warrant. *Proteſt. title of the 66.*
chapter of Iſay. ſpeaketh thus in the parſon
of God: *I will alſo take of them* (the gentiles) *for preiſts and for Leuites, ſaith the Lord.*
The learned tongues, Hebrue, Greeke, and
Latine reade, *Lachonim, eis Iiereis, in Sa-*
cerdotes, for preiſts, ſacrificing preiſts, as they
name the preiſtes of the lawe of Moyſes.
Therefore except wee ſhould deny (which
wee may not doe) there was no ſacrificing
preiſthood, or ſacrifice in that lawe, wee
muſt allow the like, though in a more excellent maner to the lawe of Chriſt. This
may ſuffice for this holy Prophet.

4. S. Auguſtine proueth the ſacrificinge
preiſthood of Chriſtians, and theire moſt
holy ſacrifice out of the books of the Kings
of reiecting the ſonnes of Hely and the old
preiſthood, and to inſtitute the new. *Au-*
guſtin. l. 17. ciuitat. cap. 5. 1. Reg. 2. Quod
addit manducare panem: that which hee ad-
deth to eate breade, doth elegantly expreſſe
that kinde of ſacrifice, of which our preiſt him-
ſelfe (Chriſt) *ſaith. Ioh. 6. the bread which*
I ſhal giue is my fleſh for the life of the world:
that

that is the facrifice, not after the order of Aaron, but after the order of Melchifedech. Anaftafius proueth the like out of Aggeus the Prophet, of the externall glory of the churches of facrificinge Chriftians there foretold. Others proue the fame from other places of the lawe, and Prophets. *Anaftas. l. cont. Iud. Agg.* 2. S. Auguftine expounding the 33. pfalme and there fpeakinge much of the holy facrifice, which Chrift inftituted of his bleffed body, and blood, vnder the formes of bread, & wine, and Gods reiecting the facrifices of the law of Mofes, writeth how this was figured by Kinge Dauid, diffemblinge and concealing himfelfe, before Kinge Achis, in the firft booke of the Kinges *cap.* 21. a figure how Chrift did fhadow his diuinitie, therby the better to alter and change the lawe, preifthood and facrifices of Moifes, and inftitute the new.

5. This was there forewarned, faith this holy Father, efpecially by two thinges, in that hiftory. Firft that the fcripture faith of Kinge Dauid, *hee chaunged his countenance before them: immutauit os fuum coram eis.* S. Auguftine readeth, *vultum fuum*. The

fecond

second is as S. Augustine readeth: *ferebatur manibus suis.* Hee was borne in his owne hands. And so the Greek in al copies, plainlie is: καὶ παρεφέρετο ἐν ταῖς χερσὶν αὐτᾶ. (*v.* 10.) as in the former, τὸ πρόσωπον. (*v. 9.*) *Hee chaunged his face or parson.* Vppon the first hee saith: *Mutauit vultum suum, quia erat ibi sacrificium secundum ordinem Aaron, et postea ipse de corpore & sanguine suo instituit sacrificium secundum ordinem Melchisedech. Mutauit ergo vultum suum in Sacerdotio, & dimisit gentem Iudaorum, & venit ad gentes.* Hee chaunged his countenance, because there was sacrifice accordinge to the order of Aaron. And after hee instituted a sacrifice of his body, and blood, after the order of Melchisedech. Therfore he chaunged his countenance in the preisthood, & forsooke the people of the Iewes, and came to the gentiles.

6. And againe speakinge how the deniers of this holy sacrifice and Chrifts reall presece there as he promised in the 6 chapter of S. Iohn were like to King Achis, condemning this for folly in Chrift, as Achis censured Kinge Dauid for his gestures in concealinge himselfe. He addeth. (*conc. 1.*)

Erat

Erat in illis regnum ignorantiæ, quaſi Rex
Achis. Id eſt regnum erroris eis dominabatur.
Ille autem dicebat: niſi quis manducauerit car-
nem meam, & biberit ſanguinem meum: quia
mutauerat vultum ſuum : quaſi furor iſte &
inſania videbatur, dare carnem ſuam mandu-
candam hominibus , & bibendum ſanguinem.
Ideo quaſi inſanus putatus eſt Dauid, quando
dixit ipſe Achis arreptitium hunc mihi addu-
xiſtis. Nonne videtur inſania, manducate car-
nem meam & bibite ſanguinem meum, & qui-
cunque non manducauerit carnem meam , &
biberit ſanguinem meum, non habebit in ſe vi-
tam? quaſi inſanire videbatur, ſed Regi Achis
inſanire videbatur, id eſt ſtultis & ignoranti-
bus. There was in them the kingdom of ignorance, as Kinge Achis, that is the kingdome of error ruled in them. For hee ſaid,
except a man eate my fleſh and drinke my
blood: becauſe he had chaunged his countenance, as fury and madnes it was thought
to giue his fleſh to bee eaten, and his blood
to bee drunken of men. Therefore Dauid
was reputed as a madd man , when Achis
himſelfe did ſay , you haue brought this
madd man vnto me, is it not thought madnes to ſay, eate my fleſh , and drinke my
blood,

blood , and whofoeuer doth not eate my
flefh and drinke my blood , shall not haue
life in him ? hee did feeme to bee as madd,
but hee did feeme to be madd to Kinge A-
chis, that is to fay, vnto fooles, and ignorant men.

7. The fecond which this holy learned
Father , expoundeth to bee propheticall of
this miftery , in that place is that which I
noted: *hee was borne in his owne hándes* : of
this faith S. Auguftine , *& ferebatur in ma-*
nibus fuis . Hoc vero fratres quomodo poffet
fieri in homine , quis intelligat ? Quis enim
portatur in manibus fuis? in manibus aliorum
poteft portari quis, manibus fuis nemo porta-
tur . Quomodo intelligatur in Dauid fecun-
dum litteram, non inuenimus, in Chriſto au-
tem inuenimus . Ferebatur enim Chriſtus in
manibus fuis, quando commendans ipfum cor-
pus fuum, ait . Hoc eſt corpus meum. Matth.
26. Ferebat enim illud corpus in manibus
fuis . Ipfa eſt humilitas Domini noſtri Iefu
Chriſti , ipfa multum commendatur homini-
bus . And hee was borne in his owne handes : ô my bretheren who can vnderſtand,
how this can bee done in a man . For who
is carried in his owne handes ? fome man
may

may bee carried in other mens hands, but
no man is carried in his owne hands. How
it can be literally vnderstood in Dauid, we
doe not finde. But wee finde it in Chrift.
For Chrift was carried in his owne hands,
when fpeaking of his owne body, he faith.
This is my body. For he carried that body
in his owne hands. That is the humility of
our Lord Iefus Chrift, that is much commended vnto men. And in his next fermon
vpon that pfalme, expounding all the gef-
tures of Kinge Dauid, before King Achis,
to bee figures of, and fulfilled in Chrift, he
writeth againe in this manner of the fame
matter. *Auguftin. conc. 2. fupr. in pfal. 33.*

8. *Et ferebatur in manibus fuis. Quomo-*
do ferebatur in manibus fuis? Quia cum com-
mendaret ipfum corpus fuum, & fanguinem
fuum, accepit in manus fuas, quod norunt fide-
les:& ipfe fe portabat quodamodo cum diceret:
Hoc eft corpus meum: And hee was carried
in his owne hands. How was hee carried
in his owne hands? Becaufe when hee recommended his owne bodie and blood, he
tooke that which the faithfull know, into
his owne handes : and hee after a certaine
maner carried himfelfe, when he faid, this

F 4   is

is my bodie. And fpeakinge plainely, that
Chrift was figured, and reprefented in that
hiftory of Kinge Dauid , hee faith : *Quis
eft? notus eft Dominus nofter Iefus Chriftus.
In corpore & fanguine fuo voluit effe falutem
noftram . Vnde autem commendauit corpus &
fanguinem fuum? de humilitate fua. Nifi enim
effet humilis, nec manducaretur , nec libare-
tur.* Who is it that was fignified by Dauid,
it is our knowne Lord Iefus Chrift. Hee
would haue our faluation to be in his body
and blood . From whence did hee recommend his body and his blood ? from his
humilitie. For if he had not beene humble,
he would neither haue beene eaten, or been
our drinke. Many fuch teftimonies more
may bee brought from the lawe and Pro-
phetes, & ar fo vfed of the beft learned holy
Saints that liued in the primatiue church,
which I muft and wittingly doe paffe ouer
to auoide tedioufnes , not fo well futeinge
with a preface or introduction: therefore I
will now laftely come to the lafte Prophet
Malachias , and his prophefie of this holy
miftery.

THE

THE VII. CHAPTER.

Wherin the same is proued at large by all ex-
positions and testimonies, euen by our prote-
stants themselues, out of the Pro-
phet Malachy.

MAny of the holy learned Fathers of
the primatiue church, demonstrate
against the Iewes, Christ to bee the true
Messias by this holy sacrifice of Masse, thē
offered by the conuerted gentiles, in all the
world: for citinge the prophesie of Malachias, of Gods reiectinge the sacrifices of
the law of Moyses, and his acceptinge of
the pure sacrifice of the gentiles, they proue therby, that whosoeuer denieth that prophesie to bee fulfilled and verified, in the
holy sacrifice of Masse, consequently denieth Christ Iesus to bee the true Messias,
and must, as yet the misbeleeuinge Iewes
doe, expect an other. S. Augustine saith:
Hoc sacrificium per Sacerdotem Christi secun-
dum ordinem Melchisedech, cum in omni loco
à solis ortu vsque ad occasum, Deo iam videa-
mus offerri, sacrificiuum autem Iudæorum qui-
bus

bus dictum est, non est mihi voluntas in vobis, nec accipiam de manibus vestris munus, cessasse, negare non possunt, quid adhuc expectant alium Christum, cum hoc quod Prophetatum legunt, & impletum vident, impleri non potuerit nisi per ipsum. When we see this sacrifice to be offered to God by the preisthood of Christ according to the order of Melchisedech, in euery place from the rising of the sunne, euen to the setting therof, and they cannot deny, but the sacrifice of the Iewes to whom it was said, I haue no will in you, neither will I receiue guift from your handas, to haue ceased, why doe they yet expect an other Christ, when this which they reade to haue beene prophesied, and see to bee fulfilled, could not bee fulfilled but by him. *Augustin. l. 18. ciuitat. cap. 35. Malach. cap. 1. Augustin. l. 1. cont. aduersar. leg. & Prophet. c. 20. orat. contr. Iudæos c. 9.*

2. The very same argument, and exposition of that prophesie, vse these holy Fathers following (to omit others too many to be cited) within the first 400. yeares: S. Clement, S. Iustine, S. Irenæus, S. Martial, Tertullian, S. Cyprian, Eusebius, S. Chrisostome, Aurelius Bishop of Carthage, and
others,

others, all against the Iewes, therby inuincibly prouing against them, that the sacrifices of that people had then ceased, and their Religion euacuated, and the Religion of Christ onely true, because according to that most vndoubted true prophesie, the sacrifice of Christians, the holy Masse was then in their times offered in all the world. And this is so euident in all antiquitie, that both the Magdeburgian protestants, Caluine, and others confesse, that S. Irenæus, S. Ciprian, S. Athanasius, S. Ambrose, S. Augustine and Arnobius doe soe expound it. And our protestants of England in their newly authorised bible, by his maiestie, doe proue as much : for thus they translate that passage, of the Prophet Malachias : *I haue no pleasure in you* (the Iewes)*saith the Lord of hostes, neither will I accept an offering at your hand* (*from your hand*) the Hebrue, as they note in the margine, *for from the rising of the sunne, euen vnto the goinge downe of the same, my name shall bee greate among the heathens, saith the Lord God of hostes. Clem. l. 7. Const. Apostolic. cap. 31. Iustin. dial. cum Tryphon. Lrenæus l. 4. c. 32. Martial. epistol. ad Burdegal. c. 3. Tertul. l. 3. cont.*

3. *cont. Marcion. c. 22. Ciprian. l. 1. cont. Iud. c. 16. Euseb. Cæsar. l. 1. demonstr. euangelic. cap. 10. Chrysostom. ad psal. 95. Aurel. Carthag. epist. ad Marcellinum. Magdeburg. cent. 2. col. 63. cent. 3. col. 83. Calv. l. de ver. ecclef. reform. Protest. Bible Malach. 1. v. 10. 11.*

3. Where the Prophet expreſsely maketh this greatnes of the name of God amonge the gentiles and the pure ſacrificing which with incenſe ſhoulde by them bee offered vnto God in all places, to bee a notion, and diſtinctiue ſigne to bee aſſured by, that the ſacrifices of the Iewes were to ceaſe, and determine, and to demonſtrate, that as the lawe of Chriſt is more excellent then the lawe of Moiſes, ſo the ſacrifice of the ſame, and the preiſts which offered the ſame, taking their dignitie from the worthines of the ſacrifice which they ſhould offer, ſhould bee more worthie, then thoſe of the Iewes, which hee did reiect. For ſo it is in all languadges, *Mincha tehora*, *a pure oblation in Hebrue*: θυσια καθαρα *a pure ſacrifice in Greek*: *in omni loco ſacrificatur*, & *offertur nomini meo oblatio munda*. In euery place a cleane oblation is ſacrificed and offered to my name: in Latine. *Fertum purum*: *a pure ſacrifice*: as

the

the proteſtant Sebaſtian Caſtalio readeth:
a pure offeringe: as our Engliſh Proteſtants
tranſlate. And it is ridiculous, for any man
to expound it of prayer, without ſacrifice
externall, for the Prophet there plainly op-
poſeth this the externall ſacrifice of Chriſtians, which was to be receaued, to the o-
thers of the Iewes which were then to ceaſe, & the cheife proteſtāts haue ſo expounded and tranſlated it before: and here hee
ſpeaketh of both prayer expreſſed in the
word *thymiama* in Greeke, *Muctar* in Hebrue, as the Engliſh Proteſtantes, together
with S. Auguſtine, S. Hierome, Euſebius
and others expound it: and externall ſacrifice in the other as is before recited. *proteſt.*
of Engl. and Fr. Maſon. of conſecrat. of Biſh.
pag. 219. 220. Auguſtin. Hierom. & Euſeb.
apud Maſon. ſupr.

4. Which being ioyned with the known
ſacrificing verbe or verball *Maggaſh*, cannot poſſibly haue any other interpretation,
but as plainely and literally expreſſeth the
publicke ſacrifice of the Maſſe, vſed by
Chriſtians, as any miſſale, or Catholicke
writer doth, or can doe in generall termes,
not deſcendinge to the particular expreſ-
ſing

sing of the blessed body and blood of the Messias there offered, which belonged onlie to the time of the lawe of Christ, and not those figuratiue dayes: yet by many attributes and properties so describeth it, that it cannot bee applied to anie other. For it termeth this sacrifice, *a pure offering, the pure sacrifice, the sacrifice wherein onely God woulde bee pleased, the sacrifice that should succeede the sacrifices of the lawe, and euacuate them, a sacrifice to bee offered in all places, as Christ was to bee honored in all,* and to continue for euer. Neuer to be abrogated by any other; all which are before remembred by the Prophet, and cannot by any possibilitie be truely spoken of any other sacrifice, then this of the most blessed body and blood of Christ, offered by his holy preistes in that sacrifice, which from the Hebrues we cal Masse in our language.

5. Neither can any thinge be so briefly spoken by God, to confute the friuolous & vaine obiections, of some protestants, allmost now quite exploded out of the world, by Catholicke arguments, about dimensions, and pluralities of places & locations

of

of this most blessed Sacrament, and sacrifice; for God here by the mouth of his holie Prophet, assuringe vs that this sacrifice
shall bee but one, and no more, as it is before expressed in all holie languages, Hebrue Greke and Latine, yet so miraculous
and extraordinary it shall bee that. *Be cal
Machom,* ἐυ παυτὶ τόπω, *in omni loco, in euerie place,* by protestant translation out of
Hebrue, Greeke and Latine iustifyinge it,
this onely pure sacrifice shall bee offered to
God: That if these men will either beleeue
naturall or supernatural reason, and authoritie, God or man, they may see the vanitie
of theire contradiction. For whereas they
would persuade their adheréts and others,
that one and the same sacrifice cannot bee
offered in many places, God himselfe testifieth the quite contrary, that this shall bee
offered in all places, and yet bee but one
pure sacrifice, as is before declared, by all
translations, and the originall text it selfe,
from the worde of God by his holie Prophet.

6. And it is as euident, from this onely
clause: *in euery place:* that this could be no
other sacrifice, then the sacrifice of Masse,

vfed in the Catholicke church of Chrift,
now dilated into all nations, and in euery
place: for there bee now in the world but
foure great profeffions of Religion, Chriftians, Iewes, Mahumetans, and Pagans.
No Chriftian will or may fay, that prophefie of the true worfhippers of God, & pure
facrifice to bee offered vnto him, is, or can
bee vnderftood of any of them; for firft the
pagans facrifices were not offered to God,
but to Idols: they were not pure and holy,
but moft wicked and abhominable: they
had not any one facrifice, that was generally offered in all places. *Eufeb. Tertul.*
cont. Iud. Iuftin cont. gent. Ariftid. Plutarch.
in vit. &c. The Mahumetans haue no externall facrifice at all to offer in any place.
Mahum. in Alcor. hiftor. Turric. and theire
whole Religion, by all Chriftians is dam-
nable, and their fect could neuer yet be called vniuerfall, in all places. And to fpeake
with proteftants, as before, in thofe contries, which the Turke poffeffeth: *The*
Chriftians make aboue two third parts of his
Emipre. Edw. Grymft. pag. 1064. Auth. of
the booke of the eftates in the great Turke in
Afia. Therfore there is nothing in that Religion

ligion that can bee called this pure ſacrifice, offered to God in euery place.

7. The ſacrifices of the Iewes were manie, and not one by one, and all of them
reieĉted by God in this place of the Prophet, as our proteſtants thus tranſlate. (*Ma-
lach.cap.1.10.*) *I haue no pleaſure in you, ſaith
the Lord of hoſtes, neither will I accept an offering at your hand.* And then immediatly
the conuerſion of the Gentiles, and their
pure ſactifice to bee offered to God. (*verſ.
11.*) *in euery place,* is ſet downe. So that not
any one ſacrifice of the Iewes, could after
this time be acceptable to God, none could
bee this pure ſacrifice, in any place, much
leſſe in euery place, when the Iewes Religion was neuer ſo extended. And as the
holy ſcriptures and Hieronymus, *à Sanĉta
fide* a Iewe. (*l. 1. contr. Iudæos cap. 9.*) proueth, the Iewes might neuer offer ſacrifice
out of Hieruſalem, and ſo this could not
poſſibly be ment of them : *oſtendit nobis in
hoc quod dicit: In omni loco: quod hæc oblatie
munda, fienda erat per vniuerſum mundum,
vbicumque per modum eſſet aſſignatum : per
contrarium ſacrificiorum antiquorum, de quibus erat prohibitum ne alibi quàm in Temple*

G   *Ieroſo-*

Ierofolymitano fierent. The Prophet sheweth
vnto vs, by that hee saith : in euery place,
that this pure oblation, was to be made in
all the world, wherefoeuer it was affigned
in the world: by the contrary of the old facrifices of which it was forbidden, that
they should not be offered in any other place, then in the Temple of Hierufalem. And
proueth there out of the Iewes *Thalmud,* often repeating, that their facrifices were to
ceafe : *quædam locutio fæpe in Talmud reite-*
rata quæ dicit fic: in tempore futuro, vniuerfa
facrificia, excepto facrificio confeffionis anni-
hilata erunt . All facrifices should be anni-
hilated but the facrifice of confeffion, called Thoda in breade and wine: meaninge
the facrifice of Chriftians, as I haue proued
in due place.

8. And *Rabbi Samuel .* (*Marrochian. l.*
de aduent. Meffiæ cap. 20.) writing to *Rabbi*
Ifaac Mafter of the Sinagogue, vppon this
prophefie of Malachie faith. *Timeo Domine*
mi , quod Deus eiecit nos à fe , & facrificium
noftrum , & acceptauit facrificium gentium,
ficut dicit per os Malachiæ : ô my Mafter, I
feare, that God hath caft vs away frô him,
and our facrifice alfo, and hath accepted
                                          the

the sacrifice of the gentiles, as hee speaketh
by the mouth of Malachy. And immediatlie citing the wordes of that Prophet, as
before, concludeth thus for the sacrifice of
Masse vsed by Christians : *sacrificium gen-*
tium, est mundus quam sacrificium nostrum.
The sacrifice of the gentils (so he called Christians converted of the gentiles) *is more*
pure then our sacrifice.

9. Thus commonly also the holy Christian Fathers, among whom S. Augustine
citinge that prophesie of Malachie, thus
speaketh to the Iewes. (*Augustin. orat. con-*
tra Iudæos cap. 9.) *Quid ad hæc respondetis?*
aperite oculos tandem aliquando & videte, ab
oriente sole vsque ad occidentem , non in vno
sicut vobis fuerat constitutum, sed in omni loco
sacrificium Christianorum offerri, non cuilibet
Deo, sed ei , qui ista prædixit , Deo Israel.
What do you answere to these things? open
your eyes sometime at the laste , and see,
that the sacrifice of Christians is offered
from East to West, not in one place as it
was appointed vnto you, but in euery place, not to euery one that is called God, but
to him, the God *of Israel, that foretold these*
thinges. Therefore seeing the word of God

G 2   pro-

proposed by his holy Prophet cannot bee
vntrue, but muft needs be verified in fome
facrifice, offered thus vnto him by fome
profeffors of Religion, and all others befides Chriftians are thus clearely excluded,
and Chriftians haue only one externall facrifice of the Maffe, conteining the oblation of Chrifts moft bleffed body & blood,
the onely moft pure facrifice and acceptable vnto God, and offered in euery place
in the whole world, it muft needs bee this
pure and generall facrifice.

10. To which our proteftants themfelues (to make all fure) do thus giue teftimo-
nie. Firft his Maieftie, as *Cafaubon* hath
publifhed by warrāt. (*Cafaub. Refp. ad Card.*
Per. pag. 51. 52.) *neither is the Kinge Igno-*
rant, nor denieth, that the Fathers of the
primatiue church did acknowledge one facrifice
in Chriftian Religion, that fucceeded in the
place of the facrifice of Moifes lawe. And both
from our Kinge, and D. Andrewes, the
Proteftant Bifhop now of Winchefter, affirmeth of this facrifice. (*pag. 50. 51. fup.*) *It*
is Chrifts body, the fame obiect and thinge
which the Roman church beleeueth. An other
diuidinge Chriftians into the Latine and

Greeke church, as the common diuision is, and telling vs, as all acknowledge, that in all contries of the Latine church, remayning still in obedience to the see of Rome, the sacrifice of the Masse is publickly in all places offered, and in the contries that haue reuolted lately from it, the same sacrifice is priuatly with many still celebrated, thus hee writeth of the Greeke church. (*Edwine Sands relation of Religion cap.* 53. *or* 54.) *With Rome they concur in the opinion of transsubstantiation, and generally in the seruice and whole body of the Masse, in praying to Saints, in auricular confession, in offeringe of sacrifice and prayer for the dead. They hold purgatory also, and worshipping of pictures. Their Liturgies bee the same, that in the old time, namlie S. Basils, S. Chrisostoms, and S. Gregories (that which the Roman church now vseth) translated without any bendinge them, to that chaunge of language, which theire tongue hath suffered.*

11. *Chytraus a German protestant, writinge de statu Ecclesiæ, of the state of the church.* (pag. 7. 8. 11. 13. 15. 18. 20. 21.) *saith: Among all the nations of Greece, Asia, Africa, Ethiopia, Armenia &c. all places are full of*

Masses,

Masses, the sacrifice of the Masse is offered for the liuing and the dead. The Georgians inhabiting old Iberia, and Albania. The Syrians name S. Basile author of their Masse. The Armenians inhabitinge most large spaces of the earth from the bounds, of Cappadocia and Cilicia vnto Iberia the Caspian sea, Media and Assiria, are moste like the papists in Religion and ceremonies, in their Masse they remember inuocation, and intercession of Saints, offering vp of the Sacrament. Also euery where in Persia, and all the east, the Christians doe the same. The Maronites at mount Libanus, are conformable to the Latine church in all thinges. The Iacobits in Asia and Africke, are more by much propagated and haue their Masses.

12. Our English Protestant translator of the author of the booke, *of the estates, Empires, & principalities of the world. (Edw. Grymston pref. to the Reader.)* although as he confesseth he altereth and addeth at his pleasure, cannot finde out any one prouince, or contry of note in al the whole world, where hee dareth to affirme, and can proue that this holy sacrifice of Masse is not there offered vnto God. The same proueth. *(pag. 102. to pag. 283. in the estate of the K. of Spaine.)*

ne.) that the Kinge Catholicke of Spaine,
by land and Sea in all parts of the worlde
Europe, Asia, Africke, and America, is the
greatest Emperour and Kinge that now
presently is, or euer heretofore hath beene
in the world, possessinge more territories,
and dominions, then all Turkes, Tartars,
Pagans, and enemies of Christianitie that
be, and yet in all these dominions this most
holy sacrifice of Masse is publickly offered
and celebrated with great honor, and glo-
rie. So that if it were receued no where els,
but in his territories, the prophesy of Malachias is fulfilled in his dominions, as well
appeareth by this, and all Cosmographers
of these dayes, that truely sett downe the
estates of great Princes. There is no maine
part, *ab ortu solis vsque ad occasum, from the
risinge of the sunne vnto the setting thereof,*
nor from the settinge to the rising againe,
but he hath some dominion there: as a late
verse is of the Enfante Mary of Spaine her
Father, and her brother is in the same condition:

G 4

Vnto

Vnto her greatnes witnes giues the sunne,
    tasked no houre, to shine at any hand,
As he his course about the globe doth runne,
    but on some part of her late Fathers land.
An homage which hee neuer did before,
    to any Prince, nor like to doe no more.

13. And yet besides these so many and
vaste countries, our protestants haue told
vs before, that all the other three parts of
the world, Asia, Africke, and Europe, are
full of Masses, and sacrificinge Christian
preists. Which this protestant also confirmeth.(*Grymston.supr. in these kingdoms pag.*
700.&c.) teaching that not only in the territories, but in *Tartaria, China, Iapan, Peru,*
Magor, Calicut, Narsing, Persia, all the Turks
estates in Europe, Africk and Asia, Monomo-
tapa, Congo, Moraco, and from the rising to
the setting of the sunne, the prophesie of
Malachie is iustified and performed, for
in all these places, *Mincha tehora, thusia*
Cathara, the pure sacrifice, hee speaketh of,
the holy sacrifice of Masse, *is offered to the*
name of God, and his name is great among the
Gentiles.

14. This is the state of thinges at this
time. Thus it was from the first planting
                                    of

of christianity in the whole known world, by the holy Fathers before : and appeareth in the most auncient Masse of S. Marke, the Euangelist, vsed among the first Christians of this nation, as I shall shew hereafter, in which thus wee finde. *Per quem (Christum) offerimus rationabilem & incruentam oblationem hanc, quam offerunt tibi Domine omnes gentes, ab ortu solis vsque ad occasum, à Septentrione ad meridiem: Quia magnum nomen tuum in omnibus gentibus, & in omni loco incësum offertur nomini tuo Sancto, & sacrificium & oblatio .* By whome (Christ) wee offer this reasonable and vnbloody oblation, which ô Lord all nations doe offer vnto thee, from the rising of the sunne, to the setting therof, from North to South, because thy name is great in all nations, and in euery place incense, and sacrifice & oblation, is offered to thy holy name. *Liturgia eccl. Alexandr. & S. Marci Euang. M. S. per antiq. tempore Britan.*

AN

AN HISTORIE OF THE
HOLY PREISTHOOD, AND
sacrifice, of the true church.
The first age.

THE VIII. CHAPTER.

Wherin is proued by all kinds of testimonies, Catholicks, Protestants, and whatsoeuer, that Christ the true Messias as his calling and dignitie required, in abrogatinge the preisthood and sacrifices of Moses lawe, institued an other more perfect sacrificinge preisthood, and sacrifice of his sacred body, and blood in Masse.

HAuing declared and proued at large out of the holy Prophets and lawe of Moses, by all learned languages, and translations, Hebrue, Greeke, and Latine, by all learned interpreters of scriptures, aswell before, as after Christ, the auncient Rabbines, and primatiue Fathers of the church of Christ, as they are allowed and receiued both by Catholicke and Protestant writers, and their consent herein. That our
blessed

bleſſed Sauiour Chriſt our Redeemer, and
high-preiſt, after a more excellent manner
accordinge to the order of *Melchiſedech*,
was to euacuate the legall preiſthood, and
ſacrifices of the lawe of *Moſes*, as in themſelues figuratiue, and vmbraticall , beeing
to ceaſe & determine at the coming of the
Meſſias, & to found and inſtitute a preiſthood and ſacrifice more perfect, effectuall,
& as S. Paul ſtileth it. *Hebr.cap.7.v.24.* and
our proteſtants tranſlate it , ἀπαράθατον τκυ
ἱερωσύνκυ, *an vnchaungeable preiſthood ,* and
conſequently a ſacrifice and law vnchaungeable , for ſo theſe men tranſlate the ſame
holy Apoſtle : *euery highpreiſt is ordeyned
to offer guifts and ſacrifices for ſinnes ,* and :
*for the preiſthood beeing chaunged , there is
made of neceſsitie a chaunge alſo of the lawe.*
(*proteſt. tranſl. Hebr. cap. 5. v. 1. Hebr. cap.
7. v. 12.*

2. Therefore the time of this moſt hap-
pie chaunge and alteration beeinge now
come, at his laſte paſſouer, or eating of the
Paſchall lambe, a figure (as I haue by greateſt allowance, and warrant formerly declared) of this moſt holy chriſtian ſacrifice,
although our Sauiour had often celebrated
that

that legall feast before, or none or smal memory thereof left in scripture, yet when in this laste hee was to end the olde , and ordeine the new, hee sent his two great Apostles and most beloued , S Peter and Saint Iohn, to prouide the first Christian church as some not vnworthly call it. (*Proclus apud Flor. Rem. l. 8. Luc. cap. 22. v. 12.*) to institute this most sacred preisthood & sacrifice in, ἀνώγεον μεγα ἱερωμένον, *a large vpper Roome furnished* (as our English protestāts translate) but as the Greeke word is , and frēch Hugonots also do read, *a great Roome strewed with carpets.* (*Hugon. gallic. apud Florim. Ræmund. supr. de origin. hæres. l. 8. cap. 12*) into which our high preist and Sauiour did enter, *vt Rabbinorum nonnulli affirmant, veste sacra , quam ipsi appellant Taleth indutus ,* as some of the Rabbines affirme , hauinge on a sacred or sacrificinge vestement, which they call Taleth . And there after hee had ended the ceremony of the lawe about the Paschall Lambe, he instituted this new sacrifice of Christians, and gaue power and commaundement to his Apostles present, to doe the same ; *Hoc facite, doe this,* which I haue done , in this mistery.

3. Wee haue heard already, and it is infidelitie to deny it, that he was a preiſt, according to the order of Melchiſedech, that hee muſt needes by that title offer a ſacrifice with ſome reſemblance to that of Melchiſedech, in bread and wine, that he was to chaunge the lawe, preiſthood, and ſacrifice: hee had not done any of theſe offices of the Meſſias, and high preiſt before, onely hee had in the ſixt chapter of S. Iohn, giuen his faithfull promiſe (which he could not violate) that he would performe it: this was the laſte day, time, and oportunitie wherein he could poſſiblie effect it, with his holy Apoſtles, to whom this charge before al others was firſt and chiefly to be recommended, hee being that very night to be betrayed, violently taken, and ſeperated from them, and neuer to communicate with them againe in the ſhort time of his life; Therefore now or neuer he was of neceſſitie to make performance of this moſt holy dutie; and if not now, the lawe, preiſthood, and ſacrifices of the lawe, had not beene abrogated and chaunged, but Iudaiſme had beene ſtill in force, and Chriſt

could

could not truely and lawfully haue enioyed the title of the true Meſſias, if ſo excellent, and euident ſigne, and propertie, of the holy Redeemer, had beene wantinge and defectiue in him.

4. Therefore all kinde of witneſſes that be or then were in the world, frends or enemies, whether Iewes Gentiles or Mahumetans, whether Chriſtians, Catholicks, either the auncient Fathers or later writers, and the beſt learned proteſtants themſelues giue euidence, that Chriſt at that time inſtituted a new ſacrifice, and ſacrificinge preiſthood. The auncient Rabbines before Chriſt, ſo expounded the ſcriptures, of the old teſtament, as I haue ſhewed before, and both Catholicks, and proteſtants ſo aſſure vs. (*Franciſc. Stancar. & Petr. Gallat. l.* 10. *cap.* 4. 5. 6. 7.) The Iewes that liued in the time of Chriſt, ſoone after, and at this day acknowledge it, hauinge proued by their lamentable experience, that after the inſtitution of the new ſacrifice, and preiſthood by Chriſt, as hee forewarned them of the ceaſing of their ſacrifices, and deſolation of the Temple of Ieruſalem, where onely by their lawe they might bee offered, they
lie

lie in that forsaké ſtate which al the world obſerueth, and the Prophet thus by proteſtants tranſlation foretold of them. (*Oſee c. 3. v. 4.*) *The children of Iſrael ſhall abide manie yeares without a Kinge, and without a Prince, and without a ſacrifice, and without an Image, and without an Ephod, and without Seraphim,* preiſtly and ſacrificing veſtures. *Iudic. cap. 17. v. 5.*

5. And al that write againſt the Iewes, as the holy Archbiſhop S. Gregentius, Iulianus Pomerius Archbiſhop of Toletum, Rabbi Samuel, Hieronymus a S. fide, Paulus Burgenſis, Petrus Gallatinus, Franciſcus Stancarus a proteſtant, and others and their owne Thalmud is witnes, that the hate of the Iewes againſt Chriſt and Chriſtians, is not ſo great for any thing, as that Chriſt at that time ordeyned a new ſacrifice and ſacrificinge preiſthood, and reieĉted thoſe of the lawe of Moyſes. The gentiles ſoone after conuerted did confeſſe it in all places, and in this kingdome of Britanie as I ſhall inuincibly demonſtrate herafter. The Mahumetans in their Alcaron and other authors giue teſtimony to this. So doe the moſte holy and beſt learned Fathers

thers of the primatiue church Greeke and
Latine, S. Denis the Areopagite conuerted
by S. Paul, S. Irenæus, S. Basil, S. Iohn Chrisostome, Theodoret, S. Martial scholler to
S. Peter the Apostle, S. Ambrose, S. Augustine, Primasius, and longe before these
S. Clement, Ignatius, Anacletus, with Pope
Alexander, liuing in the first hundred yeares, & others after, without number, plainlie some of them sayinge that Christ then
taught the new sacrifice of the new testament, *which the church receauing from the*
Apostles, doth offer to God in the whole world.
And that it is so certaine and vndoubted a
truth, that Christ did then make his Apostles sacrificing preists, that in their iudgement, *no man had called it into question. Quod*
Dominus potestatem celebrandi, & conficiendi
noui testamenti mysteria, Apostolis per hæc
verba contulerit, hoc nemo opinor in dubiū vo-
cat. Gregent. Archiep. Tephren. disput. cum
Herban. Iudeo. Iulian. Pomer. l. 1. & 2. contr.
Iudæos. Rabbi Samuel Marrochian. l. de Ad-
uent. Messiæ cap. 19. 20. 21. 22. 23. 24. 25. 26.
27. Hieronym. à S. fide l. 1. & 2. contr. Iud.
Paul. Burg. cont. Iud. Petr. Gallat. & Fran-
cisc. Stancar. l. 10. 11. Thalm. & Abraham.
Mahum.

Mahum. Rabb. Sam. supr. cap. 27. Dionis. A-
reopag. Eccles. Hierar. part. 3. c. 3. Irenæus
l. 4. c. 32. cont. hær. Victor Antiochen. in c. 14.
Marci. Basil. de sacrificijs ritu & Mis. celebr.
forma. Chrisost. de sacrificijs, & Homil. 8. &
ad cap. 26. Matth. & alibi sæpe. Theodoret. in
c. 8. ep. ad Hebr. Martial. epist. ad Burdegal.
cap. 3. Ambros. l. præp. ad miß. ad cap. 11. epist.
1. ad Cor. & alibi. August. l. 17. ciuitat. c. 20.
& quæst. 43. l. 1. quæst. in Euang. Primas. in
epist. 1. Corinth. c. 11. can. 3. Apost. Alexand.
1. epist. ad Orthodox.

6. And this sacrifice was, and is his sacred body, and blood, vnder the formes of
breade and wine , so miraculously effected
both then, and stil by the ministery of consecrated preists by his omnipotent power,
annexed by promise to this sacred and consecrating words, this is my body: this is my
blood: & that his holy Apostles were then
made such sacrificinge preists , and super-
naturally enabled to that highest and ho-
liest function . Neither can any protestant
of England bee of other opinion : for except contrary to the iudgement and testimony of all people, Iewes, Mahumetans,
Pagans, and Christians, which acknow-

H   ledge

ledge Iesus Chrift to haue beene , and ordeined a new facrifice, and preifthood, they
will caft off all nature and name of Chri-
ftianitie, and goe further then any infidell
yet hath done, moft foolifhlie and blafphe-
moufly to fay, there was neuer any fuch as
is called Iefus Chrift : they muft confeffe
with the reft, that hee ordeined thefe thinges, they muft fay , either with Turks and
Pagans his inftitution was not holy herin,
or with the Iewes, that this facrifice is, *panis polutus, poluted bread*, and not his body.
(*Hieronym. à S. fiae l. contr. Iud. 2. Iud. in
Thalm. & alibi.*) & his holy preifts, be, *tonfi,
shauelings*, as fome of them prophanely do:
or acknowledg with true Catholick Chriftians in all ages , times, and places, that
the facrifice and preifthood he then ordeyned, are the moft perfect, abfolute, and permanent for euer. For fo all teftimonies and
euidences vpon which Chriftian Religion
buildeth, the word of God deliuered in holie fcriptures, or tradition with the warrant
and practife of all the holy Apoftles , and
church of Chrift, haue already, or will in
this enfuing treatife affure vs.

    7. Therefore many of our beft learned
pro-

protestants , and with publicke warrant,
and priuiledge, haue graunted before. (*pref.
cap. 1.*) that Christ did not onely institute
and offer this most holy sacrifice , but did
giue power vnto his Apostles, *& commaundement also, to doe the same. That it succeeded
to the sacrifices of Moises lawe , that is was
from the beginning the sacrifice of the altare,
and vnbloody sacrifice, sacrifice offered for the
liuing and the deade.* (*Morton appeale l. 3. c.
13. Franc. Mason l. 5. pag. 233. 243. Middlet.
Papistom. pag.* 92. 113. 49. 137. 138. 47. 45.)
And among others to make al sure, his maiestie is auouched to be of the same minde.
(*Isaac Casaub. resp. ad Card. Peron. pag.* 51.)
that from that time of Christs institution,
there is in his Church, and hath euer beene
an externall sacrifice, wherin is conteined
the body and blood of Christ. And a protestant Bishop amonge them speakinge in
all their names. (*Morton appeale l. 3. cap. 13.*)
saith: *The protestants acknowledge in the Eucharist, a sacrifice Eucharisticall.* Which, and
more, they are all bound to doe, by an expresse statute of parlament receaued & confirmed by three protestant Princes, Kinge
Edward the sixt, Queene Elizabeth, and

our

116 *An historie of the holy priesthood, and* our present soueraigne Kinge Iames, wherin is expressely thus enacted. (*Statut. an.1. Edu- 6. cap.1.an.1 Elizabeth cap. 2. an. 1.Iacobi cap. 25.*) *The most comfortable Sacrament of the body and blood of our Sauiour Iesus Christ, commonly called of the altare, instituted of no lesse author then our Sauiour, both God and man.The institution of which Sacrament.being ordeyned by Christ,as is aforesaid, and the words,this is my body which is broken for you;This is my blood of the new testament, which is shed for you,and for many,for the remission of sinnes, spoken of it, beeing of eternall infallible and vndoubted truth, the most blessed Sacrament &c.* These bee the wordes of the statute established by his present maiestie in parlament, with publicke assent of all English Protestants,ministers or others: in which statute penalties bee decreed against al gainesayers of this holy sacrifice, and prouide an especiall writ against such transgressors. *Statut. supr.*

8. And to make all matters vnquestionable in this point,this statute was enacted when there were none but sacrificing preistes in England , diuers yeares before the booke of making ministers was inuented.

Which

Which the wordes of the abridgement of
our ſtatuts approued by his maieſty (to rei-
terate them) thus doe teſtifie. (*Abridgm. of
ſtat. an. Dom.* 1611. *Titul. ſeruice and Sacraments cap.* 1.) *the firſt makinge of this ſtatute
Was before the Maſſe Was taken aWay, When
the opinion of the reall preſence, Was not remoued from vs.* Therefore this ſtatute
wholly and without any other exception,
limitation, or reſtriction beeing publickly
made, approued, reuiued and confirmed by
three ſeuerall publicke parlaments, of three
Proteſtant Princes, cannot be contradicted by any Engliſh Proteſtant: and except
contradictions can both bee true, which is
vnpoſſible, it is not poſſible but the contents of this ſtatute of Chriſts inſtitutinge
the holy ſacrificinge preiſthood, and ſacrifice of Maſſe at his laſt ſupper, muſt needes
bee an article of faith, and infallible truth,
in the Religion and iudgement of Engliſh
Proteſtants. Therefore ſome of their beſt
learned. (*Feild l.* 3 *cap.* 29. *pag.* 138. *Couell
examin. pag.* 114.) haue with publicke ap-
plauſe, and warrant written, that it is hereſie, to bee of other opinion. For ſo they
ſhould deny and gainſay the vniuerſally receaued,

ceaued, and practised opinion, of the primatiue church. Whose custome vniuersall
and from the beginninge, was, to offer the
sacrifice of Masse, both for the liuing and
the dead. Which all men know, cannot be
performed, but by massing and sacrificing
preists, Masse and massinge preists, sacrifice and sacrificing preists, beeing vnsepe-
rable correlatiues, in al euē humane knowledge, and learninge, both of Catholicks,
and Protestants, Christians, Iewes, Mahumetans, Pagans, or whatsoeuer infidels,
professinge learninge, or followinge the
light and warrant of nature

9. And for the very vsuall name it selfe
of this most holy sacrifice, called generall-
lie in the latine church, *Missa*, or *sacrificium
Missæ*, Masse, or the sacrifice of Masse, seing
it was to be the óly external sacrifice of the
whole church of Christ, it could not possibly be named by any denomination more
aptly, then the word *Missa*, Masse, beeing
by diuers learned in the holy tongs, a name
both in Greek Hebrue and latine fittly signifyinge sacrifice, or equiualent thereof: of
the Greeke there is most difficultie, and yet
some learned gretians, as Albericus (*dictio-
ne*

ne Missa.) testifie, that *Missa* is a Greeke
word, signifyinge interpellation, or intercession, such as sacrifice to God, is, That it
is an Hebrue word, and aptly taken for sacrifice, we haue the consent allmost of all
Hebritians, both Catholicks, and protestāts, as of the first Alciatus, Hector Pintus,
Claudius Sanctus, Pamelius, Demochares,
Casalius, Capino, Cauus, Couarruuias,
Pauinus, Heruetus, and others. *Alciatus*
l. 7. parerg. cap. 10, Hect. Pint. in cap. 3. Dan.
Claud. Sainct. præf. ad Liturg. Pamel.in Ter-
tull. l. de orat. & præf.in Liturg. Græcor. De-
mochar. tract. 2. de Miss. c. 1. Casalius l. 1. sa-
crif. Miss. Io. Capr. Can. l. 12. de loc. c. 13. Co-
uarr. l. 4. Var. resol. c. 22. Pagn. v. Mitza.

10. And amonge Protestants, Sebastian
Munster, Philip Melancthon, and Iohn
Froster Professors of Hebrue ar of the same
opinion, and to iustifie our English name
of that holy sacrifice, to be taken also from
the Hebrue, where wee call it Masse, or
Mas, the worde or radix Mās in Hebrue,
signifieth tribute or due paiement, such as
wee owe in this sacrifice beeing commaunded to doe it, *hoc facite,* and the vnleuened
breade that was eaten with the Paschall
H 4   Lambe,

Lambe, and consecrated by Christ is *Maß-*
sah, in Hebrue. *Monster. in gramatica & le-*
xic, *Hebraic. Philip. Mel. Apolog. confeß. Au-*
gustan. Iohn. Froster in Lexic. Hebraic. edit.
Basil. an. 1557. *Petr. Veg. in psal.* 101. And
to come to the Latine word, *Missa*, Masse,
S. Albinus our learned countryman, expoundinge those laste wordes in Masse, *ite*
missa est, saith: *id est directa, siue missa est, id*
est perfecta est pro nobis oblatio & oratio. That
is, sacrifice or oblation and prayer for vs is
directed, or sent, or perfected. *S. Albin. l.*
de diuin. officijs. so doth Remigius Antisiodorensis, saying. *Missa dicitur, quasi transmiß-*
sa, vel quasi transmissio. Remig. Antisiodoren.
expositio. de celebrat. missæ. And Petrus
Lombardus. *Missa dicitur quia missa est hos-*
tia, cuius commemoratio fit in illo officio: vnde
dicitur: Ite missa est. Petr. Lumbard. l. 4. sent.
Where we see that it is called Missa, because it is a sacrifice sent, or offered vnto God,
and not of dismissinge the people. Which
is euident by the practise of the church in
all places, which at the ende of all Masses
dismisseth the people: but as our protestants
themselues confesse (*Foxe tom,* 2. *in Queene*
Mary,) saith not alwaies, *ita missa est*, but
som-

sometimes, *benedicamus Domino*, soometimes, *requiescant in pace*, and in the old Muzaraban Masse, in solemne feasts, where wee say in the end of Masse, *ite missa est*, they said, *solemnia completa sunt*, *the solemne sacrifice is ended*, and in other feasts : *missa acta est: masse or the sacrifice, is ended*. (*missa Muzarab. antiq. in concil. 4 Toletan. & alibi.*) And in this sence it was alwayes accepted, in all ages, from the Apostles, as our protestants themselues shall euidently confesse hereafter, in this history.

THE IX. CHAPTER.

Shewinge how the Apostles in generall being by Christ ordeyned sacrificinge preists, did accordinge to that power and commaundement giuen vnto them, offer the sacrifice of Christs body and blood in Masse, and ordered other preists to that end.

ANd by this it is also manifest, that the Apostles were sacrificinge and massinge preists, and did, as that preistly dignitie confered vpon them, required, offer this holy sacrifice, accordinge to the war-

rant

rant and commaundement of Chrift vnto
them, to doe, that which he did in that behalfe. So that if we had no further authoritie, for their facrificinge preifthood , and
dutie to offer this bleffed facrifice, but that
they were, as before is fhewed, made facrificing preifts by Chrift, feeing that preifthood and facrifice was neuer to ceafe, but
to bee continued in the church of the Meffias, vnto the end of the world , and thefe
men were the cheifeft inftruments, and rulers, which our Sauiour inftituted, to conuert the nations, and communicate this facred preifthood and power, to offer this facrifice, vnto others, ftill to bee continued,
without interruption, wee muft enforced-
lie yeelde, that they left fuch a facrificinge
power, and fome maner and order how this
facrifice was to bee folemnized, to fucceedinge generations . Which I fhall proue of
euery one of the Apoftles in particular , in
the next chapters: onely here of them all in
general, that this doctrine of confecration,
preifthood & facrifice of Maffe, they taught
and deliuered to the churches where they
liued and preached , wee haue many and
worthie arguments and witneffes.

2. S.

2. S. Chrisostome telleth vs plainly, how the Apostles practisinge and deliuering the order of this sacrifice, *decreed that the faith-full departed should bee remembred then, and prayed for. Ab Apostolis sancitum est, vt in celebratione venerandorum mysteriorum, memoria fiat eorum qui hinc decesserunt. Nouerunt illis multum hinc emolumenti fieri, multum vtilitatis, stante siquidem vniuerso populo, manus in cælos extendente, cætu etiam sacerdotali, venerandoque posito sacrificio: quomodo Deum non placaremus pro istis orantes?* (*Chrisostom. Homil. 3 in cap 1. epist. ad Philipp.*) It was decreed by the Apostles, that in the celebration of the venerable mysteries, a memory should bee made of them that were departed this life. They knew much gaine, much profit did therby come to them, for all the people standinge holdinge vp their hands to heauen, the preistlie company, and the venerable sacrifice offered: how could it bee that wee shoulde not appease God, prayinge for them? The very like hee writeth in an other place. (*Chrisost. Homil. 69. ad popul. Antiochen.*) And S. Basile setting downe many thinges deliuered by the tradition of the Apostles, saith.

faith. (*S. Basil. l. 5. de vniuersal. eccl.*) *this tradition did commend the words of long prayer, and consecration ouer the breade and chalice, set downe in order*: *multifariam digesta super panem & calicem prolixæ orationis & consecrationis verba commendauit*? Irenæus faith the church receaued this order of sacrifice, from the Apostles, and in his time offered it to God in all the world. *Oblationem noui testamenti Ecclesia ab Apostolis accipiens in vniuerso mundo offert Deo. Irenæus l. 4. cap. 32. contr. hæres.* The auncient learned Bishop Stephanus Eduensis writtinge of this holy sacrifice, setteth down the maner how the Apostles practised and preached it. (*Stephan. Eduen. Episc. l. de Sacramento Altaris cap. 20.*) *Sicut Magister docuerat Apostoli se & alios communicando consecrationem corporis & sanguinis Domini facere cæperunt, & fieri per vniuersas Ecclesias instituerunt. Primo sine aliquo ornatu fiebat canonis mysterium, postea cum canone legebatur epistola, & Euangelium. Deinde à Romanis Pontificibus, quibusdam additis ad ornatum & decoratum; Ecclesia celebranda aliqua susceperunt.* As Christ theire Master had taught them, the Apostles communicating them-

themfelues , and other began to make the
confecration of the body and blood of our
Lord , and preachinge inftituted it to bee
done throughout all churches. Firft without any ornament the miftery of the canon
of Maffe was practifed, afterward with the
canon were reade the epiftle, and Ghofpel.
After this fomethings for ornament , were
therto added by the Popes of Rome , the
churches receiued the reft to be celebrated.

3. Where wee fee the whole body and
fubftance of the Maffe , confiftinge in the
holy canon perfected, practifed, and deliuered by the Apoftles. And what was after
added by the Popes of Rome , were onely
ceremoniall for honor and ornament fake
and not neceffitie, as hee there expreffeth,
and I wil demonftrate herafter by our proteftants themfelues,and for this place their
prime man and firft proteftantlye made
Archbifhop, teftifieth as much as this holy
Bifhop hath done before.For he faith plainlie. (*Matth. Parker. l. de Britan. antiq. cap.*
17. pag. 47.) that the order and forme of
Maffe, which the Apoftles vfed, *and deliue-*
red to the church, ducētis āplius ānis in prima
Ecclefia durauit, continued aboue two hundred
*   yeares*

and
yeares in the primatiue church without alteration. And then beeing somewhat altered,
by Pope S. Zepherine, *the chaunge which
was made, was to a more excellent forme and
matter. Ad pulchriorem materiam formamq̃.*
S. Proclus Patriarch of Constantinople and
successor to S. Chrisostome there testifieth,
that Saint Clement receaued the forme of
Masse from the Apostles, and published it
to the world. (*Proclus tractat. de traditione
diuin. Liturgiæ infra. cap.*) *Quia Sacrosancta
illa mysteria à Sanctis Apostolis sibi reuelata
in lucem edidit.* And how daily after Christs
Ascension they assembled and found great comfort in this holy sacrifice of Christs body and
blood, said Masse with longe prayers. *Cum
multam consolationem in mistico illo Dominici
corporis sacrificiopositam inuenissent, fusissimè
& longa oratione Liturgiam decantabant;* and
more plainely, as hereafter, preferringe it
before all other holy duties and exercises.
And Amalarius Fortunatus maketh this
reason, why the forme and order of this sacrifice, was by our Sauiour recommended
to the care of the Apostles. (*Amalar. Fortunat. l. 3. de Eccles. offic. cap.*) *Saluator quo
vehementius commendaret mysterij illius al-
titudinem*

titudinem vltimum hoc voluit infigere cordibus & memoriæ discipulorum, a quibus ad passionem digressurus erat, & ideo non præcipit, quo deinceps ordine sumeretur, vt Apostolis per quos Ecclesias dispositurus erat, seruaret hunc locum. Our Sauiour that hee might more vehemently commend the worthines of that mistery, would haue it the last thing hee was to fasten into the harts and memorie of his disciples, from whom he was to depart to his passion, and therefore did not commaund in what order it should afterwards bee receaued, that hee might reserue that dutie to the Apostles, by whom hee was to dispose the churches.

4. To this all the holy Fathers before, that testifie Christ ordeyned this holy sacrifice, and recommended it to his Apostles, beare witnes; for none but Antichristians will say, that the Apostles taught or practised, otherwise then Christ instituted and commaunded. And they were so zelous in this holy doctrine, that as both Catholicks and Protestants haue proued before, they were wicked Hereticks by S.Ignatius testimony that then denyed this B. sacrifice to bee the body and blood of Christ, which

which were giuen and shed for the sinnes
of the worlde . (*Ignat. apud Theodoret. Be-*
zam. Whitaker. & al. supr.) And Leontius
Bizantinus writing against the Hereticks
Nestorius and Eutiches charging them first
with denyinge the Nicen creed, and producinge a pseudosimbolum of their owne inuention , taxeth the Hereticke with an o-
ther prophane impietie not inferior to the
other , to deny the holy order of the sacrifice of Masse , ordeyned and instituted by
the Apostles, receaued by the Fathers, and
that of S. Basil penned by the same holy spirit; & inuented an other Masse of his owne
to susteine his heresie full of blasphemies.
Audet & aliud malum non secundum ad supe-
riora , aliam enim Missam effutinit præter il-
lam quæ à patribus tradita est Ecclesijs, neque
reueritis illam Apostolorum, nec illam magni
Basilij in eodem spiritu conscriptum , in qua
Missa blasphemijs non precationibus mysterium
Euchariatiæ oppleuit . And this wickednes
was so great by this renowned author, that
hee calleth it Antichristianitie and the de-
nier of the Apostles Masse, Antichrist. *An*
vt alius Antichristus adhuc expectetur par est,
qui sic Christum oderit , & quæ Christi sunt
mutare

mutare nitatur? And our Engliſh Proteſtants themſelues both ſay that the ſacrifice
of Maſſe for the liuing and the dead, was a
tradition of the Apoſtles, and Aerius was
iuſtly condemned of hereſy by the primatiue church, for denyinge ſacrifice for the
dead. And this is publickly and authorita-
tiuely approued by the remembred ſtatute
of Queene Elizabeth, Kinge Eduard the 6.
and Kinge Iames our preſent ſoueraigne,
aſſuringe vs, that this holy ſacrifice of the
altare, was inſtituted by Chriſt at his laſte
ſupper with his Apoſtles, deliuered to thē,
and by them to the church and ſucceeding
Chriſtian preiſts to the end, and conteyneth the oblation of the moſt ſacred body
and blood of Chriſt. *Middleton.* ¡Papiſtom.
pag. 49. 137. 138. 47. 48. *Feild.l.* 3. *cap.* 29.
pag. 138. *ſtatut. an.* 1. *Edu.* 6. *an* 1. *Elizab.*
& an. 1. *Iacob. Reg.*

I   THE

THE X. CHAPTER.

Wherin is particularly proued of all the holy Apostles and Euangelists, that they were sacrificinge massinge preists, and did both practise and teach the same doctrines. And first the 4. Euangelists and S. Paule, who haue remēbred these misteries in holy scriptures.

THis being thus inuincibly proued, and acknowledged, both by Catholicke and Protestant authoritie, that both Chrift our Sauiour instituted this holy sacrifice, and sacrificinge preisthood; and his Apostles receauinge them from him, did all in generall both exercise and deliuer the same vnto the churches, there can bee no Christian desirous to retaine that name, that may oppose against the same; yet for a further manifestation of these truthes, vnto all, that will not desperatly dwell in error, I will now proue in particular, how euery one of the Apostles, and Euangelists, both beleeued, practised, and taught these misteries. And first to begin with the foure Euange-

uangelifts, and S. Paule, who haue committed thefe Chriftian holy fecrets, to holie writinge; I will fhew how both in thefe
their facred fcriptures, they teach and allowe the facrifice of Maffe, and a facrificinge or maffinge preifthood, by order and
facred office to offer that facrifice. And to
put vs out of all doubt or queftion that this
is and was theire meaninge in thofe holy
fcriptures, I will proue, that euery one of
them was a true maffinge preift, and ac-
tually did offer, and celebrate the moft honorable facrifice of Maffe, in effential thinges, as the holy Catholicke maffing preifts
of the church of Rome now doe, and haue
euer moft religioufly done, in all ages. The
fame I will likewife proue, of all the other
Apoftles, in their order, onely I will craue
leaue of S. Peter, the firft, and cheifeft, to
remember him lafte in this matter; for as I
haue proued at large in other places, as a-
monge the Apoftles hee was the firft, and
allmofte onely Apoftle, which planted the
faith of Chrift in thefe parts of the world:
So wee in Britanie did firft receaue from
him, our holy maffinge and facrificinge
preifts, and preifthood, neuer hitherto al-

together

together difcontinued, or interrupted, but
by him and his fucceffors in the Apoftolicke fea of Rome firft founded , and euer
after fucceffiuely in all ages preferued in
this kingdome, as will appeare hereafter.

2. Therefore to begin with the Euangelifts and S. Paule, which fpeake of thefe
mifteries in fcripture, S.Mathew the Apoftle (and firft in order amonge the Euangelifts) writeth of Chrifts deliuery of this facrifice in thefe wordes, as our Englifh Proteftants by his maiefties priuiledge tranflate them . (*Matth. cap.* 26. *v.* 26. 27. 28.)
Iefus tooke breade and bleffed it, and brake it,
and gaue it to his difciples, and faid, take eate,
this is my body . And hee tooke the cup , and
gaue thankes , and gaue it to them fayinge,
drinke ye al of it: for this is my blood of the new
teftament, which is shed for many, for the re-
miffion of finnes . The Greeke text, which
thefe men fay muft bee here preferred , is
word by word as they tranflate, fpeakinge
of Chrifts body, that it was at that prefent
giuen there , and his blood in the prefent
tence shed for remiffion of finnes ἐκχυνόμενον
ἐις ἄφεσιν ἁμαρτιῶν. Therefore if Chrifts oblation , and giuing his body , and blood,
vppon

vppon the Croſſe was a ſacrifice , as all a-
gree, ſeeing it was ſo in reſpect it was there
giuen and offered for remiſſion of ſinnes,
here beeing the very ſame body and blood,
and giuen for remiſſion of ſinnes , it muſt
needes bee alſo a ſacrifice , and not onely
euchariſticall or of thanks giuing , but ſa-
tisfactory:for whatſoeuer taketh away ſinnes , by its owne vertue, as the Euangeliſt
here ſpeaketh of this, muſt needes be ſuch,
and Chriſts body and blood beeing of in-
finite value in themſelues and of their own
nature, can not but be ſatisfactorie for ſinnes, whenſoeuer, howſoeuer, & by whom-
ſoeuer they are offered, or giuen for remiſſion of ſinnes , though the limited power
of preiſts may bringe ſome limitation to
their ſatisfaction, the ordinance and inſtitution of Chriſt, ſo diſpoſing in this ſacrifice, as it is now daily offered by conſecrated preiſts, as the common opinion is , o-
therwiſe a thing of illimited worth, ſhould
bee of like deſeruinge, and ſatisfaction.

3. And this is ſo euident, that not onely
all learned Fathers, and antiquitie do from
hence teach, that Chriſt in this place inſtituted the ſacrifice of the new teſtament, as

I haue cited diuers before, but our greateſt
enemies and perſecutors, as namly the preſent Proteſtant Archbiſhop of Canterbury
the director of Maſter Maſon, and hee alſo
with others. (*Maſon. præfat. & lib· 5. cap. 6.
pag· 235. Abb. ibidem. Magdeburgent. in S.
Iren.*) acknowledge, particularly naminge
S. Irenæus, S. Chriſoſtome, and S. Gregorie, from them concluding in theſe words:
*That Chriſt did then teach the oblation of the
new teſtament, which the church throughout
all the world doth, when ſhee ſaith, this is my
body·* And they plainly ſay . (*Maſon and D.
Georg. Abbots ſupr·pag·233.*) that theſe wordes of Chriſt recited before by S. Matthew,
*this is my body which is giuen for you, and this
is my blood of the new teſtament which is ſhed
for you* , *doe argue a ſacrifice to God·* And if
this was not a ſacrifice, then by proteſtant
Religion, admittinge nothing but ſcriptures in matters of faith , Chriſt Ieſus was
not the preiſt after the order of Melchiſedech, which was promiſed; for exceptinge
this , the whole new teſtament is ſilent of
any preiſtly act, of that order, which hee
performed in all his life, and ſo that being
a diſtinctiue ſigne, of the true Meſſias, they
would

would depriue all mankinde of Redemption , and our moste bleſſed Sauiour of the title, and honour of redeeminge vs. Therfore thus they graunt . (*Abbots and Maſon ſupr. pag. 243.*) *Chriſt hauing offered himſelf, for a ſoueraigne ſacrifice, vnto his Father, ordeyned, that wee should offer a remembraunce thereof, vnto God, in ſteade of a ſacrifice.* Which they muſt needes vnderſtand of Chriſts oblation in this place , before his paſſion, for they make this before his commaundement , and power giuen to his Apoſtles, of celebrating this miſtery, by theſe words as theſe men tranſlate. (*Luc. cap. 22. ver. 19.*) *doe this in remembrance of mee .* So that Chriſt ordeyninge, that we ſhould do what hee did , as the words bee manifeſt, and Chriſt as they confeſſe there , *offered himſelfe for a ſoueraigne ſacrifice vnto his Father,* we muſt offer Chriſt in the ſame maner, for a ſoueraigne ſacrifice vnto God.

4. And for a cleare demonſtration, that together with the cõmaundement a preiſtlie ſacrificinge power was giuen by thoſe wordes, to his holy Apoſtles , and they by them made maſſing, and ſacrificing preiſts, to ſacrifice, as Chriſt by theſe proteſtants,

and

and the scripture before, did at that time
his blessed body, and body, it is not lawfull, or validate in either Religion of Catholicks, or Protestants, for any Christian
man, or woman to intermeddle to offer,
or minister in these things, whatsoeuer we
shall name them, or iudge them to bee, but
a Catholickly confecrated preist, by the
one, or protestant minister by the other,
therfore those sacred words, do this (*Matth.
cap.* 26.*v.* 20. *Marc. cap.* 14. *v.* 17.*Luc.c.*22.
v. 14.) gaue preistly and sacrificing power
to his Apostles, only prefent, by the Euangelists: for if they had beene generally fpoken vnto all Chriftians, all Chriftians
should both haue power,& were boūd vnder dānation to take vpon them to minifter
in fuch things; for the wordes, *doe this*, to
whomfoeuer they were fpoken, conteyne
an exprefle commaundement, to bee performed.

5. And to make this matter more euident, it is manifeft by the proteftant parlament ftatute of Kinge Edward the fixt,
Queene Elizabeth,and King Iames. (*Sta-
tut.* 1. *Edw.* 6.1.*Eliz. & * 1.*Iacob. fupr.*) That
the Proteftants of England neither doe,
nor

nor by their Religion may, make it a matter of commaundement and neceffitie, for
lay parfons to communicate vnder both
kindes, but doe freely acknowledge, that
in the firft fiue hundred yeares of Chrift,
the Sacrament was miniftred vnto, and receaued of the laitie fometimes in one, fom-
times in both kindes, and yet the practife
of the church was holy in thofe dayes, therfore there neuer was a generall commaundement to al Chriftians to receaue in both
kindes: yet S. Paul fettinge downe Chrifts
ordinance, and inftitution of this holy facrifice, he faid both concerninge his body
and blood, he gaue this expreffe commaundement: *doe this in remembrance of mee* . (1.
Corinth. cap. 11. *ver.* 24. 25.) And therefore
Tatianus Alexandrinus difciple to S. Iu-
ftine the martyr, in his harmony of the
ghofpels, doth fet downe thofe wordes of
Chrift to his Apoftles. Doe this in commemoration of me, both after the deliuery of
his body and blood vnto them . (*Tatianus
Alexand. Harmon. Euang. cap.* 155.) Therfore all they being preifts, and onely prefent then, muft needs bee made preifts and
facrificinge preifts, by thofe confecratory
word

words of Chriſt, then onely ſpoken vnto
them.

6. Which is made moſte euident in the
caſe of S. Thomas the Apoſtle, who by o-
pinions Catholicke and Proteſtant was a
preiſt, and as hereafter a ſacrificinge maſſinge preiſt, yet hee was not preſent when
Chriſt ſaid to the other Apoſtles in the 20.
chapter of S. Iohns ghoſpell ; *receue yee the*
holy Ghoſt, whoſe ſoeuer ſinnes yee remit, they
are remitted vnto them: and whoſe ſoeuer ſin-
nes yee retayne, they are retayned · And as
proteſtants affirme made them preiſts; and
they themſelues in their booke of pretended conſecration, only vſe theſe in makīg
miniſters; for the ſcripture ſaith plainly, and
immediatly in the next words: *But Thomas*
one of the twelue, called Didimus, was not
with them when Ieſus came. (ver. 24.) neither when hee ſaid theſe words vnto them;
but when the reſt of the Apoſtles told him
they had ſeene Chriſt, it followeth in the
ſame place by Engliſh Proteſtants reading:
The other diſciples therefore ſaid vnto him,
wee haue ſeene the Lord. (ver. 25.) *But hee*
ſaid vnto them, except I ſhall ſee in his hands
the print of the nailes, and put my finger into
the

the print of the nailes, and thrust my hand into his side, I will not beleeue. (*v.* 26.) These be the very next words of the Euangelist, vnto the former; and then immediatly followeth, how eight dayes after, Christ appeared againe, S. Thomas beeing present, and cured his incredulitie.

7. So that it is most plaine, and euident, that S. Thomas receaued the cheife preistlie power in the last supper of Christ, and by those his powerfull wordes, when hauing celebrated the high preistly function of sacrificinge after the order of Melchisedech, in consecrating and offeringe for our sacrifice, his most blessed body and blood vnder the formes of breade and wine, and beeinge to leaue this preistly sacrificinge power in his church, hee did first communicate and giue it to his Apostles, sayinge vnto them as our protestants translate. *This doe in remembrance of mee.* (*Luc. cap.* 22. *ver.* 19. 1. *Cor.* 11. *ver.* 24. 25.) where wee may boldly reade, sacrifice this in remembrance of me, or in commemoration of me. For so both the Hebrue, and Greeke, and Latine also wil giue allowance, as I haue proued before. Yet if wee should take them onely,

onely , for the common action of doinge,
seeing in the very common sence of doing,
it conteyneth both a power & commaundement , to doe that , which Christ there
did, which by all testimonies before , and
allowance of protestants themselues , was
his moste holy offeringe , and sacrificinge
his sacred body,and for sinnes;It must needes giue both power, and precept to his A-
postles, to doe the same, *doe this* , or , *this
doe* : otherwise neither the Apostles , nor
preists truely consecrated after them , had
done that, which Christ did , and which
he gaue power and commaund vnto them
to do;but some other thing,not commaunded,and which they had no authoritie, or
warrant to doe;which is the transgressing,
vncōmaunded,and vnwarranted lamentable condition of all those , that deny this
holy sacrifice, and presume to practise any
other thing in place thereof.

8. Therefore seeinge no man doth , or
can pretend , but there was onely one true
consecrator, time, place,maner, and order
of consecratinge, both S. Thomas,and the
other Apostles,for holy preists, it euidentlie followeth, they were all consecrated by
Christ

Chrift in the action, time, place, and order as is before remembred; and that they were fo confecrated facrificinge maffinge preifts. Which our learned Proteftants of England plainely teach vs to bee fo. The great Archbifhop, champion for the Englifh Proteftants, when he fo profeffed him felfe, writing with their greateft applaufe, and priuiledge, fpeakinge of the time, place, and maner, when, where, and how the Apoftles were made preifts, and of theire two fpirituall powers, iurifdiction, and order, hee faith of this. (*Marcus Anto. Reipub. Ecclefiaft. l. 2. cap. 1. num. 3.*) *Ordinis ego poteftatem intelligo nunc ad conficiendam Eucharißiam, & facrificij in cruce per Iefum Chriftum peracti memoriam celebrandam: ad quod Sacerdotium quoddam eft neceffarium. Ad hoc Sacerdotium promoti funt Apoftoli à Chrifto Domino, in vltima cana, quando eis dixit: hoc facite in meam commemorationem.* (*Luc. 22. & 1. Cor. 11.*) By power of order, I now vnderftand power to confecrate the Eucharift, and celebrate the memory of the facrifice, which Chrift perfected vpon the Croffe, to which a certaine preifthood is neceffary; to this preifthood the Apo-

stles

ftles were promoted in the laft fupper, whē
hee faid vnto them, do this in my commemoration.

9. And againe. (*Marcus Anto. fupr. l. 2.
cap. 4. pag. 19.*) *Quando Euchariſtiæ confi-
ciendæ ipſis dabat poteſtatem , dixit eis : hoc
facite in meam commemorationem: nimirum id
quod me videtis nunc facere, & vos facite: hoc
eſt ſumite panem, benedicite, frangite, & por-
rigite : ſimiliter & vinum . Et conſeqnenter
Apoſtoli ex ipſo facto Chriſti inſtructi , certē
diuina Chriſti inſtitutione dabant Euchariſtiam.* When Chriſt gaue vnto his Apoſtles
power to confecrate the Euchariſt, he faid
vnto them : doe this in my commemoration: That is, what you fee mee now to do,
doe you the fame; that is take bread, bleſſe
it, breake, reach: likewiſe alfo wine. And
confequently the Apoſtles armed by that
fact of Chriſt, certainely by the diuine inftitution of Chriſt, did giue the Euchariſt.
And in an other place . (*Marc. Anton. l. 2.
cap. 4. pag. 118.*) *de Sacroſancta Euchariſtia:
Ipſius neceſſitatem toties inculcauit: niſi man-
ducaueritis carnem filij hominis , & biberetis
eius ſanguinem, non habebitis vitam in vobis.
Panis quem ego dabo caro mea eſt , pro mundi
vita*

vita. (*Ioh. 6. Luc. 22.*) *postea in vltima cæna:*
accepto pane gratias egit, & fregit, & dedit
eis, dicens, hoc est corpus meum, quod pro vo-
bis datur : hoc facite in meam commemoratio-
nem. Panis consecrationem in corpus Christi,
& vini in sanguinem, ipse coram Apostolis fe-
cit: eandem ipsi quoque vt facerent, frange-
rent, & darent, expresse mandauit. Concerninge the holy Eucharist, Christ did very
often inculcate the necessitie of it : except
you shall eate the flesh of the sonne of man,
and drinke his blood, you shall not haue
life in you. The food which I will giue, is
my flesh for the life of the world. After in
his laste supper, when he had taken bread,
he gaue thankes, brake, and gaue to them
saying, this is my body which is giuen for
you: doe this in my commemoration. Hee
made the consecration of breade into the
body of Christ, & of wine into his blood,
before the Apostles, and expressely-com-
maunded, that they also should do the same
consecration of bread & wine into Christs
body and blood.

10. And in an other place he teacheth,
with S. Chrisostome, whom he followeth
therein, and other holy auncient Fathers.
(*Marc.*

(*Marc. Anto. l. 1. cap. 1. pag. 9. Chrisostom.
hom. 17. in epist. ad Hebr.*) That the sacrifice which the Apostles were here commaunded to offer by Chrifts wordes, *doe
this*, and which by that power they did offer, *and which all truely consecrated preists did
after offer, was the same body & blood of Christ,
which hee himselfe offered, the same, and no
other sacrifice.* Hoc facite in meam commemorationem. *Quid ergo nos? ait Chrisostomus,
nonne per singulos dies offerrimus? offerrimus
quidem. Et vna est hostia, & non multæ. Quomodo vna est, non multæ? quia semel oblata est
in Sancto Sanctorum: hoc autem sacrificium
exemplar est illius: idipsum semper offerrimus.
Pontifex noster ille, qui hostiam mundantem
nos obtulit: ipsam offerrimus & nunc, quæ
tunc oblata quidem consumi non potest.* And
much more to as great effect, or greater,
and yet at his pleasure hee doth maine, and
make lame the sentences of that holy Author. And to auoide the friuolous cauill of
some about the wordes, *in my remembrance,*
or, *commemoration of mee*, whereby they
would haue it gathered, that this is onely a
commemoratiue sacrifice, or commemoration of that sacrifice, this man with all
other

other Proteſtants. (*Marc. Ant. l. 1. cap. 12,*
pag. 146 147. Mumer. 26. 27.) and the expreſſe ſcriptures are witnes, that the preiſts
and ſacrifice of the lawe of nature and
Moiſes, of Adam, Seth, Enoch, Noe, Sem,
Abraham, Iſaac, Iacob, and his twelue ſonnes, Iob, Melchiſedech, Aaron and all in
the lawe were true preiſts, and ſacrificers;
yet they were in all Chriſtian learninge,
but figures of the truth in the time of the
Meſſias.

11. Therefore if this were onely a commemoration, it ſhould at leaſte by as great
reaſon and authoritie, bee alſo a ſacrifice,
and the parſon that celebrateth it, a ſacrificinge preiſt, both beeing farr more excellent then thoſe preiſts, and ſacrifices. And
the words, *in remembrance, or commemora-*
tion, are ſo far from hindering the truth, of
theſe preiſts and ſacrifice, that they rather
giue a ſecond power, & vertue vnto them,
euen by theſe proteſtants themſelues; for
they haue told vs before, that by theſe wordes, *doe this,* Chriſt gaue power to conſecrate the bread and wine into his body and
blood, and doe what hee did in that ſacrifice, then addinge after the wordes, *in re-*

mem-

membrance, or commemoration, he gaue them
a second power, and commaundement different from the other, yet both of them
preistly and sacrificall: otherwise Christ
himselfe should bee said (which cannot be)
that hee did consecrate and offer this remembrance of himselfe, and his owne action: Therefore the words must needs con-
teine a double virtuall power and comma-
und to the Apostles, the one part and principall beeing, to doe that Christ did, expressed plainely in the powerfull wordes,
doe this, the other in remembrance or commemoration, conteyned in the same terms.
Which was by a (then) publick protestant
preachinge minister both preached publickly, and with publicke allowance after printed in this maner. *Edw. Maie serm.*
of the communion of Saints, printed by Iohn
Dauson an· 1621. pag. 6.

12. *God hath giuen to preists a power ouer*
his owne naturall bodie, which is himselfe: for
to them onely was it said: doe this in remem-
brance of mee: by which words they haue com-
mission to dispose of that very body, which was
giuen for the life of the world, and of that in-
naluable blood, which was shed to redeeme sin-
full

full soules : for which cause the Bishops and presbyters haue, as antiquitie can tell, beene honored with an honor, which no Kinge, no Angel had euer giuen him. They are the makers of Chrifts body, they doe a worke which none but the holy Ghoſt beſides them euer did. And in the margine hee thus citeth Iſodor Peluſota, l. 2. epiſt. 5. ἐξꜳσίαν οἴσαν ꜳ ꜳ οι τῆς γῆς βασιλεῖς ἔχꜳσι. *ſuch a power the Kings of the earth haue not. An other ſpeakinge of the conſecratóry preiſtly power, by thoſe words of Chriſt, ſpoken in his parſon: This is my body : This is my blood, concludeth. (Couel def. of Hooker pag. 116. 117. 276.) The omnipotency of God maketh it his body. And of preiſts: To theſe parſons God imparteth power ouer that naturall body, which is himſelfe, a worke which antiquitie calleth the making of Chriſts body. And of preiſtly power: By bleſſing viſible elements it maketh them inuiſible grace, it hath to diſpoſe of that fleſh which was giuen for the life of the world, and that blood which was powred out to redeeme ſoules. Others ſay: The ſacrifice of the altare, and vnbloody ſacrifice, were vſed in the primatiue church. The primatiue church did offer ſacrifice at the altare for the deade, ſacrifice*

K 2

*for the deade was a tradition of the Apostles
and auncient Fathers . Ærius was iustly condemned of heresie by the primatiue church, for
denying sacrifice for the dead . Middlet. Papistom. pag. 51.91. 113. 49. 137. 139. 47. 48.
Feild. l. 3. cap. 29. pag. 138.*

13. And to put vs out of doubt, that this
is, or should bee the common doctrine and
Religion of all English Protestants , their
chosen champion, with greatest allowance
amonge them , as hee affirmeth , writeth
plainely . *Hæc est fides Regis , hæc est fides
Ecclesiæ Anglicanæ* : this is the faith of the
Kinge , this is the faith of the church of
England. (*Io. Casaub. resp. ad Card. Peron.
pag. 51. 52.*) And their publicke statute of
al the Protestant Princes of England saith
so, and so decreeth to be obserued of all, authentically prouinge in protestants Religion , that this most holy sacrifice of the
altar, was instituted by Christ, *that it is his
body and blood, broken and shed for remission
of sinnes, & by the omnipotent words of Christ,
This is my body this is my blood, being of eternall infallible and vndoubted truth, so consecrated by truely and duely ordeyned preists
vnto the end of the worlde .* Therefore most

euident

euident it is, by all kinde of Arguments
and teſtimonies, that the holy Apoſtle and
Euangeliſt S. Matthew, as the reſt alſo,
did, and of dutie was bound to offer the
moſt holy ſacrifice of Maſſe. And that hee
thus did, as the reſt of the Apoſtles alſo did,
it is manifeſt by diuers antiquities, which
wee haue of this holy Apoſtle.

14. Firſt it is commonly agreed vppon,
both by Catholicke and Proteſtant writers, that hee preached, and ſuffered Martyrdome in Ethiopia, hauing firſt conuerted the Kinge and many others, and that
of all nations the Chriſtians of Ethiopia
were euer moſt deuout to the holy ſacrifice
of Maſſe, the proteſtants themſelues ar witneſſes, and as they haue had that holy ſacrifice from their firſt receauinge the faith
of Chriſt, which in all things as tranſſub-
ſtantiation of bread and wine into the bodie and bloody of Chriſt, according to the
doctrine of S. Matthew, before and offeringe of the ſaid bleſſed body, and blood,
with inuocation of Saints, and prayer for
the deade, ſo their tradition aſcribeth it,
to S. Matthew the Apoſtle, as ordinarily
it is referred vnto him. And not onely S.

K 3   Abdias

An historie of the holy preisthood, and Abdias which liued in that time, by his workes vsually receaued, Iulius Africanus, and others be witnesses, that he said Masse, and was martyred at the holy altare by Kinge Hirtacus, but that vndoubted historie of his life and death, which the vniuersall church of Christ followeth, approueth and proposeth vnto vs, so testifieth: *Origen. in Genes. Euseb. histor. lib. 3. cap. 1. Socrat. lib. 1. c. 15. Doroth. in Synops. Magdeburg. cent. 1. l. 2. col. 777. 776. Edw. Grimston. in Presbyter. Iohn Pag. 1088. 1089. Missa Æthiopum siue S. Matthæi Apostoli Biblioth. SS. Patr. Tom. 6. Iudoc. Cocc. Tom. 2. Sebastian. Munster. Cosmograph. l. 6. cap 57. Abdias & Iul, Afr. c. l. de vita Apost. in S. Math. Metaphrast. in S. Matth. Anton. part. 1. Petr. anot. l. 8. cap. 100.*

15. *Rege mortuo, Hirtacus eius successor Ephigeniam Regiam filiam, vellet sibi dari in matrimonium: Matthæum, cuius opera illa virginitatem Deo vouerat, & in Sancto proposito perseuerabat, ad altare mysterium celebrantem, iussit occidi vndecimo calendas Octobris. Vita S. Matth. Apostoli in Breuiario die 21. Septembr.* Kinge Aeglippus whome S. Matthew had conuerted to the faith being deade,

deade, Hirtacus his successor desiringe to
Mary his daughter Ephigenia, shee by the
helpe of S. Matthew, hauinge vowed virginitie to God, and perseueringe in her holie purpose, hee commaunded S. Matthew
to bee killed, as hee was celebrating Masse
at the altare, on the eleuenth of the calends
of October. Which history and relation,
must needs bee approued by the Protestant
church of England, keeping his festiuitie
with the former histories, the church of
Rome, the auncient Martyrolodges of
Rome, S. Bede, Vsuardus, and others vpon
the same day. (*Engl: Protest. Comm: Booke
in fest. S. Matth. Apostol. & calend. 21. Septembr. 11. cal. Octobr. Martyr. Rom. Bed. &
Vsuard. eod. die & Ado Treuer. 16.*) To which
the auncient Manuscript of an author A-
nonimus, published in print, all most an
hundred yeares since by Fredericus Nausea
Bishop of Vienna, writtin as hee saith, *cha-
racteribus plusquam vetustis, in exceedinge
old characters, in a most auncient library,* giueth this ample testimony, hauinge before
related the history of S. Matthewes preachinge there: *Cumque omnes respondissent
Amen, & mysteria Domini celebrata fuis-*

sent,

fent, & Miffam fufcepiffet omnis Ecclefia, re-
tinuit fe Sanctus Matthæus iuxta altare, vbi
corpus ab eo fuerat Chrifti confectum, vt illic
Martyrium expectauit: nam expanfis manibus
orantem, fpiculator miffus ab Hyrtaco, à tergo
puncti ictu feriens, Apoftolum Dei, Chrifti
Martyrem fecit. And when all had anfwe-
red *Amen*, and the myfteries of our Lord
were celebrated, and all the Chriftian af-
fembly had heard Maffe, S. Matthew kept
himfelfe ftill by the altare, where the body
of Chrift was confecrated by him, and ex-
pected Martyrdome. For as hee was praying with his hands ftretched forth, the exe-
cutioner beeing fent from Kinge Hyrtacus
cominge behinde him, thruft the Apoftle
of God throughe, and made him a Martyr
of Chrift. *Anonymm antiq. l. in vitas, mira-*
cula & pafsionis Apoftolorum.in paf.S.Matth.
Apoft. cap. 6.

16. And this may fully fatisfie for S.
Matthew the Apoftle, that he was a facrificinge and maffinge preift, and did both
fay Maffe, and ordeyne other holy maffing
and facrificinge preifts, and deliuered a
forme of that holy facrifice to the Chriftians of Ethiopia. I haue bene more large

in him, becaufe hee was the firft amonge
the Apoftles which in his ghofpell wrote
of thefe facred myfteries, and beeinge an
Apoftle, and confirmed in grace, neither
did, nor could in this, or any article of
Chriftian Religion, beleeue, or practife o-
therwife, then Chrift commaunded, and
inftituted, and the reft of the Apoftles and
Euangelifts did alfo beleeue, teache, and
exercife, as I haue taught in generall of
them all. Now in particular of euery of
them with fo much breuitie as I may, the
difficultie beeinge already cleared, vntill I
come to S. Peter, in whom beeinge befides
his primacy amonge the Apoftles, and in
the whole church of Chrift, our protopa-
rent Paftor and Father in Chrift, I muft
fpend fome longer time, in that refpect to
deduce our holy facrificinge, and maffing
preifthood from him.

17. The next of the Euangeliftes, and
fcripture writers, which entreateth of this
bleffed miftery, is S. Marke, whofe words
in his ghofpell as our proteftants tranflate
them, concerninge Chrifts inftitution of
this facrifice, are thefe : *Iefus tooke breade,
and bleffed, and brake it, and gaue to them*
and

and said, take, eate: This is my body, and hee tooke the cup, and when he had giuen thanks, hee gaue it to them: and they all dranke of it, and hee said vnto them, this is my blood of the new testament, which is shed for many. (*Marc. cap.* 14 *ver.* 22. 23.) Where wee see, as in S. Matthew before, so heare S. Marke doth assure vs, that the misteries there celebrated, were Chrifts body and blood, shedd for many; and so accordinge to that which is already proued in this matter, must needes bee an holy sacrifice in the iudgement of this Euangelist: and that by his owne continual vse and practise of saying Masse, and deliueringe a perfect forme and order thereof, vnto the churches where hee preached and liued, we haue many testimonies.

18. Firft the very Masse it selfe which hee deliuered to the church of Alexandria, and others which hee founded, is yet vsed in those parts, and knowne to all antiquaries. (*Missa S. Marci, seu Ecclesiæ Alexandrinæ. in Biblioth. patrum.*) and it doth agree in all matters of subftance, with the Masse of the Latine church. And he himselfe had so reuerent opinion of this most holy sacrifice, that hee thought himselfe vnworthie

to

to offer it; and therfore as S. Hierome writeth, cut off his Thombe, but it was miraculously restored, and hee vsually offered
that holy sacrifice, as wee haue testimonies
euen of this our owne nation, farr beyond
exception: to omit others S. Bede S. Marianus and Florentius Wigorniensis, al which
affirme in these same words : *Marcus disci-*
pulus & interpres Apostoli Petri, mittente
Petro porrexit in Ægiptum, & primus Ale-
xandriæ Christum annuntians, constituit Ec-
clesiam, & postquam constitutis & confirma-
tis Ecclesijs per Lybiam, Marmoricam, Ammo-
nicam, Pentapolim, Alexandriam atque Ægip-
tum vniuersam, ad vltimum tentus est à Pa-
ganis qui remanserant Alexandriæ, qui vi-
dentes eum die sancto Paschæ Missas facien-
tem, miserunt funem in collo eius. Marke the
disciple, and Interpreter of Peter, beeing
sent by Peter, went into Egipt, and was the
first that preached Christ at Alexandria,
and founded that church, and after foun-
ding and confirming the churches through
Lybia, Marmorica, Ammonica, Penta-
polis, Alexandria and all Egipt, at the last
was apprehended by the Pagans, which
remayned at Alexandria, who seeinge him
saying

faying Maſſe, on the holy feaſt of Eaſter,
caſt a rope, about his necke, and ſo put him
to death. *Beda in Martyrolog. 7. cal. Maij.*
Marian. Scot. l. 2. ætat. 6. pag. 233. in Ne-
rone. Florent. Wigorn.

19. Thus theſe three auncient & learned
Engliſh writers, with others. And this forme of Maſſe which he vſed & deliuered to
theſe churches, ſeemeth by Antonius Sa-
bellicus, to haue beene written by him at
Aquileia in Italy, whether he was firſt ſent
by S. Peter before hee went to Alexandria:
for hee tellinge with the common opinion
how hee wrote his ghoſpell at Rome, by
the warrant and approbation of S. Peter,
and his coming to Aquileia, ſaith he wrote
there alſo ſomethinges, *hic quoque aliqua*
ſcripſiſſe creditur, and moſt likely his Maſſe
becauſe wee finde no mention of any other
his works, but his ghoſpel writté at Rome,
and that.

20. And to make all ſure by our Engliſh
Proteſtant antiquaries, and other writers,
who aſcribe the greateſt credit in theſe
matters to the brittiſh Authors, their Religion and practiſe, before the vniting themſelues with the ſucceſſors of S. Auguſtine,
and

and the Romane church , there is yet extant a very old manuscript , written by a Brittish Christian , before that vnion allmost a thousand yeares since , which our protestants intitle, *prima institutio ecclesiastici seruitij, the first institution of the ecclesiasticall seruice.* (*M. S. Britan. antiq. pr. Stores in exordio, prima institutio ecclesiastici seruitij.*) in which manifestly mention is made that S. Marke the Euangelist did write a forme therof, and that very forme of Masse vsed and penned by S. Marke, was practised here in Britanie, when it was first conuerted, in or nere the Apostles time : of this I shall speake more at large when I come to S. Peter. And this will suffice for S. Marke.

21. S. Luke the next of this holy company , is moste plaine of them all for holye sacrifice , for first hee doth plainelie distinguish the consecrated cup , from the other which he calleth by protestants translation, the fruite of the vine. (*Luc. cap. 22. ver.* 18.) an exception with vnlearned protestants · And then by their owne translation, he thus writeth of Christs action herin· (*ver.* 19·) *And hee tooke breade, and gaue thankes, and brake it , and gaue vnto them, saying,*

saying, this is my body which is giuen for you,
doe this in remembrance of mee. (ver. 20.)
likevvise also the cup after supper, saying, this
is the nevv testament in my blood, vvhich
is shed for you. Where as I haue proued before, both by protestants and all witnesses, our holy sacrifice of Masse is plainely
instituted, which our protestants proue by
one of the most auncient antiquities of our
Christian Britans, a sermon as Master Foxe
saith. (*Act. and monum. pag.* 1142. *sermon.*
translat. by Ælfricus.) so auncient and of so
great authoritie in this kingdome, that it
was vsually reade in the church here in the
yeare of Christ 366. aboue two hundred
yeares before S. Augustines cominge hither, and translated into the Saxon language out of Latine by Kinge Aelfricus in the
yeare 996. Which speaketh of Christ in
these words: Hee blessed breade before his
,, suffering and diuided it to his disciples thus
,, saying: eate of this, it is my body, and doe
,, this in my remembrance. Also hee blessed
,, wine, in one cup, and said: drinke yee all
,, of this, this is my blood that is shed for ma-
,, nie in forgiuenes of sinnes. The Apostles
,, did as Christ commaunded, that is, they
blessed

they bleſſed bread and wine to howſell a- „
gaine afterward in his remembrance: euen „
ſo alſo their ſucceſſors and all preiſtes by „
Chriſts commaundement doe bleſſe bread „
and wine, to howſell in his name with the „
Apoſtolicke bleſſinge. „

22. And againe: In the old lawe faith- „
full men offered to God diuers ſacrifices „
that had foreſignification of Chriſts body, „
which for our ſinnes he himſelfe to his hea- „
uenly Father hath ſince offered to ſacrifi- „
ce , certainly this howſell which wee doe „
now hallow at Gods altar, is a remembran- „
ce of Chriſts body which heé offered for „
vs: and of his blood which heé ſhed for vs: „
So heé himſelfe commaunded , doe this in „
my remembraunce . And ſhewinge how
Chriſt is wholly and truely preſent in euerie parcell of this bleſſed ſacrifice of Maſſe,
it addeth : That innocent Lambe which „
the old Iſraelites did then kill , had ſignifi- „
cation after ghoſtlye vnderſtandinge of „
Chriſts ſufferinge, who vnguiltie, ſhed his „
holy blood for our redemption. Herof ſinge „
Gods ſeruants at euery Maſſe , *Agnus Dei* „
qui tollis peccata mundi miſerere nobis: That „
is in our ſpeach: Thou Lambe of God that
takeſt

takeſt away the ſinnes of the world haue
mercy vpon vs.

23. Where is plainely proued by theſe
proteſtants antiquitie, that Chriſt did in
thoſe wordes of S. Luke, both inſtitute the
moſte holy ſacrifice of Maſſe, for that E-
uangeliſt, and all preiſts to offer, and that
the Lambe of God that taketh away the
ſinnes of the world (onely Chriſt Ieſus) is
preſent there, and was publickly prayed
vnto as preſent, in our firſt Britane primatiue church in this kingdome. Therefore
no Chriſtiã of Britanie can make it a queſtion, but S. Luke an holy Euangeliſt, did
in this holy miſtery, as Chriſt had inſtituted, by his owne ghoſpell, and the other
Euangeliſts and Apoſtles, did preach and
practiſe: Which is farther confirmed out of
the hiſtory of his life, wherin we finde that
hee erected altars, and conſecrated ſacrificing and maſſing preiſts, no others known
to Chriſtians in that time. This will more
appeare when I come to S.Paul whoſe both
companion, and ſcribe and ſecretary in
ſome ſort hee was, and ſo could not bee of
an other opinion, or practiſe in this point,
then that great Apoſtle. *Metaphraſt. in vit.*
S.

S. Luc. Gul. Eisengren. cent. 1. part. 5. dist.
7. Hieron. l. de vir. illustris. in S. Luca.

24. The holy Apostle and Euangelist
S. Iohn bringeth Christ speakinge in these
wordes, as our protestants translate them,
(*Ioh. cap. 6, v. 51.*) *I am the liuinge breade
which came downe from heauen. If any man
eate of this breade, hee shall liue for euer: and
the breade that I will giue, is my flesh vvhich
I vvill giue for the life of the vvorlde. The
Ievves therefore stroue amonge themselues,
saying hovv can this man giue vs his flesh to
eate? Then Iesus said vnto them, verelye
I say vnto you, except yee eate the flesh of the
sonne of man, and drinke his blood, yee haue
no life in you. Who so eateth my flesh, and
drinketh my blood, hath eternall life, and I
vvill raise him vp, at the last day. For my
flesh is meate in deede, and my blood is drinke
in deede. Hee that eateth my flesh, and drinketh my blood, dvvelleth in mee, and I in him.
As the liuinge Father hath sent mee, and I
liue by the Father: so hee that eateth me, euen
hee shall liue by mee. This is the bread vvhich
came dovvne from heauen: not as your Fathers did eate Manna and are deade: hee that
eateth of this breade, shall liue for euer.*

L   25. These

25. These words bee so euident, for the reall presence of Christ in the sacrifice of Masse, by all testimonies of antiquitie, that as I haue shewed before, none but incredulous people, and like Kinge Achis will denie it. And for Britanie the lately cited antiquitie that was publickly reade, in our churches here so longe before S. Augustines cominge hither, doth with the whole cōsent of our church, in or before the yeare of Christ 366. so approue it, citing all these words of S. Iohn which I haue related, to that purpose. (*the old Britt. serm. supr. apud Foxe pag. 1142. & alios.*) and no man can better expound S. Iohn, then S. Iohn himselfe, who as wee are assured both by Catholicke and Protestant antiquaries, and authorities, did both say Masse, and consecrated sacrificinge and massinge preists, to doe the same. So wee are taught by *Eusebius Emissenus,* or *Faustus Reginensis, S. Bede, Haymo, the author of the scholasticall history, Smaragdus, Durantes, Honorius, Vincentius, Nicolaus Methonensis,* and others. *Euseb. Emis. seu Faust. Regin. hom. in fest. S. Ioan. Bed. homil. in id. dixit Iesus Petro sequere me. Haymo Homil. 2. in festo S. Ioan & Homil.*

mil. 1. *hiſtor. ſcholaſtic. cap.* 106. *Smarag.*
Abb. in collect. in Euangel. in feſt. S. Ioan:
Duran. l.7. c.42. de diu. offic. Honer. ſerm. in
feſt. S. Ioan. Vincent. l.11. c.44. Nichol. Me-
thon. l. de corp. Chriſti. And we haue both
Catholick & Proteſtant teſtimony for this,
of our own nation, a preiſt of Eaton in his
holy trauailes aboue 200. yeares ſince, and
a proteſtant miniſter thus approuinge and
relatinge from them : *Ad occidentalem par-*
tem Eccleſiæ, quæ eſt in monte Sion, eſt lapis
rubens præ altari, qui quidem lapis portatus
erat de monte Sinay per manus Angelorum ad
preces S. Thomæ reuertentis ab India: ſuper
quem celebrabat ſanctus Ioannes Euangeliſta
coram beatiſsima virgine Maria Miſſam, per
multos annos, poſt Aſcenſionem Domini. At
the Weſt ende of the church which is in
mount Sion, there is a redd ſtone ſtanding
in ſteade of an altare, the which ſtone was
tranſported thither from the mount Sinay
by the hands of Angels, at the prayers of
S. Thomas, when he returned from India:
vpon this ſtone S. Iohn the Euangeliſt did
celebrate and ſay Maſſe, before the bleſſed
virgin Mary, many yeares after the Aſcenſion of our Lord, *Gulielm. Way Etonenſis*

L 2   *pres-*

presbyter. l. Itinerar. cap. loca sancta montis Sinay. an. D. 1420. Hackluyts. booke of trauailes in Gul. Way cap. mount Sinay. And he was so daily deuoted to this holy sacrifice, that as the auncient Anonymus writer of his and the other Apostles liues doth witnes, hee celebrated it, the very day he died, and was buried by the altare. *Anonimus antiq. in vit. miracula & pass. Apostolorum in Ioanne cap. 10.*

26. S. Paule the laste of our holy writers of these mysteries, saith plainely by our protestants translation. (*1. Corinth. cap. 11. 23. 24. 25.*) *I haue receaued of the Lord, that which also I deliuered vnto you, that the Lord Iesus the same night in which he was betraied, tooke bread, and when hee had giuen thankes, hee brake it, and said; Take, eate, this is my body which is broken for you : This doe in remembrance of mee , and after the same maner also hee toke the cup, when he had supped, sayinge ; This cup is the new testament in my blood: this doe yee as often as yee drinke it, in remembrance of mee.* Where wee see a double power & commaundement also of Christ vnto his Apostles, both to consecrate and comunicate, both his body and blood: And
yet

yet there is no commaundement in any Religion Catholick or Proteſtant, for any but preiſts to doe all theſe thinges, and to them onely when they offer the holy ſacrifice of Chriſts body and blood in Maſſe, for if at any other time in ſicknes or otherwiſe they communicate, they doe it only as other Catholick lay parſons doe; And many caſes there bee in the Religion of Proteſtants, in which communicants are not bounde to receaue in both kinds: and it is approued and enacted by the publicke ſtatute of all our Proteſtant Princes that euer were in England, Kinge Edward the ſixt, Queene Eliſabeth, and our preſent ſoueraigne King Iames, that euen in the firſt primatiue and vnſpotted times of Chriſtianitie the Chriſtians did very often communicate in one onely kinde. (*Statut. parlament. 1. an. 1. Eduard. 6. 1. Eliſabeth. & an. 1. Iacob*) which could not bee tolerable, if the commaundement of Chriſt had beene generall vnto all to communicate in both, as it was to his Apoſtles, and all maſſinge or ſacrificinge preiſts in them.

27. And to make it moſt euident in all proceedings, that the powers & commaun-

dements

dements were communicated and giuen to
preifts onely, no parfons whatfoeuer Kinge
or Cæfar but preifts onely, and with proteftants their minifters which in their Religion cypher the places of preifts, doe or
may intermeddle with any of thofe powers
or commaunds of Chrift, doe this, either
in refpect of his bleffed body or blood, or
howfoeuer wee will terme thofe myfteries,
and yet to them to whome they were committed, they are plaine commaundements
imparatiue in all laguages Greeke, Latine,
Englifh, ποιῆτε, *facite*, doe this, in the imparatiue and commaundinge moode, and
maner of fpeach : and fo all men of whatfoeuer Religion doe vnderftand them, and
cannot poffibly truely vfe them in any o-
ther meaninge. And after prouinge how
the mifteries there deliuered, are the very
body and blood of Chrift, (1. *Corinth. cap.*
11. *ver.* 27. 28. 29. 30. 31.) although he had
faid before, that hee had deliuered vnto
them, that which hee receaued of Chrift,
and entreateth of the fame, diuers verfes before, and in 11. or 12. after euen to the end
of that chapter, yet not hauinge therein fet
downe the forme and order fully, how this
facri-

sacrifice was to bee celebrated, he concludeth thus in that chapter: *The rest I vvill
set in order vvhen I come.* (1. *Corinth. c.* 11.
v. vlt 34.) reseruing it to tradition, beeing
to longe a worke to bee comprised in an
epistle.

28. Whereuppon S. Augustine expoundinge those very words: *catera cum venero
ordinabo.* The other thinges I will order
when I come, as hee readeth, writeth in
these words. (*Augustin. epistol.* 118. *ad Ia-
nuarium cap. 6. Tom 2. operum eius.*) *vnde
intelligi datur, quia multum erat, vt in epistola totum illum agendi ordinem insinuaret,
quem vniuersa per orbem seruat Ecclesia, ab
ipso ordinatum esse, quod nulla morum diuersi-
tate variatur.* Whence wee are giuen to
vnderstand, that it was to much for him
to insinuate in an epistle, all that whole order of celebration, which the vniuersall
church obserueth in all the worlde, to bee
there ordered of him, which is not varied
with any diuersitie. Where wee see plainlie, that by the testimony of S. Paul himselfe warranted with this great authoritie,
hee deliuered a forme of Masse vnto the
church, and the church in S. Augustines

L 4 time

168 *An historie of the holy preisthood, and*
time still continued it without any diuersitie or difference to bee excepted against.

29. And where S. Paul writeth to S. Timothy according, to our protestants transl-
lation : *I exhort therefore , that first of all,*
supplications, prayers, intercessions, and gi-
uinge of thankes bee made for all men: for
Kings and all that bee in authoritie . (1. *Ti-*
moth. cap. 2. v. 1. 2.) it is the common interpretation of the holy Fathers, and expositors of scriptures , that hee there alludeth
to the order vsed in the holy sacrifice of
Masse , where these things were obserued,
as appeareth in the moste auncient Masses
wee haue extant . So S. Remigius , S. Augustine, S. Bede, S. Bruno , S. Anselme,
Haymo , Petrus Lombardus and diuers o-
thers writinge vppon that place, expound
them of the holy Masse. S. Remigius saith :
Apostolus dirigens hæc verba Timotheo, & in
illo tradidit omnibus Episcopis & presbyteris
omnique Ecclesiæ, quando deberent Missarum
solemnia celebrare, & pro omnibus orare. The
Apostle directinge these wordes to Timothie , and in him deliuered to all Bishops
and preists, and to the whole church, when
they shoulde celebrate the solemnities of
Masse,

Masse, and pray for all. *Remigius in* 1. *Ti-moth. cap.* 2. *Augustin. epistol.* 59. *quæst.* 5. *Beda in* 1. *Timoth. cap.* 2. *Bruno, Haimo, Petr. Lombard. & alij in eund. loc.*

30. And a little after: *Quam formam vel exemplum, omnes Ecclesiæ modo retinent: nam obsecrationes sunt quicquid præcedit in Missa-rum solemnijs, vbi incipit Sacerdos consecrare mysteria corporis & sanguinis Domini.* Which forme or example all churches doe still re-taine: for obsecrations are all whatsoeuer is said in the solemnities of the Masse, vntill that place where the preist beginneth to cō-secrate the misteries of the body, and blood of Christ, sayinge: *Te igitur clementissime Pater.* (Which bee the first words of the ca-non.) *Orations or prayers are those which the preist vttereth in the consecratiō of the Eucha-rist, euen to the fractiō of the body of our Lord: that is, when the preist putteth one part of the host into the chalice. Postulations are the bles-sings, which the Bishop saith ouer the people inuocating vpon them, the name of God. The giuing of thanks are prayers which the preist, after the people haue receaued, doth render vnto God the Father, who hath offered vnto them, the mistery of the body and blood of his*
                                                      sonne

sonne for theire saluation. Which all moste
word by worde and in the same sence is deliuered by S. Augustine in his 59. epistle.
quæstione 5·*Tom* 5 where he setteth downe
the whole order, and maner of the sacrifice
of Masse, as wee now vse it, and expoundeth S. Paules wordes to that purpose, as
the other holy and learned recited Father
likewise doth.

31. And to make all sure by our protestants themselues, they assure vs that S. Tro-
phimus mentioned by S. Paul, was his disciple, and left by him at Arles in Fraunce,
when hee passed from Rome to Spaine, al-
thoughe Eisengrenius proueth from the
french Annals and diuers antiquities, that
he was disciple both of S. Peter and S. Paul,
B. Petri & Pauli discipulus. (*Guliel. Eiseng.*
renten. 1. *part.* 1. *dist.* 3. *fol.* 53·) And was
of such fame and renowne as Pope Zosi-
mus 1200. yeares since the Romane Martyrologe. (*Zosimus To.* 1.*concil. Martyrol. Ro-*
man. in S. Trophimo die 29. *Decembris*, the
Magdeburgian Protestants with others testifie:) *ex eius prædicationis fonte, tota Gallia*
fidei Riuulos accepit : out of the fountaine of
his preaching all Fraunce receauing the chan-
nels

nels of faith . (*Magd. ecntur. 1. l. 1. in Tro-*
phimo.) yet the auncient Brittish antiquitie
suppressed by our protestants (of which before, and more herafter) is a sufficient warrant and witnesse , that hee deliuered and
obserued in Fraunce, a certaine forme and
order of the holy sacrifice of Masse, and the
same was vsed and practised , also both at
Rome and here in Britanie likewise at that
time. *M. S. Britan. antiq. pr. Stores in exor-*
dium.

32. And the same is as euidently proued, from his renowned scholler S. Denis
the Areopagite; Who in his booke of the
ecclesiasticall Hierarchie. (*cap. 5. 7. & epist.*
ad Demophil.) setteth downe the whole order of the sacrifice of Masse , and how the
preist behaued himselfe at the holy altare,
both before and after consecration , how
the catechumens , energumens, and publick penitents , were not permitted to bee
present , but onely to the prayers which
were before the oblation of the sacrifice:
He setteth down how bread and wine was
proposed on the altare, how blessed , consecrated into the body & blood of Christ,
and offered in sacrifice , How greate reuerence

rence and prayer was also vsed vnto Christ
vnder the externall species. *O tu diuinum
sacratissimumque Sacramentum , obducta
tibi per signa obscuritatum , quasi vela & in-
tegumenta , patefacta perspicuè nobis ostende,
mentisque nostræ oculos singulari , & qua ob-
tegi non potest, luce comple.* . Hee sheweth
how a memory of Saints is there made,
mystica Sanctorum recitatio sit. He teacheth
how the preist or Bishop , prayed for the
dead, for remission of their sinnes , and to
come to glory . *Precatur oratio illa diuinam
clementiam, vt cuncta dimittat per infirmita-
tem humanam admissa peccata defuncto, eum-
que in luce statuat,& regione viuorũ.* Which
is as much as the Romã church now vseth,
in that holy sacrifice of Masse. And hee re-
membreth how in the ende the preist acknowledgeth the dignitie of that holy sacrifice, to bee so great, that he was vnwor-
thy to offer it, but that Christ did both giue
power and commaund to doe it, when hee
said to his Apostles, *doe this in commemoration of mee. Religiosè simul, & vt Pontificem
decet, post sacras diuinorum operum laudes de
sacrificio , quod ipsius dignitatem superat , se
purgat, dum primò ad eum clamat, tu dixisti,*
hoc

hoc facite in meam commemorationem.

33. And how carefull, and diligent an obseruer, and practiser of this massing do-ctrine hee was, in act and deed, daily in his whole life, we may be assured by the wor-thie writers of his life and death, Hildui-nus Abbot of S. Denis in Fraunce where hee was buried, about 800. yeares since, Roswita or Roswida, not longe after and others, who confidently and from publick testimony, write, that neither his strict im-prisonment in a dungeon could hinder him from performing this holy dutie, but there both persuadinge the people present, and writinge vnto others absent, to confirme them more, said Masse in that vnfit place: & to proue how acceptable it was, Christ Iesus with a multitude of Angels appeared vnto them all, with such a light from hea-uen, as had beene seene, at the very time when they were to communicate, & com-forted his holy Martir. *Sed nec carcereis prae-sul praeclarus in antris desinit obsequium Do-mino persoluere dignum: sed docuit plebem studiosè conuenientem, ac celebrat sacrae solitò solemnia Missae: Est vbi caelestem debebat fran-gere panem, lux noua tristifico subito fulge-*
bat

bat in antro, in qua sidereæ regnator splendidus aulæ scilicet angelica pariter comitante caterua apparens, charum consolabatur amicum. Trithem. l. de scriptorib. in Hildonio. & Rosswida. Hilduinus Abb. in vita S. Dionisij Areopag. cap. 29. Rossvita l. de vit. S. Dionis. Areopag. & alijs.

THE X. CHAPTER.

How all the rest of the, Apostles in particular S. Andrew, Iames the great, Thomas, Iames the lesse, Philip, Bartholomew, Symon, Thaddæus, and Matthias, were sacrificinge Preists, and Apostles, and vsually offered the sacrifice of Masse.

N Ow let vs come to the rest of the holie Apostles which haue not in scriptures written of these misteries, and proue of them all, and in order (except S. Peter the first, whom I haue promised to put in the last place) that in their sacred functions, they offered the most holy sacrifice of Masse. And first to begin with S. Andrew. It is a receaued opinion. *Iodoc. Cocc. Tom. 2. l. 7. artic. 5. de purgator.* that this holy Apostle
did

did firſt deliuer that forme of Maſſe, which
was auntiently and from the beginninge
vſed in the church of Conſtantinople, and
after called the Maſſe of S. Iohn Chriſoſtome, the great and learned Patriarke of
that place, becauſe it was enlarged by him,
and is ſtil, as our proteſtants acknowledge,
vſed to this day in the churches of Greece.
Edwin. Sands relation of Religion. cap. 53. or
54. And that hee himſelfe did vſually and
daily offer this moſte ſacred oblation of
Chriſts body and blood , wee haue moſte
auncient and vndeniable teſtimonies, whether we will profeſſe our ſelues Catholicks
or proteſtants in Religion ; for both theſe
agree in this, that S. Andrew was martyred
by Aegeus Procoſull of Achaia in the citie
Patras: and they celebrate his day of feſti-
uitie, vppon the laſte of Nouember . And
they doe, or ought if they make not fictions
of theire owne , deduce the hiſtory of his
paſſion from the auncient penners and re-
lators thereof , which bee the preiſts and
deacons of Achaia , which were eye witneſſes and preſent at the ſame. S. Cyprian,
or whoſoeuer was the auncient Author of
the booke amonge his workes , *de duplici*
Mar-

Martyrio. The old Anonimus who wrote
the booke of the Apostles liues, published
by the learned Bishop of Vienna Fredericus Nausea, S. Simeon Metaphrastes himself, a learned grecian and auncient of those
parts, S. Iuo, S. Bernard, Algerus, the aun-
cientwriter of the liues of Saints, the whole
latine church in the publicke seruice of the
feast of S. Andrew the Apostle, the auncient Breuiary of the church of Salisbury
in England, and others are witnesses, that
S. Andrew beeinge persuaded and threat-
ned by Aegeus the Proconsull, to sacrifice
to the Pagan Gods, answered publicklie
vnto him in these wordes: *Ego omnipotenti
Deo, qui vnus & verus est, immolo quotidie,
non taurorum carnes, nec hircorum sanguinem, sed immaculatum Agnum in altari: cuius
carnem posteaque omnis multitudo credentium
manducauerit, Agnus qui sacrificatus est, integer perseuerat & viuus*. I doe daily sacri-
crifice to God almightie, the onely true
God, not the flesh of bulls, nor blood of
goates, but the immaculate Lambe vppon
the altar, whose flesh after all the multitude
of beleeuers haue eaten, the Lambe that is
sacrificed, remayneth whole and liuinge.
Breuiar.

Breuiar. & Missale Rom. Martyrolog. Rom.
Bed. & Vsuard. vlt. Nou. Protestant comm:
Booke in calendar. Nouem. & in fest. vlt. No-
uem. Cooper v. Andreas Godw. conuers. Mag-
deb. cent. 1. in Andr. Apostolo. Act. S. An-
dreæ per Presb. & Diacon. Achaiæ. Ciprian-
l. de duplic. Mart. Anonim. in mirac. vit. &
Pass. Apost. in S. Andrea. Sim. Metaphr. in
S. Andr. S. Iuo Carnoten. Episc. serm. de Sa-
cram. dedicat. ser. 4. Algerus contra Beren-
gar. S. Bernard. apud Francisc. Feuarden. an-
notat. in Frenæum l. 4. contra hær. cap. 32. pag.
361. Iacob. Genuen. Epis. in vit S. Andreæ vlt.
Nouem. Breu. Ecclesiæ Salisbur. ibidem.

2. Thus it is euident that S. Andrewe
the Apostle did offer this holy sacrifice of
Masse, and euery day: and that the sacrifice
was Christ himself the true Lambe of God
that taketh away sinnes. Amonge the holy
auncient and renowned witnesses, S. Iuo
supr. ser. 4. speakinge of this holy sacrifice
of Masse thus writeth: *In memoriam veniunt*
verba beati Andreæ Apostoli, quibus asserit &
in cælis esse corpus Domini, & de altari posse
sumi corpus Domini. Cuius inquit carnes cum
sint comestæ in terris à populo, ipse tamen in
cælestibus ad dexteram Patris integer perse-
M *uerat*

uerat & viuus . The wordes of S. Andrew
the Apostle doe come to memory, in which
hee affirmeth, that the body of our Lord is
in heauen, and yet may his body bee receued from the altare . Whose flesh saith hee,
when it is eaten of the people on earth,
yet he perseuereth whole and aliue in heauen , at the right hand of his Father . And
this giueth full satisfaction for S. Andrew,
that hee was a sacrificinge and massinge
preist.

3. The next in order is S. Iames the brother of S. Iohn the Apostle , and Euangelist, martired by Kinge Herode as we reade
in the 12. chapter of the Acts of the Apostles , where our protestants thus reade :
About that time, Herod the Kinge stretched
forth his hand to vexe certaine of the church.
And he killed Iames the brother of Iohn with
the sword. (Actor. cap. 12. *ver.* 1. 2. *)* Which
his timely death hath taken from him such
ample memory as is deliuered of some o-
ther Apostles that liued longer , in histories. But beeing assured before by all kinde
of testimonies, that he was one of them to
whom our blessed Sauiour gaue power, and
commaundement to offer the holy sacrifice

of

of his body and blood, that he there being
consecrated a preist, and one of the three
Apostles which our Sauiour most loued,
and hee him, it would be more then impietie to thinke, hee either neglected the
power, or brake the commaundement of
his Master, whome he so much loued, and
loued him againe; for so he should not haue
beene so principall a frend and louer of
Christ, but his professed enemy, in continually violatinge his lawe, and commaundement. And being both brother to S. Iohn,
and consecrated and ordeyned preist at the
same time, in the same maner, and order as
hee was, how could S. Iohn be a massinge
and sacrificinge preist, so vndeniably as is
proued of him, except S. Iames were also
in the same degree?

4. Further it is proued that S. Iames liued sometime before his death & was martired in Hierusalem, where the publick sacrifice of the Christian church at that time
was the holy Masse: for as Hieremias Patriarke of Constantinople proueth against
the Protestants in his censure, and others.
The holy Masse is a sacrifice instituted of
Christ. (*Hierem. in censura Concil. 6. Con-*

stantinop.)in memory and commendation of all his mercy and humilitie sustained for our soules. Saint Iames the Apostle, called our Lords brother, first reduced into order that liturgie, and sacrifice, beeinge so instructed of Christ to doe it, in all parts of that holy sacrifice, nothing els is handled, but an vniuersall order of thinges, which our Sauiour vndertooke for our redemption. Then this S. Iames also a cheife Apostle of the same Christ, consecrated with the same solemnitie the other was, and liuinge and dyinge in the same place, a great Saint and Martyr as the other was, could not possibly differ from him in this point: nor from the rest of the Apostles, all of them by all consent before, agreeinge in these misteries. And it is an historicall approued veritie, by all antiquities, that these few disciples which this S. Iames conuerted in Spaine, and brought with him to Hierusalem, were directed and sent thither againe by S. Peter the Apostle, that great massinge preist (as hereafter)and they were such as he that sent them in that respect.

5. S. Thomas followeth next in Apostolick order, how hee was a sacrificinge and

and maſſinge preiſt I haue ſhewed before
in S. Iohn. And this holy Apoſtle preachinge in India, altares and diuers other
pregnant arguments of his ſaying Maſſe in
thoſe parts are found amonge them there.
Chriſtiani qui Indias frequentarunt, quas o-
lim diui Thomæ prædicatio peragrauit, alta-
ria Chriſtiana cum reliquijs quibuſdam Ima-
ginis Virginis in ſpeluncis inuenerunt. Flori-
mund. Ram. de origine Hær.l.8. cap.12. And
Franciſcus Aluares. (*de reb. Ind.*) that liued
longe in thoſe parts, writeth, that their Annals teſtifie, they had a church built in their
contry within ten yeares of Chriſts Aſcenſion, which church there ſtill remayneth,
and beareth the name, as euer it did, the
church of our Lady of Mount Sion, and the
reaſon why it is ſo called, is becauſe the
ſtone where of the altar was builded, was
brought thither from Mount Sion. The
ſame is proued by others, and proteſtants
themſelues, further declaringe the maner
of their ſaying Maſſe, ſtill continued with
great réuerence, and deuotion; teachinge
how they neuer ſay Maſſe without incenſe,
and three cleargie men, a preiſt, deacon,
and ſubdeacon, and they deriue their Re-

M 3　　　　ligion

ligion from S. Thomas the Apostle. An
other, an English Protestant minister from
experienced trauailers, and antiquitie writeth: *est Capella Indorum: there is a Chappell*
of these Indians conuerted by S. Thomas in
Mount Caluary at Hierusalem, where onely
the pilgrims of India, by theire preists singe
Masse, after their order consecrating and ma-
*kinge,*conficientes,*the Sacrament of the body*
and blood of Christ, of bread and wine · They
behaue themselues with greatest attention,
reuerence, humilitie, and deuotion. Therfore
wee cannot doubt but S. Thomas taught,
and practised these misteries, both there,
and wheresoeuer hee liued and preached.
Edw. Grim. booke of estates pag. 1088. 1089.
201. 203. *Sebast. Munster. l. 6. cap. 57. vide*
multos apud Gul. Eisengr. centen. 1. fol. 168.
Rich. Hackluits booke of trauailes in mount
Sinay. Sir Iohn Mandeuil pag. 36. cap. 14.

6. Concerning S. Iames commonly called S. Iames the lesse, and brother of our
Lord, whose place is ordinarily numbred
next, I haue spoken before, how, and by
Chrifts appointment, as the greeke writers
say, hee composed a forme of Masse, and
deliuered it to the churches, where hee liued,

ued, and so must needs bee a professor and
practiser of that, which he taught to others;
and consequently consecrated massing and
sacrificinge preists, to performe the same.
His Masse approued of in the sixt generall
councell held at Constantinople, as our
protestants allow, is stil extant, and known
to all learned men, in all things of substance agreeing with the vsuall present missale
of the Roman churche. *Censura Oriental.
Hieremias Patriarch Constantinapol. ib. cap-
10. Proclus S. Nichol. Methon. & Bessarion
apud Gul. Eisengr. cent. 1. fol. 186. Concil-
general. 6-can. 52. can. Apost. 3. Missa 5. Iacobi in Biblioth. Patr. & al. Morton apol. part.
2. pag. 8.*

7. Now followeth S. Philip, which followed the same opinion, and practise of the
holy sacrifice of Masse: for wee doe not onlie often reade in generall, that hee founded churches, and consecrated Bishops,
preists, deacons and other inferior cleargie
men, which none but they which hold a
sacrificinge preisthood, and sacrifice of
Chrifts body and blood in holy Masse, allowe: But S. Simeon Metaphraftes liuinge
where S. Philip preached, with others testi-

M 4   fieth

fieth in particular: *Sacerdotes & altaria v-*
bique in illis locis statuit & construxit , pro
sacrificijs illis quæ fiebant in dæmonum alta-
ribus , sacrosancti fecit in eis peragi sacram
misterij celebrationem. Hee appointed preistes and builded altars , euery where in
those places, and for those sacrifices which
were vsed to bee offered vppon the altars
of deuils , hee caused the holy celebration
of the sacred mistery to bee perfected . *A-*
nonimus. supr. l. in Pass. Apostol. in S. Phi-
lippo Gul. Eisengr. centur. 1. fol. 157. 158. *&*
alibi. Simeon Metaph. in S. Philippo Apo-
stolo Sur. die 1. *Maij.* And the protestant Sebastian Munster with others teacheth, how
the Abissines testifie from their Apostolick
antiquities, and constitutions of the Apostles themselues , preserued by continuall
tradition with them , that amonge other
misteries of Christian Religion deliuered
by them, this of the holy sacrifice of Masse,
and Christs sacred body and blood offered
therin, was one, and that S. Philip the A-
postle was principally theire Apostle, and
preached these things to them. *Asserunt im-*
primis Philippum Apostolum apud eos prædi-
casse Euangelium. Sebastian. Munst. Cosmo-
graph.

8. Touchinge S. Bartholomew, we read
that hee preached in India, where that
knowne maſſinge Apoſtle taught, and left
that holy ſacrifice, ſo that two Apoſtles if
they had not beene confirmed in grace, &
free from error (as all agree they were) no
Chriſtian will thinke they could preache
and practiſe contrary doctrines, in ſo great
miſteries, to, and in one people, place, and
time, and wee further reade, that S. Bartholomew cōſecrated many preiſts, which
(as before) muſt needs be ſacrificing maſſing preiſts. And he made Kinge Polimius
a maſſinge Biſhop, and maker of maſſinge
preiſts, continuinge ſo 20. yeares, beſides
others. *Breuiar. Rom. in feſt. S. Bartholom.*
Abd. cert. Apoſtol. l. 8. Antonin. part. 1. ti-
tul. 6. Petr. de natal. l. 7. cap. 103. Martyro-
log. Rom. die 24. Aug. Dion. Areopag. l. miſ-
tic. Theolog. Euſeb. l. 5. hiſt. c. 10. Origen. in
Gen. Hieron. l. de ſcript: in pauten.

9. S. Simon and Iude could not bee of
any other profeſſion opinion or practiſe in
this point, beeing both with the reſt of the
Apoſtles conſecrated ſacrificinge preiſts,
and S. Simon ſo zelous a louer of Chriſt,

as

as our protestants write, that hee thereby
was named Zelotes, by a kinde of excellency, and S. Iude as he himselfe is witnes,
in his epistle, was *frater Iacobi*, *brother to*
S. Iames, that notorious massinge preist,
and Apostle as is before declared: and S.
Simon is generally taught, to haue conuersed most in those contries, where S. Marke
that massinge Euangelist practised, and
plated that doctrine. And S. Iude first preached in Iury diuers yeares, where his massing Brother S. Iames was so renowned for
writinge the forme of this holy sacrifice,
and both practising it himselfe, and deliueringe it to others. And they consecrated
Abdias Bishop of Babilon, who by his
owne, and all testimonies, was a massinge
and sacrificinge preist, and Bishop, who
could make and consecrate no others but
such as hee was, and had authoritie to doe.
Socrat. l. 1. cap. 15. Niceph. hist. l. 4. c. 32.
Fortunat. Godwin. Conuers. of Britanie. Iud.
Episc. c. 1. v. 1. Martyrolog. Rom. die 28. Oc-
tob. Bed. & Vsuard. ib. Stowe histor. Godwin.
Conu. of Brit. Nicephor. l. 2. cap. 4. Ado Tre-
uer. & Bed. 5. cal. Nouemb. Nicephor. lib. 2.
cap. 40. Guliel. Eisengr. centen. 1. part. 5. dist.
7.

7. *fol.* 168. *Abd. certam. Apost. l.* 4. *Antonin.*
part. 1. *Petr. de natal. l.* 9. *cap.* 115. *Abdias*
l. de certam. Apost. l. 6. *Iul. African. præfat.*
histor. Apostol. Anonym. in S. Bartholom.

10. S. Matthias beeing chosen into the
place of Iudas the traitor, by the other A-
postles, could bee of no other iudgement,
and Religion herein, then they were. And
the places hee preached in, giue testimony
vnto this: for whether wee will say with
Sophronius, Dorothus, and Nicephorus,
that hee preached in Aethiopia, wee haue
heard that massinge Apostles and preists
preached there: or with our auncient Mar-
tyrologes, that hee was martired in Iury, S.
Iames and the other Apostles before haue
proued hee must needs bee a massinge and
sacrificinge preist, and execute that holy
function, liuing and dying there. *Sophron.*
apud Hier. l. de scrip. Eccles. Doroth. in Sy-
nops. Nicephor. l. 2. c. 40. *Martyrolog. Rom.*
24. *Febr. Bed. Ado. & Vsuard. ib. Isidor. l. de*
vit. & obit. Sanct. cap. 81.

11. To conclude with S. Barnabas, extraordinarily called to bee an Apostle, as
S. Paul, hee is commonly taken to bee the
first composer of the Masse of Milane, in
Italy,

Italy, named S. Ambrose his Masse, in respect of certaine additions of his vnto it, &
vsed with great priuiledge in that church,
to this day, not differinge in any materiall
point from the present order of saying Masse vsed in the rest of the Romane Latine, or
Greeke church at this time, or wherfoeuer.
Traditio Eccl. Mediolanen. in Ital Iodoc. Cocc.
l. 6. To. 2. articul. 9. lib. 7. artic. 5. And this
Masse was, as our protestants themselues
acknowledge, in such vse and credit in the
Latine church, that it was more vsuall then
that called S. Gregories Masse, vntill the
time of Pope Adrian the first about the
yeare of Christ 780. Their words bee these.
(*Io. Balæus in act. Roman. Pont. lib. 3 in Ha-*
drian. 1.) *Missarum ritus à magno Grego-*
rio editus, occidentalibus Ecclesijs imperauit.
Pope Adrian commaunded the order of the
Masse publithed by Gregory the greate, to
bee vsed of the west churches, till which
time S. Barnabas and S. Ambrose Masse
still vsed at Millane were more vsuall, as
an other thus writeth. (*Foxe Tom. 1. act. and*
Monum. pag. 130.) *Pope Adrian the first ra-*
tified and confirmed the order of Saint Grego-
ries Masse, aboue the order of S. Ambrose Mas-
se,

se , for vnto this time , which was about the yeare of our Lord 780. the Liturgie of S. Ambrose was more vsed in the Italian churches. Therefore there is no difficultie but S. Barnabas as the reft of the Apoftles, was alfo a facrificinge maffinge preift.

THE XI. CHAPTER.

How S. Peter the cheife Apoſtle , and firſt founder of the church of Chriſt in this our kingedome , was a facrificinge , maſſinge preiſt , deliuered a forme of Maſſe to the church, confecrated many maſſinge preiſts in this part of the world nere vnto vs , and fome of this kingdome.

NOw laſtely to come to S. Peter , the prime and cheife of the Apoftles, hee could not bee at difference with the reft in this , but muft needs bee a maffinge preift as they were , and fo for this purpofe is it little, materiall whether this contry receaued the faith from him, or any other of the Apoftles. But becaufe both Catholicks, and proteftants agree. (*Gul. Cambden in Britan. Theatr. of great Brit. l. 6. controuerſ. hiſtor.*

To.

To.1. in S. Petro.) that both Greeke and Latine antiquities giue that vnto him, as is
lately proued at large, hee must also bee the
first institutor of our ecclesiasticall Hierarchie, in consecratinge vnto vs, diuers holy
Bishops, and preists, which that is deliuered already, proueth to haue beene massing
Bishops, and preists, and by those sacrificinge Bishops, and his sacrificinge successors, our preists and Bishops were euer sacred massinge Bishops, and preists vnto
these daies, of innouation, as will manifest-
lie appeare in all ages, herafter by this treatise. For, besides that, which is said before,
how all the Apostles were massing and sacrificing preists, and all the other Apostles
and Euangelists besides S. Peter, wee haue
of him in particular, more and moste credible witnesses, then are needfull to be al-
leadged. S. Isidor saith. *Ordo Missæ vel ora-*
tionum, quibus oblata Deo sacrificia consecran-
tur, primum à S. Petro est institutus, cuius
celebrationem vno eodemque modo vniuersus
peragit orbis. The order of Masse, or of the
praiers by which the sacrifices offered vnto
God are consecrated, was first instituted by
S. Peter, whose celebration the whole world
ob-

obserueth in one, and the same maner. *Isodor. l. 1. de officijs cap. 15. de Missa & orationibus.*

2. Our holy auncient learned contriman, S. Albinus, or Alcuinus by others, purposely entreatinge of this most blessed sacrifice, and the ceremonies thereof, thus writeth: *Celebratio Missæ in commemorationem Passionis Christi peragitur, sic enim ipse præcepit Apostolis, tradens eis corpus & sanguinem suum, dicens hoc facite in meam commemorationem, hoc est in memorian Passiones meæ. Tanquam diceret, quod pro vestro salute passus sum, ad memoriam reuocate. Hanc Petrus Apostolus primus omnium Antiochiæ dicitur celebrasse.* The celebration of Masse is done in commemoration of the Passion of Christ, for so hee gaue commaundement vnto his Apostles, when he deliuered vnto them his body and blood, saying doe this in commemoration, which is in memory of my passion: as though hee had said, recall vnto memory that I suffered for your saluation. This Masse S. Peter the Apostle is said first to haue celebrated at Antioche. *Albinus alij Alcuinus l. diuin. offic. cap. de celebrat. Missæ.*

3. Egber-

3. Egbertus writinge how the court of the Kinge, *Regalis aula*, at Antioch was in the time of S. Peters beeinge there made a Christian church, amonge other holy functions S. Peter exercised in it, *hee* saith hee *ordinarily said Masse , in qua communiter populum docuit, & Missas celebrauit .* (*Egbert. Abb. serm. de incremento & manifestat. Cathol. fide.*) And againe. (*serm. 10.*) *Sacerdotalem ordinem nos accepimus à Romana Ecclesia, Romana autem Ecclesia, ab Apostolo Petro, Petrus à Christo , Christus à Deo Patre, qui vnxit eum oleo lætitiæ, hoc est Spiritu Sancto præ participibus suis , & iurauit dicens ad eum, tu es Sacerdos in æternum, secundum ordinem Melchisedeih. Verus Sacerdos erat Dominus noster Iesus Christus. Ipse inuisibiliter dedit corpus & sanguinem suum , quando coram discipulis panem & vinum in cana benedixit benedictione cælesti ; & fecit sua admirabili potestate vt sub specie eiusdem panis, & vini sumerent de manibus ipsius corpus & sanguinem eius . Ipse quoque sicut pollicitus est, cum Ecclesia sua est , vsque ad consummationem sæculi , & quotidie inuisibiliter offert per manus Ecclesia Deo Patri pro salute mundi, corpus & sanguinem suum sub specie panis & vini.*

vini. Propterea dictus est Sacerdos secundum ordinem Melchisedech, qui erat Rex Salem, & Sacerdos Dei summi, & oblationem fecit Deo ex pane & vino. Dominus Iesus Christus discipulos suos fecit veros Sacerdotes. Dedit eis potestatem conficiendi corpus & sanguinem suum sub specie panis & vini, quando dixit ad eos. (Luc. 22.) hoc est corpus meum quod pro vobis tradetur; Hoc facite in meam commemorationem. Omnem denique potestatem quae ad Sacerdotij officium, & ad episcopalem dignitatem spectat, ab illo acceperunt. Eandem autem potestatem singuli successoribus relinquerunt, in illis terris, & in illis Ecclesijs, quas eis Dominus conuertendas, & gubernandas delegauit. Et vt nunc de reliquis taceam, Beatus Petrus princeps Apostolorum in Romana vrbe, presbyteros, & Episcopos ordinauit, & omnem potestatem quae ad officia eorum pertinebat, eis dedit, sicut ipse à Domino Iesu Christo acceperat.

4. We haue receued preistly order from the church of Rome, and the church of Rome receaued it from the Apostle Peter, Peter receaued it from Christ, Christ receaued it from God his Father, who anointed him with oyle of gladnes, that is with

N   the

the holy ghost aboue his partakers, and
swore, saying vnto him. (*psal.* 10.) thou art
a preist for euer, after the order of Melchisedech. Our Lord Iesus Christ was a true
preist. Hee did inuisibly giue his body and
blood, when before his disciples at his supper hee blessed breade and wine, and made
by his admirable power that vnder the species of the same bread & wine, they should
receaue from his hands, his body and blood.
Hee also, as hee hath promised, is with his
church vnto the ende of the world, and
doth daily inuisibly offer by the hands of
the church, to God the Father for the saluation of the worlde, his body and blood
vnder the forme of bread and wine. Therfore hee is called a preist after the order of
Melchisedech, who was Kinge of Salem,
and preist of the high God, and made offeringe vnto God of breade and wine. Our
Lord Iesus Christ made his disciples preistes. Hee gaue them power to make his bodie and blood vnder the forme of breade,
and wine, when hee said vnto them. (*Luc.*
22.) this is my body, which shall bee giuen
for you : doe this in my commemoration.
Finally they receaued from him all power,
which

which belongeth to the office of preisthood, and episcopall dignitie. And euery one of them, left the same power to their successors, in those contries, and in those churches, which our Lord commended to them to conuert and gouerne. And at this time to bee silent of the rest, S. Peter cheife of the Apostles in the city of Rome ordeyned preists, and deacons, and gaue them all power which apperteined to their offices, as hee himselfe had receaued from our Lord Iesus Christ.

5. And thus from S. Peter deduceth a continuall succession of sacrificinge massinge preists, and Bishops in all this West part of the world; And amonge others teacheth how particularly this our kingdome of England had our massinge preists, and Bishops by that deduction from S. Peter, and his successors in the Apostolicke see of Rome. Stephanus Eduerists. (*l. de Sacramento Altaris.*) a learned Bishop many hundred yeares since, saith: *sicut Magister docuerat, Apostoli se & alios communicando consecrationem corporis & sanguinis Domini facere cæperunt, & fieri per vniuersas Ecclesias prædicando instituerunt.* As Christ theire

N 2   Maister

maister had taught, so the Apostles communicatinge themselues, and others, began to make the consecration of the body
and blood of Christ, and by preachinge
instituted it to bee done through all churches: and sheweth how the canon of the
Masse was vsed by S. Peter, & the rest from
the beginninge. *Primo fiebat canonis myste-*
rium. Before any thinge was added by the
Popes of Rome. And Paschasius Ratbertus
plainely faith, it was the common opinion
in his time, that S. Peter was the Author
of the canon of Masse: *respice in Sacramen-*
torum celebratione, instituente beato Petro,
vt credimus, quid orat Sacerdos in canone.
And then hee addeth particularly, that by
S. Peters institution, the preist praieth, *vt*
fiat corpus & sanguis dilectissimi filij tui Do-
mini nostri Iesu Christi : That it may bee
made the body, and blood of thy moste beloued sonne, our Lord Iesus Christ. *Pascha-*
sius Rathert. l. de corpore & sanguine Christi.

6. I reade in an auncient Anonymus
Manuscript history of this kingdome. (*M.*
S. hist. incipit in principio creauit Deus cap no-
mina summorum Pontificum.) *post Passionem*
Christi anno sequenti beatus Petrus Apostolus
tenuit

tenuit cathedram sacerdotalem in partibus o-
rientis annis quatuor, vbi primam Missam ce-
lebrauit. Deinde venit Antiochiam, vbi ca-
thedram adeptus, sedit annis septem, inde ve-
nit Romam. The next yeare after the Paſſion of Chriſt, S. Peter the Apoſtle held his
preiſtly chaire in the parts of the eaſt foure
yeares, where hee firſt celebrated Maſſe.
From thence hee came to Antioch, where
obteyning the chaire, hee ſat ſeuen yeares,
from thence hee came to Rome. The auncient Engliſh hiſtory, commonly called
Caxtons hiſtory, becauſe printed by him,
thus teſtifieth: *Peter the first Pope was a bleſ-*
ſed man, and glorious Apostle of Christ, hee
was head of the church (after S. Hierome) 37.
yeares, and he held his Bishoprick in the easte
fiue yeares, and hee said Maſſe. hee made our
Lords body, then after hee came to Antioch.
Old English histor. published by Caxton. part.
4. an. D. 34.

7. Martianus Polonus hath the ſame
words, with our Manuſcript hiſtory before
cited. Walfridus Strabo 800. yeares ſince
writeth, *how the Romans receaued the vſe*
and obſeruations of their Maſſe (common to
the weſtern world) *from S. Peter the chei-*

feſt

fest of the Apostles. Martin. Polon. *in supputat. tempor. col.* 27. *in S. Petro. Walafrid. Strab. l. de obseruat. cap.* 22. The like hath S. Clement scholler and successor to S. Peter, Comestor, Ioannes Belethus, Pope Innocentius the third, Polychronicon, Ioannes Cantabrigiensis, Petrus de natalibus, Hesichius, Nicholaus Cabasilla, Germanus S. Beda, S. Hierome, Theonas, Cassianus. S. Anacletus, who was made preist by S. Peter, as hee himselfe witnesseth, S. Epiphanius, Ionas Aureliensis, our learned cotryman, with diuers others, cited by Eisengrenius and others. And to take the warrant of Protestants with vs, for this veritie: first wee haue the testimony of the Magdeburgians from Martinus Polonus, and others, *in quibusdam chronicis vt Martini & aliorum*, not onely that S. Peter said Masse, but in some sort the order thereof. Our first English Protestant Archbishop of Canterbury expressely acknowledgeth, *that S. Peter said Masse both in the easte*, *Missam dicta à Petro in orientalibus regionibus*, and after hee came into the west also, and that, *illius traditio à Christi primo instituto ducentis amplius annis in prima Ecclesia durauit*. The order

der of Maſſe which S. Peter vſed & taught,
continued in the primatiue church aboue
200. yeares from the inſtitution of Chriſt
vntill the time of Pope Zepherine. *Clem.*
Rom. l. 10. *Recognit. hiſtor. ſcholaſt. cap.* 7.
in act. Apoſtol. Io. Belethus l. de offic. diuin.
cap. 124. *Innocent.* 3· *præfat. l.* 1. *Polychronic.*
l. 4. *cap.* 6. *Ioannis Cantabrigien. in pupill.*
oculi. c. 8. *Petrus de natalib. l.* 4. *cap.* 108. *He-*
ſichius Hieroſol. in act. cap. 20. *& cap.* 23. *Le-*
uit. l. 6. *Nichol. Cabaß. c.* 28. *de Miſſ. Germ.*
Conſtantinp. in can. Miſſ. Anaclet. epiſt. 2. *&*
al. apud Eiſengren. centen. 1. *fol.* 116, 117.
Magdeburg. cent. 1. *l.* 2. *cap.* 6. *col.* 500. *Math.*
Parker. antiquit. Britannic. pag. 47. *cap.* 17.

8. And this Pope by this great proteſtants confeſſion, was ſo far' from chaun-
ginge any eſſentiall thinge therin, to make
it worſe, that to inſiſt in his wordes : *donec*
eam Zepherinus 16. *Romanus Pontifex quo-*
rundam ſuaſionibus ad pulchriorem materiam
formamque mutare voluit: vntill Zepherine
the ſixteenth Pope of Rome by the perſua-
ſions of ſome would chaunge that Maſſe to
a more excellent matter and forme. And
to put vs out of doubt that Pope and S. Zepherine did make no chaunge or alteration
N 4   of

of this S. Peters Masse, now after two hundred yeares, in proteftants iudgement, but that which rather honored, then in any refpect difgraced this holy facrifice, all the chaunge which this Proteftant Archbifhop findeth made herin by this holy Pope, is this, by his owne teftimony, that where before woddé challices were vfed in fome places, in thofe times of perfecution and neceffitie, this Pope (to vfe this proteftants words the 16. Pope of Rome) *conftituted that Maffes should bee celebrated with patens of glaffe. Zepherinus* 16. *Romanus Epifcopus, patenis vitreis Miffas celebrari conftituit.* (*Matth. Parker fupr. cap.* 18. *pag.* 47.) Which an other Englifh Proteftant purpofely entreating of fuch thinges, thus expreffeth: *fanguinis Chrifti confecrationem in vitreo calice, non ligneo, vt antea, fieri debere ftatuit.* Pope Zepherine conftituted, that the confecration of the blood of Chrift fhould bee made in a chalice of glaffe, & not of wood, as before was vfed. *Robertus Barns in vita Pontific. Roman. in Seuer. alij Zepherin.* And further : *Cum Epifcopus celebraret Miffæ facra, iufsit omnes presbyteros adeffe.* Hee commaunded that all the preifts fhould be prefent, sent, when the Bishop celebrated the sacrifice of Masse.

9. This is all S. Zepherine altered in this Masse of S. Peter, by these protestants own graunt : Therefore it is sufficiently agreed vpon both by Catholicks and the best learned protestants, that according to the common opinion in that respect, S. Peter did not onely and vsually say Masse, beeinge a massing and sacrificing preist, by his preistlie consecration, but as the great Apostle of Christ composed an order, or forme of saying Masse, and deliuered it to the church to practise, and it was so accordingly receaued, and practised with the best learned & most holy men, the glorious lights of Gods house, in that primatiue and freely confessed vnspotted dayes of Christianitie. What this holy order was, and how it did not differ in any substantiall or essentiall matter from that Masse which the present Roman church now vseth, I shall sufficiently proue, with the good leaue, and likinge, both of Catholicke, & learned protestant authors, hereafter.

10. In the meane time, to make that which is already said vnquestionable, S. Peter

Peter euer left in the renowned places where hee liued, this holy doctrine, and practise of saying Masse. And whether soeuer he sent any Apostolick men to preach the ghospell, this was a principall charge, & power bequeathed vnto them. For Hierusalem where S. Peter first preached I haue spoken sufficiently in S. Iames before, so for S. Marke at Alexandria, & the African parts. For Antioch also I haue written what might suffice, yet will I add somewhat of the glorious successor of S. Peter there, S. Ignatius, whome S. Chrisostome the great ornament of that very church S. Felix, and Theodoret doe allowe mee to call, the immediate substitute or successor of S. Peter there, *and that by S. Peter hee was consecrated Bishop, dextera beati Petri fuisse ordinatum Episcopum Ecclesiæ Antiochenæ,* and *per magni Petri dexteram Pontificatum suscepit.* Though I doe not deny, but as S. Clement did to S. Linus, and Cletus at Rome, so S. Ignatius might and did giue place to Saint Euodius at Antioche. Whome great Authors therefore name S. Peters first successor there. (*S. Io. Chrisostom. orat. de translat.corp. S. Ignaty Antioch. Eelix. Rom. Pont. epist.*

epist. ad Zenon. Imper. in S. Synod. Const. act.
1. Theodoret. dialog. 1. Immutab. Euseb. chr.
& hist. l. 3. c. 16. Hieron.l. de scriptor. in Ig-
nat. Ignat. epist. ad Antioch.

11. This holy Saint and learned Father
consecrated by S. Peter, was so farr a massing preist, and earnest practiser and patron
of this holy sacrifice of Masse, wherein
Christs sacred body and blood ar offered,
that as not onely Theodoret and al Catholicks with him teach, but as the grand protestants Beza, Peter Martyr, Scultetus, Whitaker, and others as enforced doe graunt,
that S. Ignatius did condemne Simon and
Menander for hereticks, because according
to theire knowne heresie against Christs
true humanitie, they did reiect the sacrifice
of his body and blood in the sacrifice of
Masse : (*Theodoret. Dial. 3. Beza Dial. Cy-*
clops. Peter Mart. loc. 12. Missa. Scutlet. part.
1. Medull. patr, l. 1. Whitaker contra Camp.
& al.) *They doe not receaue* (saith S. Ignatius) *Eucharist and sacrifice, because they doe*
not confesse the Eucharist to bee the body of
our Sauiour Iesus Christ, which suffered for
our sinnes, which his Father by his bountie
raised againe. (apud Theodoret. supr.) ευχαρι-
σίας

ξίας καὶ προσφορας ἔκ ἀποδ'έχονται, δ'ιὰ τὸ μὴ
ὁμολογεῖν τὴν ευ καρισίαν σαρκαἔναι τᾶ σωτήρ⊙
ἡμῶν Ιησᾶ χρισᾶ τὴν οπερ τῶν αμαρτιῶν ἡμῶν
παθᾶσαν, κο χρησότητι ὁ πατερ ἐγειρων,

12. The proteſtants of Magdeburg. (*cent.*
2. *col.* 113. *cap.* 6.) acknowledge (which no
man can deny) *in epiſtolis Ignatij vt hodie*
extant vtrimque legitur & ſacrificium immo-
lare, & Miſſas facere. Wee reade both to offer ſacrifice , and ſay Maſſes In the epiſtles
of Ignatius, as they are extant at this day,
And our Engliſh Proteſtants confeſſe in
theſe termes . (*Sutcliffe ſubu. pag.* 32.) Wee
reade *in Ignatius this phraſe, offerre, and, ſa-*
crificium immolare, to offer, and, immolate ſa-
crifice. And not to inſiſt vpon the words of
S. Ignatius. (*Ignatius epiſtol. ad Smirnenſ.*)
δοχὴν ἐπιτελειν which the olde tranſlation
turneth , *Miſſam facere* , to ſay Maſſe , the
other Greeke wordes of this holy Saint
which the Magdeburgian proteſtants doe
allowe for his (*Magdeburg ſupr.*) προσφερειν,
and θυσίαν προσκομιζειν do in all lexicons and
Greeke Authors , properly ſignifie ſacrificinge, or offering ſacrifice; and yet as that
holy Father witneſſeth, this was in his time
the act and office of Chriſtian preiſts. *And*
ſaith

saith: *this preisthood, is the toppe or cheife of*
all good things amonge men, and hee that ra-
geth against it, doth not reproach mã, but God
and Christ his onely begotten Sonne, who by
nature is the highest preist of God his Father,
and hee teacheth how an externall sacrifice offered vppon an externall materiall altar, is a proper act of this holy preisthood.
(*Ignat. epistol. ad Hieron. epistol. ad Ephes.*)
And that this sacrifice in particular is, *a*
medicine of immortality, a preseruatiue against
death, and procuringe life in God. The bread
of God, *heauenly food, which is the flesh of*
Christ, and blood of Christ. Ignat. epist. ad
Trallian. ad Ephes. & ad Roman.

13. And if wee attend S. Peter in his
iorney from the east to these western parts,
as Rome, & from thence to this kingdome
of Britanie, wee shall still finde antiquities,
and monuments, though so many ar loste,
that hee still continued his holy function
in sayinge Masse, and neither there, nor
here did or could consecrate any but sacrificinge massinge preists. This holy Apostle cominge in his iorney to Rome to Pisa
a famous citie of Hetruria in Italy, vppon
the Sea coaste, with his disciples, we finde
auncient

auncient euidence , that he there said Maſſe, & in honor & memory of him a church was there builded , and after his death dedicated vnto him, yearely frequented with great reſorte of pilgrims . (*Martin. Pereſ l. de diuinis & Apoſt. traditionib. part.* 3. *fol.* 70.) *and part of the very altar whereon hee ſaid Maſſe is there ſtill kept in the ſacrarie of that church, with an antiquitie in authenticall old characters, teſtifying the truth herof. Certa parte altaris vbi celebrauit in ſacrario templi maioris venerabiliter recondita , vna cum teſtimonio literis valde authenticis & vetuſtis, hinc rei fidem minimè ſuſpectam facientibus.* Alſo there is at Naples , as both Catholicks and proteſtants witnes, an old church, where S. Peter ſaid Maſſe, and the church thereuppon called : *Ad diui Petri aram :* At the altar of S. Peter. (*Benedict. Fulco l. de locis antiq. Neopolitan. Lindan. Apolog. Iacob. Gualier. tabula chronographic. ſeculi.* 1.*pag.* 44.) at the entrance of the dore whereof, this inſcription ſtill remayneth to keepe it in remembrance.

Siſte fidelis.

Et priuſquam templum ingrediaris,
   Petrum ſacrificantem venerare.

O

O faithfull man stay, and before thou enter into the church, worship Peter sacrificinge.

14. For Rome wee haue still the portable and remoueable altare whereon S. Peter and many of his successors there in persecution said Masse. (*Antiquitat. Eccl. Lateran. Rome. Breuiar. Rom. die 9. Nouembr. in dedica. Basilic. Saluatoris.*) wee haue all his successors holy Saints and Martyrs allmost 300. yeares by protestants confession, all of them sacrificinge, and massing preistes, as shall bee manifest in their times and places, and the foure first of them S. Linus Cletus, Clement, and Anacletus, consecrated and ordered massing and sacrificing preists, by their holy Master and predecessor S. Peter himselfe, as both they themselues and other auncient authors testifie. We are warranted by our protestants with others before, that the forme and order of the sacrifice of Masse which S. Peter composed, vsed, and deliuered to the church, was without any chaunge or alteration, continued in that church of Rome & these westerne nations aboue 200. yeares: from whence it appeareth consequently & plainlie by these protestante writers, that this

king-

kingdome of Britanie receauing the faith
from Rome in the Apostles times, and generally in the times of Pope Eleutherius &
Victor, who both werebefore S. Zepherine,
in whose dayes they suppose some addition
to haue beene vsed in that Masse, inuincibly proueth, that this kingdome with o-
thers did not onely admit Masse, and massinge preists in the first conuersion thereof,
but the very vnchaunged and vnaltered
Masse of S. Peter himselfe. We haue the Catalogues and histories of the successions of
Bishops in all renowned churches in this
part of the world, which receaued theire
first Apostles and Bishops from S. Peter,
that are preserued, testifyinge that these
their first Apostles, Preists, and Bishops
sent vnto them from S. Peter, were massinge and sacrificinge preists, and Bishops.
If I could exemply but in halfe the number
of them which were so ordered, and sent
by S. Peter into Italy, Spaine, Germanie,
and Fraunce, I should make to longe a di-
gression from the question of Britanie,
which I cheifly handle, write a forreine
historie, and entertaine my reader ouer
much in such affaires: therefore I will only
infist

infist in fome few of the cheifeft, thofe that came nearest vnto vs, and with whom our Britans in al probable iudgement had most intercourfe, commerce, or acquaintance.

15. I begin with S. Maximinus, and S. Lazarus whom Chrift raifed to life, feeing to the firft one of the 72.difciples of Chrift S. Peter commended S. Mary Magdalen, becaufe fome proteftants thinke S. Iofeph of Aramathia that buried Chrift, and liued, died, and was buried with vs in Britanie, came into Fraunce with them. (*Guliel. Eifengren. centenar. 1. part.5. dift.3. fol.148. Theater. of great Britanie l.6.* That the firft faid Maffe we are taught, becaufe we read, *that hee did minifter the holy Euchariſt, to S. Mary Magdalē after Maſſe was ended. Quod morienti S. Magdalenæ poſt Miſſarum ſolemnia Sacroſanctam Euchariſtiam adminiſtraſſe legimus. Anton. Democh.l. 2. de Miſſ. contra Caluin. Petrus de natal. l.5. Antonin. part.1. Volater. l. 7. Guliel. Eiſengr. cent. 1. fol. 148. pag. 2.* This for Aqueus where he was Biſhop. For S. Lazarus his beeing a maſſinge preiſt, and his ſaying of Maſſe, at Marſſiles in Fraunce, where hee was Biſhop, *the holie veſtiments in which hee ſaid Maſſe beeing*

O

to this day preserued and to be seene in the ca-
thedrall church there, ar sufficient witnes. In
Cathedrali Ecclesia, *vestes in quibus Missam*
celebrabat, *adhuc hodie conseruantur & mon-*
strantur. Demochar. *l.* 2. contr. Caluin. c. 32.
Petr. de natal. l. 1. c. 72. Antonin. part. 1. tit.
6. cap. 19. Guliel. Eiseng. centen. 1. fol. 149.

16. How famous S. Martial disciple of
S. Peter, and sent into Fraunce by him, was
in many parts of that nation so wel known
to our British Druides in those dayes, it is
not vnknowne to any antiquarie of these
contries: And as little ignorance can any
man pretend, that hee was a massinge sacrificinge preist, for so renowned hee was
for this, that the infidels themselues then
knew it, amonge whome the cheife idolatrous preist or Druid of Limogen, as the
french Annales tel vs, forsooke the towne
by reason of an Hebrue called Martiall,
who being come into Gaule, *vseth not wine,*
nor flesh, but when he offereth sacrifice to God:
si non que au sacrifice de Dieu. Who buildinge
a chappel there, celebrated Masse in it. Celebré
le Sainct sacrifice de la Messe. S. Aurelian. in
vct. S. Martialis. Doctor. Puel. D. Tigeon. Cl.
March. Ro. *Seigneur de Faux Augenin hi-*
stor.

Flor. Gallic. in S. Martial. Vincent. in specul.
hist. cap. 41. *Io. Gualt Chronolog. ecclesiasti-*
copol. an. Do. 56. And in that citie still remayneth the holy altar, on which hee vsed
to say Masse whereof hee himselfe maketh
mention in his epistle, *ad Burdegalenses,* &
for that cause so honored , *that it is by pu-*
blick edict of parlament examining and appro-
uing the truth of that history , from auncient
time, decreed, that seuen candels should conti-
nually bee kept burninge before it, the body of
that their Apostle beeing buried neare vnto it.
Florimund. Remund. de Origen. haref. l. 8.
cap. 12. *edict. inter log. parlam. Gallia de hac*
re. Annon videtis S. Martialem ad Burdega-
lenses nostros scripsisse , se aram Deo Israelis
& martyri ipsius Stephano dedicasse? ea ara in
ciuitate Lemogicum, vbi Apostolus ipse Aqui-
taniæ quiescit, conspicitur, ædificata à Principe
Stephano , quem ad Christianismum ipse con-
uerteret : ante eam noctes diesque ardent sep-
tem candelæ, iuxta antiquam istam fundatio-
nem, in parlamento nostro, & disceptatam, &
confirmatam.

17. And this holy Saint, and Apostle of
Aquitaine, himselfe teacheth , what great
honor and reuerence is due to Christian sa-

O 2   crifi-

crificing preists, and what an excellent sacrifice they offer of Chrifts facred body &
blood in holy Maffe: thus he writeth to his
late conuerted Chriftians. (*S. Martial. E-*
pifc. ad Burdegalef. cap. 3.) *honorabatis Sa-*
cerdotes qui decipiebant vos facrificijs fuis qui
mutis & furdis ftatuis offerebant, qui nec fe
nec vos iuuare poterant: nunc autem multò ma-
gis Sacerdotes Die omnipotentis, qui vitam
vobis tribuunt, in calice & pane vino, hono-
rare debetis. Before you were conuerted to
Chrift, you did honour your preifts, which
deceaued you with their facrifices, which
did facrifice to dumbe and deafe ftatues,
who could neither helpe themfelues, nor
you . But now much more you ought to
honour the preifts of God almighty, which
giue vnto you life in the chalice, and liue-
lie breade. And a little after, fpeaking more
plainely of this holy facrifice, offered vnto
God, vppon the altar, hee faith: *Sacrificium*
Deo Creatori offertur, in ara Chrifti corpus &
fanguinem in vitam æternam offerrimus. Quod
Iudæi per inuidiam immolauerunt, putantes
fe nomen eius à terra abolere: nos caufa falutis
noftræ, in ara fanctificata proponimus, fcientes
hoc folo remedio nobis vitam præftandam, &
mortem

mortem effugandam: hoc enim Dominus noster misit nos agere in sui commemorationem . Sacrifice is offered to God, our Creator, vppon the altar. We offer the body and blood of Christ for euerlasting life . That which the Iewes did offer through enuy, thinking to abolish his name from the earth; wee offer this vppon an hallowed altare, knowinge that by this onely remedy, life is to be giuen vnto vs, and death to bee auoided. For this our Lord Iesus commaunded vs to doe in his commemoration.

18. Thus this holy Saint, that stilleth himselfe. The Apostle of Iesus Christ, who as hee saith was present with Christ in his life, when hee was buried, and see him after his resurrection. (*Martial. epist. ad Bardegal. epestol. ad Tholosanos.*) was one of his 72. disciples, & was by speciall commaund of Christ vnto S. Peter, whose disciple hee after was, sent by him to bee the happy Apostle of that contrie . And I haue rather amonge many others in the like condition, cited this history of S. Martial, because morally to speake, the best learned Druids & others of this our Britanie, where the cheifest and commaunders in that sect remayned,

ned , could not bee ignorant of these thinges ; for both S. Aurelianus successor immediate to S. Martial at Limogen , and S.
Martial also himselfe are most worthy witnesses, that Sigebertus the *summus Sacerdos,*
high preist, Arch-flamen, and cheifest of
the Druids sect, in those partes, was by S.
Martial conuerted, to this his holy, sacrificinge and massing Christian Religion. (*S.*
Aurelian· in vit· S· Martial· & Martial· epi-
stol· ad Burdegal·cap· 3·) And S· Aurelianus
doth make this his holy conuersion so famous, that it could not be concealed, from
the rulers of the Druids Religion in Britanie, whom it so much concerned . (*Aure-*
lian· supr· & annotat·in S· Martial·) for presently after, *Benedicta*, wife of the Prince of
that Prouince, was conuerted by S·Martial,
this high preiste of the Druids : Sigebert
being also conuerted, *did breake in peeces all*
their Idols , destroyed their Temples , except
the Temple dedicated to the vnknowne God,
and shiuered the altars of the diuils into dust.
Ipsemet Sigebertus Pontifex Idola omnia con-
fregit minutim , & Templa euertit , excepto
Templo ignoti Dei,& altaria dæmonum in pul-
uerem. Which S·Martial himselfe doth sufficiently

Sacrifice, of the true church. the 1. age. 215
ficiently infinuate, when hee faith: *dum al-*
taria dæmonum, in puluerem redigerentur,
aram ignoti Dei ad confecrationem referuari
iufsimus. Quia dedicata in nomine Dei Ifrael,
& teftis ipfius Stephani, qui pro eo à Iudæis
paffus eft. (*S. Martial fup, cap. 3*) when the
altars of the deuils were beaten into duft,
wee commaunded the altare of the vnknowne God to bee referued for confecration. Which was dedicated in the name of
the God of Ifrael, and Martir Stephen, who
fuffered for him by the Iewes.

19. And if wee come to the nearer parts
of Fraunce, Paris, Rouen, Britany, Normandy, Picardy, and all the fea coafte, we
fhall euidently fee, that no other doctrine
or practife of this holy facrifice of Maffe,
could poffibly haue entrace into this kingdome: for in thofe parts wee finde S. Denis
the Areopagite, that glorious maffinge, and
Maffe teaching Father, S. Pauls fcholler,
fent thither by the maffinge Pope, S. Clement, with his maffinge companions, S.
Rufticus, and Eleutherius, and S. Nicafius
fent a maffinge preift, and Bifhop, by the
fame maffinge Pope. (*Gregor Turonen. l. 1.*
hift. Sur. in vit. Genouefuæ. Metaphr. 3. Oc-
tob.

tob. Bed. & Vſuard. 7. id. Octob. Volater. l.15.
Breu. Rom. in S. Dioniſ. Arnold. Merman. l.
Britones, Normandos, Rothomagenſes, Picar-
dos, omnemque maris Oceani tractum inſtru-
xit, formauitque fide S. Nicaſius à S. Clemen-
te illuc Apoſtolus delegatus imperante Nerone.
Conuerſ. gent. tabul. Eccleſ. Rothomagen. And
ſome thinke he preached and practiſed this
doctrine alſo, in this our Britanie. *Harris*
Theatr. l. 1.

20. If we circuite further, and come to
Gallia, Belgica, Collen, Mentz, Treuers,
Lothoringia, Alſaſia, Heluetia and thoſe
parts, wee ſhall finde in theſe daies of the
Apoſtles ſent thither by S. Peter, S. Clement vncle to S. Clement the Pope, his glorious companions S. Manſuetus our contriman, Celeſtius, Felix, and Patiens: wee
ſee ſent thither alſo by the ſame Apoſtle &
his authoritie, S. Maternus, one of the 72.
diſciples of Chriſt, with S. Eucharius, Valerius, our noble Britan, S. Beatus, and o-
thers. *Arnold. Mohu. ſupr. Io. Scomer. Gul.*
Eiſengren. cent. 1. Antonin. part. 1. Petr. de
natal. l. 10. cap. 113. Ant. Democh. lib. 2. de
Miſſ. Sebaſt. Munſter. in Coſmograph. Bed.
18. cal. Octobr. Wolfg. Bawr. in vit. præſul.

Memetocern. Annal. Colonien. & Treueren.
And that these were massinge, and sacrificinge preists, wee haue many authorities:
onely I will exemplify in the two cheifest,
to which the others were subordinate in
such affaires, and taught and practised as
those two their superiors, S. Clement and
S. Maternus did.

21, Of these it is euident, not onely because they were both consecrated preists,
and directed by that great massinge preist,
and Apostle S. Peter, whose commaund &
order, and their owne institution beeinge
holy Saints they neither did nor could violate, but also that they vsually said Masse,
as first of S. Clement it is testified, of his
publicke, and solemne sayinge of Masse,
Missarum solemnijs celebratis, wherewith he
armed himselfe before hee wrought that
great miracle, in destroyinge the horrible
dragon which had killed at Metz, so many
men, & other creatures; by which publick
miraculous deede many were conuerted to
the faith of Christ. *Antonin. part. 1. tit. 6.*
cap. 26. Anton. Demochar. l. 2. de Missa. c. 42.
Gulielm. Eisengren. centen. 1. fol. 147.) And
to performe this holy solemnitie and sacri-
                                          fice

fice of Masse, hee ordered cleargie men, *in diuers degrees, and orders, in diuersis gradibus,* which no Christians but such as allow the sacrifice of Masse, admit, and builded churches there. (*Antonin. supr. Petr. de natal. l. 10. c. 113. Vincent. l. 9. cap. 42.*) S. Maternus also the disciple of the same massing Apostle, S. Peter, and sent into Germany by him, who preached in many prouinces thereof, buildinge diuers churches to holy Saints, as S. Iohn Baptist, his Master, S. Peter, and others, was so renowned a massing preist, that among other his wonderful miracles. (*Petrus Messaeus Cratepol. Catalog. de Archiepiscop. Treuern.*) it is commonly deliuered, and written of him, *that he said three Masses in one day, in far distant places. Diuersis ac longè distantibus locis.* So renowned were these men for that most holy function, and office, so zelous and deuoute in the performance thereof, and God so well pleased, and serued in that so sacred an exercise, that he did so miraculously concurre vnto it.

THE

THE XII. CHAPTER.

Wherein is proued euen by protestants, that whatsoeuer Apostle or other, first preached Christ in Britanie, brought sacrificinge preisthood hither: and S. Peter first founded here our ecclesiasticall Hierarchie, of sacrificinge massinge preists and Bishops.

NOw we may hope that no man being by name a Christian, will bee so opposite an Antichristian, to thinke, that Christ which could not teache errors, or contrary doctrines, and deliuered but one, and the same true, and infallible Religion to the whole world, for all places, people, and ages, had one Religion for the rest of the world, in Europe, Asia, and Africke, all of them as before, embracing in the Apostles time the holy sacrifice of Masse, and sacrificinge preisthood: and an other for Britanie, quite different, and neuer heard of in any antiquitie, neuer practised in any other forme, or order, neuer registred in any monument. And seeing all the Euangelists, and Apostles of Christ, together with their

dis-

disciples, were massinge and sacrificinge
preists, and there were no other to preach,
and propagate true Religion, in this, or
any other nation, vnder heauen, but they,
how could any Caluinistical communion,
or other new deuise bee imagined to haue
had beeinge here? For whosoeuer it was,
which any protestant doth, or will affirme,
to haue beene the first preacher of Christianitie in this kingdome, S. Peter, S. Paul,
or S. Simon Zelotes, who onely among the
Apostles are reported in histories to haue
beene in this kingdome, as our best learned
protestant antiquaries with others truely
acknowledge, or S. Ioseph of Aramathia,
for which many contend, or whosoeuer, if
they were preists (as preists they must needes bee in all opinion Catholicke or Protestant, that should found our church) they
must needes also be massing and sacrificing
preists, no other Christian preists beeinge
in the whole worlde at that time, as before
is euident. *Theater of great Britanie lib. 6.*
Camb. in Britan Godw. conuers. of Brit. Stowe
hist. Holinsh. hist. of Engl.

2. And for those three Apostles, I haue
particularly proued in euery of them, that
they

they all, as also all the rest of that holy
order of the Apostles which diuided the
world among them to conuert it to Christ,
were without any exception, massing preistes. And if any man will persist in S. Ioseph and his holy company, seeing none of
these were Apostles, but directed by them,
as all other disciples either of the 72. or o-
thers were at those daies, whosoeuer among
them were preists, must needs also be massing and sacrificing preists, no others being
either to consecrate, or direct them in their
holy labours, but those which are manifestly proued such. And seeing wee do not
finde in any antiquary, Catholicke or Protestant, but S. Iosephs both conuersation
and direction was either with, or by S. Peter, S. Iohn, S. Iames, or S. Philip, Apostles, all these beeing acknowledged to bee
massinge preists, whosoeuer in S. Iosephs
company were consecrated, or directed by
any of them, could not receaue any other
consecration, or direction.

3. But to do some honor vnto this kingdome, of great Britanie more expressely in
this kind, though the generally complained
of, and lamented amonge antiquaries losse
of

of our auncient records, and histories of
these matters, will forbid mee to write so
fully as I could wishe, of this subiect, I will
set downe some of the cheifest, and first
massinge and sacrificinge preists, and Bishops in this nation, and shew plainly, how
wee had and euer continued, an holy and
hierarchicall succession of such sacred parsons from S. Peter, that greatest Apostle of
Christ in all ages, offeringe the blessed bodie, and blood of Christ in the sacrifice of
Masse, vnto these times. So that it shall euidently appeare, although this kingedome
hath for situation beene called an other
world, yet it did neuer from the beginning
of Christianitie here, differ frō the known
Catholick Christian world, in these holy
misteries, vntill these times.

4. For the truth and veritie of this first
plantinge the sacrificinge Christian preisthood, and sacrifice of Masse in this kingdome, it is little or nothing materiall whether it was S. Peter, S. Paul, or S. Simon
Zelotes, or S. Ioseph of Aramathia, or any
others, disciples to any of those, or any others of the Apostles, because as before is
proued, they all agreed in these holy thinges;

ges; yet to know who was our firſt founder
and Father in Chriſt, to whome wee owe
for that the greateſt reuerence, dutiful children ſhould, and ought to performe, to deriue from him, our happy Hierarchicall
ſucceſſion in holy things, and to know the
truth which ſome haue veiled and obſcu-
red to much, it is a thing moſt worthy our
knowledge, and our ſhame if wee ſhoulde
dwell in ignorance thereof. Therefore to be
breife, becauſe it is lately and largely proued, that S. Peter was this our firſt parent
in Chriſt, by all teſtimonies, for this place
it will ſuffice, to ſhew how the beſt learned
Engliſh Proteſtant antiquaries moſt back-
ward in this buſines, by certaine Maximes
or vndoubted grounds in antiquitie, doe
conſequently and by an euident neceſſitie,
binde themſelues and al others to be of this
opinion. *Stowe and Howes hiſtor.*

5. Firſt they ſay the twelue Apoſtles diuided the world amongſt them, to conuert
it. Secondly, which followeth from the former, that this kingdome fell in diuiſion to
one of theſe Apoſtles. Thirdly, that there is
a ſilence in hiſtories, that any Apoſtle, but
S. Peter, S. Paul (this none of the twelue)
and

and S. Simon Zelotes were here. Fourthly, that this kingdome receaued the faith (if not sooner) in the beginninge of the Empire of Claudius. Fiftly, that in his time many Christians came hither from Rome, and diuers here were in that time conuerted to the faith of Christ. Sixtly, that S. Paul came not to Rome, nor any of these western parts, while longe after the death of Claudius, in the dayes of Nero, as the scripture it selfe with all histories is witnesse therof. Seuenthly, none of them doth affirme, that S. Simon Zelotes was here at all, but if hee were here, they incline to thinke hee came not hither vntill the cominge of S. Ioseph of Aramathia, in the 63. yeare of Christ, when in all opinions diuers of this kingedome were Christians allmost 20. yeares, and some preists of this nation very longe before that time.

6. From hence an halfe blind man must needs make this vndoubted, and infallible conclusion, that S. Peter was our first Apostle and Father in Christ. These protestant antiquaries of Englād giue vs further warrant both from themselues and antiquitie, *that S. Peter did in euery Prouince appoint*

one

one Archbishop, whom all other Bishops of the same Prouince should obey. Peter preached in no place, but hee there ordeyned Bishops and teachers, and founded churches. And that it is confirmed almost 800.yeares since by Simeon Metaphrastes (a learned Saint of the Greeke church) out of the Greeke Antiquities, and diuers others that S. Peter preachinge the word of life in this Iland, hee here founded churches and ordeyned preistes and deacons. And except S. Peter himselfe, S. Iohn, S. Iames, S. Marke and S. Timothie with whom they Paralel S. Aristobulus our first Archbishop, were not Archbishops, this great Saint was by theire allowance our Archbishop in Britanie, and as before so constituted by S. Peter, no other being then to ordeine him to that dignitie in this nation, all which our protestants thus write with publick warrant and priuiledge. *Iohn Whitguift answere to the admonition pag. 65. sect. 1. and def. of the answ. pag. 318. Clem. Rom. apud eund. & Polydor. Virg. l. 4. de inuent. c. 12. 13. Sutcliff. Subuers. pag. 3. Theater of great Britanie l. 6. cap. 9. Sim. Metaphrast. die 29. Ian. Eisengrencentem. 1. Thom. Rogers in artic. Relig. of Engl.*

P
articul.

7. Therefore except this great massing preist and Apostle S. Peter should bee of an other opinion and practise in these thinges in this our Britanie, then hee and all the other Apostles had beene in all other times and places before (which no Christian can once imagine) he also consecrated massing and sacrificing preists, and Bishops in, and for this kingdome. And although our losses of such sacred monuments haue beene great, yet wee haue not altogether loste the memory of al their names: one and the first which I finde in histories, was *S. Mansuetus natione Scotus*, borne in this kingdome of great Britanie, and by the antiquities of the church of Toul in Lorraine claimed to bee the first Bishop of that citie, so likewise of the church of Treuers, except the identitie of the name deceaueth mee, to be afterwarde liuinge very longe Archbishop there, because hee made much stay or residence in those places, yet both our learned contriman S. Marianus, and Methodus, nere the Apostles times affirme, that hee as others which they there name, S. Clement, Felix, Rusticus, Moses, Martinus &c. preached
ched

ched both , *in propria prouincia & exterius,* both in their owne and other nations . *Annal. Tollens. Arnold. Mirman. in Theatr. conuerſ. gent. Belliforeſt Coſmograph. Petr. Merſſaus Catalog. Archiep. Treuerenſ. in S. Manſueto. Marian. Scot. l. 2. ætat. 6. col. 254. Method. apud eundem ſupr.*

8. This holy contriman of ours beeinge consecrated preiſt by S. Peter , that greate maſſinge preiſt, and Apoſtle, muſt needes himſelfe also by that , if wee had no other argument, bee a maſſinge preiſt . But wee ar not ſo ſtreightned of proofes in this matter, for wee haue warrant by the French & German hiſtories, that hee was one of the companions of S. Clement vncle to S. Clement the Pope, that great maſſinge Archbiſhop of Metz , ſent thither as Arnoldus Mirmannius thinketh in the time of Caius Caligula: ſo auncient a maſſinge preiſt he maketh this our glorious contrimā. *Arnold. Mirm. ſupr. Annal. Tullen. Bellifor. ſupr. Gul. Eiſengren. centur. 1. Petr. de natal. l. 11. Demochar. l. 2. de Miſſ. contra Caluin. Caio Caligula Imperante , Tullenſes habuere Apoſtolum, ſuaque in Chriſtum fidei primum Antiſtitem S. Petri Apoſtoli diſcipulum S. Clemen-*

tis

tis Collegam origine Scotum. The inhabitants of Toul had for their Apostle & first
Bishop of their faith in Christ, S. Mansuetus disciple of S. Peter the Apostle, companion of S. Clement, hee beeinge a Scot by
natiuitie. Eisengrenius, and the Authors
hee followeth, hath the same, onely saying
he was made Bishop of Toul Anno Christi
49. in the 49. yeare of Christ in the Empire
of Claudius. *Guliel. Eisengr. centur. 1. fol.*
56. cit. Petr. de natal. l. 11. & Demochar. l.
2.) so that if this Britanie had a massinge
preist made by S. Peter, whose disciple he
was, in the 40. yeare of Christ, and the
same a massinge Bishop within 9. yeares
after, the sacrifice of Masse, beeing of continuance here aboue 1580. yeares, it maketh
a sufficient time of prescription to claime
title of continuance. And hee was one of
the oldest massing preists and Bishops, that
I finde of this nation, onely S. Kentigern
equall perhaps vnto him therin, for the annals of Treuers say that this S. Mansuetus (I
finde no other in that time) was successor
to the greate massinge Archbishop of that
city S. Maternus, of whome I haue spoken
before, *Anno Domini* 160. in the 160. yeare
of

of Chrift: at which time, by many authors
Kinge Lucius and this kingdome was conuerted ; and befides many fuch preifts had
28. maffing Bifhops, as I fhall demonftrate
in the next age . *Petrus Merſſeus Catalog.*
Archiep. Treuer. an. 160.

9. And very probable it is, euen by our
Englifh Proteftants . *The Proteſtant Thea-*
ter of great Britanie l. 6. teaching that about
this time betweene the 40. and 50. yeare of
Chrift, many in Britany became Chriftiãs,
as namely *Pomponia Græcina,* the wife of the
Romans Lieutenant, Aulus Plautius , and
about the fame time *S. Beatus,* and his holie companion Anonymus, but that a German writer calleth him *Achates,* made maſ-
fing preifts by S. Peter, & directed by him,
this holy maffinge preift S. Manfuetus had
fome cooperatiõ in that happy bufines. And
that thefe our two renowned contrimen S.
Beatus and his companion, were facrificing
maffing preifts, it is euident: firft becaufe
they were here firft inftructed in the faith
of Chrift by thẽ, which of neceffitie (no o-
thers being here, or els where at that time)
were maffinge preifts: fecondly becaufe as
thefe proteftãts both Germã & Englifh tell

as they were further instructed & directed
by S. Peter a massing preist and Apostle, &
if perhaps (which these men doe not insinuate, S. Peter was martired before they
were consecrated preists, yet beeing consecrated at Rome, without all question,
where none but massinge Bishops and consecrators were, S. Linus, Cletus or Clemens,
they must needs bee consecrated massinge
preists. which is further proued by the places of their moste aboade after, S. Beatus
liuinge in and beeinge the Apostle of Heluetia, where abouts many massinge preists
before remembred consecrated by S. Peter,
as S. Eucharius, Valerius, Clemens, Mansuetus, his contryman, with others were.
The other came into his owne contry of
Britanie here, where (as before) as he could
finde none but massinge preists, so hee left
behinde him no others, as I shall proue herafter.

10. And manifest it is, that our Christian Britans which were conuersinge at
Rome, when and where they were consecrated, and with whome they also at their
beeing there conuersed, were for their qualities, sayers, or hearers of Masse. Which is
clearely

clearly proued by the Christian family of
our noble contriwoman Claudia, or Sabi-
nella, wife to Aulus Pudes; whose house by
the Romane antiquities, as it was the first
lodginge of S. Peter the Apostle, that great
massinge preist, so it was their cheifest place of saying, and hearinge Masse: *Maiorum*
traditione præscriptum est, domum Pudentis
Romæ fuisse primum hospitium Sancti Petri,
illicque primum Christianos conuenisse ad Sy-
naxim coactam Ecclesiam. Martyrolog. Rom.
in S. Pudente, Praxede, Pudentiana, Donato
& Timotheo. Baron. ib. annotat. die 19. Maij.
Where wee see, it the first and principall
massinge church in Rome, both for the Britans & Romans also, that were Christians,
and the best residency S. Peter or his successors which were the consecrators of preists
there had at that time. And hee had such
care of this house and family, that not onlie the parents, Pudens, and Claudia, but
all their children S. Nouatus, S. Timotheus,
Pudentiana, and Praxedes were by him instructed in the faith, and S. Timothie was
made massinge preist, as the auncient Roman Martyrologe and others witnes. *Romæ*
depositio S. Nouati, filij beati Pudentis Sena-
P 4   *toris,*

tories , & fratris S. Timothei presbyteri , &
sanctarum Christi virginum Pudentiana, &
Praxedis, qui ab Apostolis eruditi sunt in fide.
Martyrolog. Rom. die 20. Iunij. Vsuard. eod.
die. Baron. annotat. in 20 diem Iun. act. S. Nouati & S. Iustine. Therefore this S. Timotheus our holy côtriman by his blessed Mother S. Claudia , beeinge instructed by S. Peter a massinge preist, and consecrated by a massinge preist and Pope, and resigninge his house to be a massinge church , as will euidentlye appeare in the beginninge of the next age , when I come to that notorious massinge preist and Pope S. Pius by our protestants confessions, who dedicated that house for a massing church, must himselfe also by these protestants bee a massing preist , and his holy parents brother and and sisters sacred Virgins ; with the rest of our Christian contrimen there , bee reuerencers and frequenters of holy Masse.

11. The like I might without reprofe write of others , whose names I haue els where remêbred , that probably they preached in Britanie , in this age , and out of question were massinge preists, but hauing so many certaine and euident examples without exception ; I neede not the assi-

stance of probabilities, onely because wee
are assured by great English Protestants Bishops and others, that as the truth is, *there
is a mutuall relation and dependance, betweene
an altare and sacrifice, and that an altar doth
as naturally, and as necessarily infer a sacrifice,
as a shrine doth a Saint, a Father a sonne.*
(*Morton. Apolog. part. 2. pag. 82. Morton appeale l. 2. sect. 1. pag. 162.*) these protestants
confesse vnto vs againe, which they cannot deny, that longe before they imagine
any alteration of Religion in the church of
Rome, this kingdome had Christian altars,
(*Theater of great Britanie l. 6. Gildas l. de excid.*) and amonge others they iustifie vnto
vs the antiquities of Glastenbury, which
assure vs, there was an altare in the olde
church there builded by S. Ioseph of Aramathia, and his holy company; and this
altar and holy place was of such reuerence,
that the holy Saint Patrick with others, de-
sired to bee buried by that holy altar, and
an Angel from heauen did assigne him that
place of buriall. *Sepulturam Angelo mon-
strante, flamamque ingente de eodem loco cunctis videntibus erumpente in vetusta Ecclesia
in dextera parte altaris promeruit.* Where we
see

see an Angel from heauen, and with a great
figne, and miracle, openly before all people
prefent, *cunctis videtibus*, to giue teftimony
to the worthines of the holy altar, & place
in refpect therof. *Io. Leland in affert. Arthur.*
Math. Park. antiquit. Britan. Stow hift. Godw.
conuerf. of Brit. antiquit. Glafto apud Capgrau.
in S. Patric. Gul. Malm. l. antiq. canob. Glaft.

12. And not without iuft caufe & deter-
uing by thefe our proteftats who in Gildas
as they allowe him, & who wrote as they
comonly teach, when the Britans ftill held
the Religion deliuered vnto them in the
Apoftles time, without alteration, doe teftifie, that the altars here from the beginning
were, *facra altaria, Sacrofancta altaria, facri-*
ficij cæleftis fedes, holy altars, facred altars, the
feate of the celeftiall facrifice, altars at which
preifts did facrifice and fay Maffe, Sacerdotes
facrificantes inter altaria ftantes. Altars fan-
ctuaries and priuiledges, refuge for fuch as
fled vnto them, teftified by our proteftants
themfelues. *Gildas epiftol. de excid. & con-*
queft. Britan. edit. per proteftant. who further witneffing that the firft general councell of Nice was receaued here in Britanie
in the da ies of Conftantine, and now by
                                        our

our proteſtant ſtatute is of high authoritie,
and vndeniable in England, witneſſe alſo:
The Nicen councell in that canon which Cal-
uine and all other receaue, ſaith plainely, that
the Lambe of God offered vnbloodely, is layed
vpon the holy table. Stowe and howes hiſtor.
an. 542. theater of great Britanie l. 6. ſtatut.
an. 1. Eliz. Regin. & 1. Iacob. Regis. Fraunc.
Maſon with direct of the proteſt. Archb. Abbots booke of conſecrat. pag. 243. and the ſacrifice of Chriſtians beeing as is inuincibly
proued, the moſte holy body and blood of
Chriſt, and the altar the place whereon it
is offered, by that connexion in Greeke,
θυσία θυσιαϛήριον, mutuall correlatiues, and
inſeparable, & nomine & re, it cannot poſſibly bee otherwiſe. So that if any teſtimonie of heauen or earth, men or Angels, Catholicks or Proteſtants will ſatiſfy in this
matter, it is manifeſtly conuinced, that S.
Peter preached and eſtabliſhed a ſacrificing
preiſthood, and the doctrine and practiſe
of holy Maſſe in this our nation.

13. And yet if any man is deſirous to
heare S. Peter himſelfe confirme that from
heauen, which hee ſo approued on earthe,
wee may add ſuch his teſtimony alſo to the
holy

holy Angels before, and bringe other A-
postles from heauen also, that were mafsinge preists when they liued here, to iu-
stifye the same, in, and to this kingedome. Wee reade in the aunciently written
life of S. Sampson Archbishop of yorke,
when our protestants say the Britans still
kept their Apostolick first receaued Religion, a man so holy and miraculous that S.
Iltutus prophesied of him beeing but a boy
of seuen yeares old, that he should be a light
to this nation, the cheife of all, and Archbishop very profitable to the church of
God. *Cum septem esset annorum ad S. Iltutum*
Abbatem discendi gratia adducitur: qui vi-
dens puerum osculatus est eum, dicens: gratias
Deo agimus qui lumen hoc nobis indignæ de
gente nostra accendere dignatus est in terra.
En caput omnium nostrum: en Pontifex sum-
mus multam Ecclesiæ Dei profuturus. Manuf-
cript. antiq. & Capgrau. in Catalog. in vita S.
Sampsonis Ep. & Confess. he was made a deacon, and after a massing preist by the great
massing preist and Bishop S. Dubritius the
Popes Legate, consecrated by the massinge
Bishop S. Germanus, who was sent hither
from S. and Pope Celestine, to settle the
church

church of Britanie; both whē he was made
deacon and preist, a doue descended vppon
him and staied immouably vntill the office
was ended. *Beeing made a preist, hee was so
glorious and renowned a massinge preist, that
alwaies in his life he had Angels assisting and
ministring vnto him whensoeuer he said Masse. Omni tempore vitæ suæ Angelos dum celebraret, sibi assistere & in sacrificio ministrare
videre meruit.* Yet this man aboue all of
this nation, was in such fauour with God,
S. Peter, S. Iames called the brother of our
Lord, S. Iohn the Euangelist and the court
of heauen, that these three great Apostles,
with a great company of celestiall citi-
zens, *densissimis candidatorum turmis*, appeared vnto him, and S. Peter told him,
*that our Lord Iesus Christ had chosen him to
bee a Bishop:* and soone after an Angell appeared to *S. Dubritius*, and commaunded him to
consecrate S. Sampson a Bishop: in whose consecration they, that were present did see a
Doue sent from heauen to stand immouably vppon him. *Nec multo post Angelus Domini beato Dubritio apparens, Sampsonem ordinari Episcopum præcepit, in cuius consecratione qui aderant columbam cælitus emissam
immo-*

14. And in the time of S. Mansuetus, the first Bishop of London in the Saxons time, when S. Peter did miraculously appeare about the dedicatinge of the church of westminster, as many both holy and aunct̄ Catholicke writers, and protestants antiquaries assure vs, and the circumstances of the historie demonstrate it to bee true, hee sent this charge and commaund to S. Mellitus Bishop of London, who had determined to dedicate it the next day followinge: *I haue dedicated the church, and by authoritie of my sanctification preuented the episcopall benediction. Therefore tell the Bishop what thou hast heard and seene, and the signes remayninge will iustifie thy wordes to bee true. Therfore let him absteine from dedication, and supply that which wanteth, to offer there the holy sacrifice of our Lords body and blood. Ego sum Petrus qui cum meis ciuibus construct̄am in meo nomine basilicam dedicaui, episcopalem-que benedictionem meæ sanctificationis authoritate præueni. Dic ergo Pontifici quæ vidisti & audisti, tuoque sermoni signa parietibus im-pressa testimonium perhibebunt. Supersedeat igitur dedicatione, suppleat quod omisimus Do-*

minici

*minici corporis & sanguinis Sacrosancta my-
steria. S. Alured. Riuall. M.S. in vita S. Eduardi Regis & confess. Iacob. Gen. Episc. in eius
vit. & M. S. antiq. Sur. in vit eius & Cap-
gran. in eius vit. Franc. Mason l. of consecrat.*
here wee see, that S. Peter now in glory,
both allowed and commaunded the sacrifice of Masse, which when hee liued and
conuersed on earth, hee had practised, frequented, and instituted with so great dili-
gence and deuotion.

15. So likewise when in the time of the
Danish fury here, hee appeared to comfort
this afflicted contry, where hee had preached and taught this holy doctrine, hee did
not chuse any man to reueale his glad ti-
dings vnto, and the deliuery of this kingdome, but S. Brithwold, that great and famous massinge preist, and Bishop of Winchester, or Wilton, and in the most known
massinge place of England, the Abbey of
Glastenbury, and did fortell, how S. Edward Kinge and confessor, that most great
reuerencer of holy Masse, perhaps yet vn-
borne, and borne in exile in Normandy,
should bee Kinge in England, and deliuer
it from those floods of miseries, wherewith
is

it was then surrounded, and longe time had
beene. And to assure vs this was a true vision, and prophesie of S. Peter, and hee an
approuer of all louers of holy Masse, as God
also is, this hee addeth : *Erit cum dormieris*
cum patribus tuis, visitabit Dominus populum
suum, & faciet Dominus redemptionem plebis
suæ. Eliget enim sibi virum secundum cor suum
qui faciat omnes voluntates suas, qui me opi-
tulante regnum adeptus Anglorum Danico
furori finem imponet. Erit enim acceptus Deo,
gratus hominibus, terribilis hostibus, amabilis
ciuibus, vtilis Ecclesiæ, laudabilemque vitam
sancto fine concludet. It shall come to passe,
when thou shalt sleepe with thy Fathers,
our Lord will visit his people, and our Lord
will cause a redemption of his people. For
hee will chuse vnto himselfe a man, accordinge to his owne hart, which shall doe all
his desires, who by my helpe obteyninge
the crowne of England, shall make an end
of the Danish fury. For hee shall bee acceptable to God, gratefull to men, terrible to
his enemies, amiable to his citisens, profitable to the church, and hee shall conclude
his laudable life, with an holy end. And
the holy and learned writers of his life thus
imme-

immediatly add : *all which things the euent of the thinge proued to bee fulfilled in S. Edward . Quæ omnia in beato Eduardo completa rei exitus comprobauit .* Therefore this muſt needs bee a true viſion, and propheſie of S. Peter. *Alured Riuall.l.de vit.S. Eduardi Iacob. Epiſc. Gen. in vit. eius M.S. antiq. ibid. Capgrau. in Catal. in S. Eduardo Rege & Confeſſore Sur.in vit eius & Lippom.Godwin Catal. of Biſhops in B. Brithwild.*

16. This is that holy Kinge that left the hereditary miraculous power of curing the diſeaſe called the Kings euill obteyned by his piety, to his ſucceſſors. This is that great reuerencer of maſſinge preiſts , this is hee who at the time of eleuation at holy Maſſe in England , vpon Whitſunday did ſee by reuelation the Kinge of Denmarke drowned in the ſea by the coaſte of Denmarke, as hee was takinge ſhip to come to inuade England, and his nauy diſperſed, which, *peractis Miſſarum ſolemnijs,* as ſoone as Maſſe was ended, hee confidently related. *This holie Kinge,* to ſpeake in proteſtants and their authors words. (*Stowe hiſtor.in Edward Cōfeſſor.*)*before the day of his natiuitie was elected of God, who perſeuering in chaſtitie, ledd*

Q   *a*

all his life dedicated to God in true marriage,
wherefore as wee haue knowne proued by good
and sufficient men being witnesses, God great-
lie glorified him in his life with wonderful sig-
nes . Therefore it is euident that S. Peter,
and God himselfe, with the whole court of
heauen, did , and doe allowe of massinge
preifts, and the holy sacrifice of Masse, not
only as it was celebrated in the beginning,
but after all additions which protestantes
write, or imagine, were put vnto it; for after all thefe added and longe after , as wee
see, both S. Peter and God himfelfe did thus
approue, and honor the both reuerent sayers, and hearers of that blessed sacrifice.

THE XIII. CHAPTER.

Wherein is proued, how after the death of S.
Peter, in the time followinge commonly af-
cribed to S. Linus and Cletus in the fee of
Rome , and to Marius Kinge in Britanie,
the Britans both at home and abroade vfed
the facrificing preifthood, preifts and Masse.

Hitherto wee haue spoken of S. Peter,
who being martired by Nero the Emperor,

peror, it is a question whether S. Linus, whom (and S. Cletus) he had consecrated Bishops at his beeinge at Rome before hee came into these West parts, or S. Clement did immediatly succed him; S. Leo the second with our renowned contrimen, S. Marianus, Florentus Wigorniensis, and to speake in Martinus Polonus wordes. (*Leo Papa 2. epistol. decretal. Marian. Scot. lib. 2. etat. 6. in Nerone. Florent. Wigorn. an 50. al. 72. Martin. Pol. supputat. col. 33. in Lino.*) *They which searched more diligently concerning the chaire of the Romane church, doe say, that Linus and Cletus did not sitt as Popes, but as coadiutors of the Pope, to whome S. Peter in his life onely committed the dispensation of ecclesiasticall things: for which beeing endowed with so great authoritie, they deserued to bee placed in the catalogue of the Popes, but S. Peter appointed S. Clement his successor.* Dicunt qui de cathedra Romanæ Ecclesiæ diligentius perscrutati sunt, quod Linus & Cletus non sederunt vt Pontifices, sed vt summi Pontificis coadiutores, quibus in vita sua beatus Petrus vnam tradidit ecclesiasticarum rerum dispensationem: propter quod tanta authoritate dotati, meruerunt in catalogo Pontifi-

cum

cum poni . *Clementem vero ipse beatus Petrus succefforem conſtituit* . Which S. Clement himſelfe as he is commonly receaued, doth alſo likewiſe affirme of himſelfe, and S. Leo ſaith: *Linum & Cletum nihil vnquam legi-bus ſuis ex pontificali miniſterio , poteſtatiuè egiſſe, ſed quantum eis à beato Petro præcipie-batur, tantum ſolumodo agebant* . Linus and Cletus did nothinge at any time by theire lawes by papall miniſtery or power , but how much was commaunded them by S. Peter, ſo much onely they did. *Clem. Roman. epiſtol.* 1. *Leo Papa* 2. *epiſt. decretali ſupr. apud Marian. Wigorn. & alios.* which wee finde in their liues that the firſt , *ex præcepto Pe-tri Apoſtoli conſtituit, vt mulier in Eccleſiam velato capite intret:* conſtituted by the com-maundement of S. Peter , that a woman ſhould haue her head couered , when ſhee entred the church . *The other by the precept of S. Peter ordeyned* 21. *preiſts in the citie of Rome.Cletus , hic ex præcepto Petri, vigin-ti & vnum presbyteros ordinauit in vrbe Ro-ma. Martin. Polon. ſupputat. in Lino & Cleto & alij.*

2. But becauſe many others , and great authors incline to thinke they were Popes,

I

I meddle not to discusse this matter, little
pertinent to my present purpose, because
very little is written of them. But this most
certaine it is, that whether they were Popes, or no, being consecrated by S. Peter
that knowne massing preist, and Pope, and
hauinge S. Clement their successor, that
knowne, massinge Pope, they must needs
bee also massinge preists, and Popes, if they
were Popes. And for S. Linus who as both
Catholicks & Protestants testifie, did write
the acts of S. Peter in the same sort as they
are published, giueth plaine testimony, to
the daily saying of Masse, & offering therin the blessed body and blood of Christ,
and sheweth how the signe of the Crosse
was vsed in the celebration thereof euerie
day : *ô crux quæ quotidiè carnes immaculati
Agni fidelibus diuidis populis. Linus in histor.
pass. S. Petri.* And it is proued not onely by
histories, but S. Paul himselfe doth sufficiently incline vs to knowe, that his cheife
lodginge was in the then cheife massinge
houle of our Christian Britans, at Rome,
and not onely of him, and other the Popes,
but such holy disciples as came to Rome
vnto them: for writing vnto S. Timothie.

Q 3 (2.

2. *Timoth*. 4.) hee remembreh onely to falute him, but fower parfons, *Eubulus*, *Linus*,
Pudens, and *Claudia*, which feeme to haue
had all , or the mofte of their permanency
in that houfe , where S, Timothy alfo had
beene entertayned when hee was at Rome:
and therefore they alone falute him, beeing
as S. Chrifoftome and Theodoret wel note
vppon this place, the moft eminent Chriftians then in Rome. *S. Chrifoftom. & Theo-*
doret. in 2. Tim. 4. for S. Linus was a Bifhop
there ordeyned by S. Peter , and the other
three renowned for their harbouring of the
Chriftians, there at that time, as moft certaine it is of Pudens and Claudia , and not
vnprobable as I haue fhewed in other places that Eubulus was our noble contriman
and Father to Claudia , and fo for his hof-
pitalitie to the Saints of God, firft remembred in this falutation, all hiftories beeinge
filent of him and no other nation claiming
him to bee from them.

3. Therefore this beeing then fo renowned a receptacle, and maffinge houfe , although S. Linus did not intermeddle in fen-
dinge preifts, or preachers into this, or any
other countrie , yet the Chriftian Britans
which

which liued at home, could not bee ignorant what was done in such things, in this
holy house of our so eminent Christians at
Rome, seeing there was continuall traffick
and intercourse betweene Rome and Britanie at that time, and so much euen in spirituall things by our best protestant antiquaries of this kingdom. (*Theater of great Brit.
l. 6. Matth. Parker antiquitat. Britan. pag.
2. 3. Godwin. conuers. of Britanie pag. 17. 18.
Cambd. in Britan. Stowe histor.*) that they as-
scribe a great part of the labours and meanes of plantinge the faith of Christ in Britanie, to our holy Brittish Lady Claudia,
and those of that house in Rome. All of
them beeing Christians, as both Catholicks and Protestants write, *totamque suam
familiam Christi fidem amplexos*, and that
number so greate, that there were in it in
the beginning of the next age an hundred
men, wantinge foure, *nonaginta sex homines*, that were Christians, and not fewer in
this time by probable opinion, the owners
of the house beeing both so honorable and
religious, all of them hearers at the leaste,
and frequenters of this most holy sacrifice.
*vit. S. Pudentiana in Breuiar. Rom. die 19.
Maÿ.*

4. And to speake in a Protestant Arch-bishops, & great ātiquaries words: (*Matth. Parker. antiquitat.Britan.pag.3.*) *Nec verisimile solum sed verum iudicandum est , in tam nobili familia fuisse cum Claudia gentiles suos Britannos qui vna baptisati fuerunt, à quibus Euangelij ignicula per totam gentem Britannicam dispersa,viritim ad multos peruenerunt.* Neither is it onely to bee iudged likely, but true , that in so noble a family with Claudia , there were Britans her countrimen, which were baptised with her , by whome the smale fiers of the ghospell dispersed throughout the whole nation of Britanie from man to man, did come to many.And not onely those reuerencers of holy Masse which were of the family of Lady Claudia,but many others in Rome,at that time, both Romane and Brittish Christians , in theire owne parsons cominge from thence into Britanie , parsonally performed these holy offices , as our Theater protestantes, thus assure vs. *Theater of great Britanie l. 6. cap.9. it hath also passed with allowance among the learned Senate of our antiquaries , that when Nero began (a little before this time)to banish*

banish and persecute the Christians in Rome, many Romans and Britans beeing conuerted to the faith, fled thence into these remote parts of the earth, where they might, and did more freely enioy the libertie of their professions. Which an other Protestant Bishop and antiquary speakinge of these dayes of Claudia, thus cōfirmeth. (*Godwin conuers. of Britanie pag. 18. cap. 3.*) *Of these times wee speake of, I doubt not wee may vse the words of Cassiodorus, it was not counted vnlawful for those to bee Christians, that dwelt beyond Italy and Fraunce, as in Britanie. Whereby vndoubtedly it came to passe, that many professing Christ, not daringe to abide nere vnto the hart of the Empire, made choice of our Britanie, vvhere to leade their liues in such sort, as they might enioy libertie of conscience.* And hee noteth in the mergine : *Britanie a refuge for Christians.*

9. Therefore although wee should follow their opinion, that say S. Linus and Cletus executed the papall function, excluding S. Clement vntill after their death, though wee finde no preists purposely, sent by them vnto this kingdome, or other nation, yet the protestants themselues do freelie

lie

lie graunt. *The English Protestant Margin.
annot. in Matth. Westm. an. 59. Robert. Barnes in vit. Pontif. in Lino Damaf. feu Anastaf.
in S. Lino & Cleto. Breu. Rom. die. 26. April.
& 23. Septemb. Martin. Pol. in S. Lino &
Cleto.* that they were both made preists by
the great maffinge preist and Apostle S. Peter, *Petrus Apostolus Linum & Cletum presbyteros ordinauit,* and both of them did alfo
make preists, S Linus 18. as both Catholicks and proteftants teach, and diuers Bishops: and S. Cletus by S. Peters commaund
confecrated in the citie of Rome 25. preifts,
which beeing commaunded by a maffinge
Apoftle, and performed by a maffinge Bishop, muft needs bee maffinge preifts, and
all thofe fo many Chriftians of thefe times
by our proteftants before either Britans or
Romans, which either by their concurréce
at Rome ftill ftaying there, or by perfonall
prefence beinge come, and ftayinge here,
gaue affiftance and helpe towardes the inftruction and conuerfion of this our Britanie, muft needes bee either fayers, or hearers of Maffe, and practifers and approuers
of that holy facrifice, and fo ioyned themfelues with thofe maffinge preifts, and Bishops

shops in this kingdome, which I named before and liued longe after this time, as I
shall shewe hereafter. Or if wee will rather
incline to them that say, these two were
onely coadiutors and not Popes, but giue
the papacy in this time to S. Clement as
some Protestants with many Catholicks
before, and others hold, to speake in a protestants words (*Robert. Barnes l. de vit. Pontif. Romanor. in Petro. Petrus ordinauit Clementem, sui officij vices ei committens:*) Peter
ordeyned Clement, committinge the place
of his office vnto him: It must needs euen
by that title bee, that as hee was sacred and
receaued this charge and power from that
great massing preist, and Bishop S. Peter,
so hee also receaued from him that holy sacrificinge preisthood, and power, and succeeded him in that; as other sacred papall
functions, of whome I am to speake in the
chapter followinge.

THE

THE XIV. CHAPTER.

How duringe the time of S. Clement his papacy , and all this first hundred yeares of Christ , our Christian Britans , together with all others continued these holy doctrines and offices of sacrificing preisthood, preistes, and the sacrifice of the blessed body and blood of Christ in Masse.

THis holy and learned Pope , and successor to S. Peter, S. Clement, whether hee presently executed that highest pastorall function, or of humilitie gaue place to S. Linus, and Cletus more aunciently consecrated Bishops, at and for Rome by S. Peter , beeing himselfe consecrated as before a massinge preist , and most deuoutly and religiously as I shall demonstrate , continually executinge that holy massinge and sacrificinge preistly power, and duty, did not onely in generall impart it to this nation , as hee had care and charge of the whole church committed vnto him, nor in particular because hee had residence and much continuance with our Christian Britans

tans at Rome as S. Cletus, Linus and Peter
before had, but becauſe in all probable iudgement, hee was longe time here in Britanie with S. Peter, and after by the ſame
greate Apoſtle charged in one of his laſte
admonitions vnto him, to haue an eſpecial
care of this kingdome of Britanie in particular, both which are eaſely proued by the
words of S. Peter vnto S. Clement, as hee
himſelfe thus relateth them, and produceth
them, as one amonge other reaſons, why
aboue all others ſo manie worthie men, hee
made choiſe of S. Clement to bee his ſucceſſor. *Clemens Rom. epiſtol. 1. ex verb. S. Pe-*
tri. mihi ab initio vſque ad finem comes itine-
ris & actuum fueris, quæque per ſingulas ci-
uitates, me diſputante ſolicitus Auditor exce-
peris. Thou haſt beene a companion of my
trauailes, and deedes from the beginninge
vnto the end. Thou as a carefull Auditor
haſt obſerued what I haue preached in euerie citie.

2. And to him againe: *If I had any other*
better then thou, or any had beene ſo diligent
helper of mee, or any had ſo fully receaued my
doctrine, and learned my eccleſiaſticall diſpo-
ſitions, if I had any ſuch other, I woulde not
compell

*compell the vnwillinge to vndertake this good
vvorke: Si eſſet alius melior, ſi quis mihi alius
adiutor tam ſedulus adſtitiſſet, ſi quis tam plenè doctrinæ meæ rationem capiſſet, ſed & ec-
cleſiaſticas diſpoſitiones à me tam plenè didiciſ-
ſet, habens alium talem, non te cogerem opus
bonum ſuſcipere nolentem.* And to the Chriſtians at Rome in this maner. When hee
was to die. *Audite me fratres & conſerui
mei, quoniam vt edoctus ſum ab eo qui me mi-
ſit, Domino & Magiſtro meo Ieſu Chriſto,
dies mortis meæ inſtat, Clementem hunc Epiſ-
copum vobis ordino, cui ſoli meæ prædicationis
& doctrinæ cathedram trado: Qui mihi ab initio vſque in finem comes in omnibus fuit, &
per hoc veritatem totius meæ prædicationis
agnouit: Qui in omnibus tentationibus meis
ſocius extitit, fideliter perſeuerans.* Heare
mee ô my brethren and fellow ſeruants, becauſe as I am taught by him that ſent mee,
my Lord and Maſter Ieſus Chriſt, the day
of my death is at hand, I ordeine this Clement to bee your Biſhop, to whome alone
I commit the chaire of my preachinge and
doctrine, who hath beene a companion
vnto mee in all thinges, or places from the
begining to the end, and thereby knoweth
the

the truth of all my preachinge . Who hath beene my fellow in al my tentations, faithfully perseueringe. *Clem. supr. epist.* 1. *Marian-Scot. in S. Petro. Flor. Wigorn. in chron. in S. Petro. Leo Pap.* 2. *epistol. decretal. Alexander* 1. *epist.* 1. *ad omnes orthodox. To.* 1. *Concil.*

3. Therefore seing S. Peter was in Britanie as I haue shewed before, and our protestant antiquaries allowe of those auncient recordes, which almost 800. yeares since were alleaged for reuerende antiquities, and say, *that S. Peter stayed longe time in this our Britanie, conuerted many, founded churches, and ordeyned Bishops, preists, and deacons* ; *quo in loco cum longo tempore fuisset moratus, & verbo gratiæ multos illuminasset, & Ecclesias constituisset, Episcoposque, & presbyteros, & diaconos ordinasset . Protestant Theater of great Brit. lib. 6. cap. 9 antiquitat. græc. apud Sim. Metaphrasten die 29. Iunij. Laurent. Sur. 29. Iunij*: and was such a massinge preist and Apostle, as I haue shewed before, S. Clement this his vnseparable companion, in all times, and places, from the beginning to the end, and the best learner, follower, and obseruer of his doctrine,

and

and practife in holy Religion , must needs
bee here in Britanie, with him staying here
longe time , *longo tempore* , and bee as his
Master S. Peter was, a massing preist. And
S. Peter hauinge confecrated for the Romans two Bishops , S. Linus, and Cletus
before, S. Clement could not bee onely for
that place. And the commissionall wordes
of S. Peter to S. Clement, are generall for
all Christians , without limitation of place, or parsons, to supply the place, and parson of S. Peter, who was cheife of all . So
this must needs include our Britans, beinge
so many of them then Christians at Rome,
and his bretheren and fellowe seruants in
Christ , as the wordes bee , equally as the
Romans, or any others were: and our noble contriwoman S. Claudia her house hauinge many more Christians in it, then any
other in Rome, and the principall place of
S. Peters residence , when hee conuersed
there , it cannot seeme vnprobable , that
this great charge was committed to S. Cle-
mēt by S. Peter in that house, where the or-
dinarie assemblies of Christians were kept.
And so of all nations , this our Britanie
could not bee left out, in that charge , and
com-

commiſſion : which S. Clement himſelfe
doth ſufficiétly proue, in that epiſtle, wherwith others thus hee writeth of S. Peters
charge vnto him. *S. Clem. Rom. epiſt. 1. Leo
2. epiſtol. decretal. Marian. Scot. in S. Clemente. Florent. Wigorn. in eod.*

4. *Epiſcopos per ſingulas ciuitates, quibus
ille non miſerat, perdoctos & prudentes, ſicut
ſerpentes, ſimplicesque ſicut columbas, iuxta
Domini præceptionem, nobis mittere præcepit.
Quod etiam faſere inchoauimus, & Domino
opem ferente, facturi ſumus, vos autem per
veſtras dioceſes Epiſcopos ſacrate & mittite,
quia nos ad alias partes, quod idem iuſſet,
agere curabimus. Aliquos vero ad Gallias, Hiſ-
paniasque mittemus, & quosdam ad Germa-
niam, & Italiam, atque ad reliquas gentes dirigere cupimus. Vbi autem ferociores & rebelliores gentes eſſe cognouerimus, illic dirigere
ſapientiores, & auſteriores neceſſe habemus.*
S. Peter commaunded vs, to ſend Biſhops
very learned, and wiſe as ſerpents, and ſim-
ple as doues according vnto the commaū-
dement of our Lord, to all cities, to which
hee had not ſent. Which wee haue begun
to doe, and by the helpe of our Lord will
doe hereafter and conſecrate you (*writinge*

and send Bishops, throughout your diocesses, because wee will haue care to doe it to other parts, as hee commaunded. Wee will send some to Fraunce, and Spaine, and some to Germany, and Italy, as wee desire to the other nations:and where the people ar more feirce and rebellious,thither we haue need to send more wise and austere men.

5. Where wee euidently see, by S. Clements owne testimonie, & consent of manie auncient learned men embracinge it, that he was charged by S. Peter to send Bishops, not onely into Italy, Spaine, Fraunce, and Germany, but into all these other nations, *atque ad reliquas gentes*, in which Britanie must needs bee comprehended: & consideringe in what state of barbarousnes this kingdome was in respect of Italy, Spaine, Fraunce, and Germany also, before it became more ciuill by the Romans rulinge and abidinge here, and receauing the faith of Christ, there was no nation in this part of the world,knowne then to the Romans, that might bee so truely termed, *ferociores & rebelliores gentes*, more feirce and rebellious nations, then these of Britanie, as not

onely

onely the Roman historians of those times
but S. Gildas himselfe, a Britan, moste lamentably bewaylinge it , their owne Brittish history, and others ar sufficient witnesses. *I nl. Cæsar. l. de bell. Gallic. Cornel. Tacit.*
Sueton. Diod. Sicul. Gild. l. de excid. & con-
quest. Britan. Galfrid. Monum l. 3. 4. and yet
S. Clement plainely saith, that hee then already had , or would by the grace of God,
send Bishops into al those contries, and that
it was S. Peters commaunde vnto him to
send to all cities , where hee himselfe had
not ordeyned Bishops. Therefore wee cannot doubt , but S. Clement did performe
this commaundement of S. Peter, and his
owne promise in sending some learned Bishops , and preists into this kingdome . S.
Antoninus, Philippus Bergomensis, diuers
in the opinion of Harrison a protestant,
and Master Harris a late Catholicke writer
thinke hee sent S. Taurinus hither . *S. An-*
tonin. Florent. Archiep. histor. part. 1. Phi-
lipp. Bergom. histor. in S. Taurino. Will. Har-
rison descrip. of Britanie, Harris theatr. l. 1.
and this laste affirmeth the same of S. Nicasius citing also Arnoldus Mirmannius, who
plainely, saith that amonge other people, *S.*

Nica-

*Nicasius instructed the Britans in the faith,
beeinge sent thither Apostle by S. Clement:
Britones , formauit fide S. Nicasius à S. Clemente illuc Apostolus delegauit. Arnold. Mirmann. theatr. conuer). gent.* at which time there were no Britans, but of this Britanie.

6. The same I may and not vnprobably say, of S. Martine, to whome a church was dedicated at Canterbury in the time of Kinge Lucius, and S. Marcellus, or by some Marcellinus, a Brittish Bishop of this Land, or the nere ensuinge time. And if any man obiecteth, three of these S. Taurinus, Nicasius and Martine by diuers writers preached in Fraunce, this hindereth nothinge, but rather proueth, seeing others affirme it , that they preached here also , S. Marcellus , or Marcellinus which was certainly a Britan, both preached , and was Bishop in a forreine contry, so was S. Mansuetus , and S. Beatus in the same case before, and it is euident by *Methodius,* and *Marianus* already cited , that this was vsuall in those daies, for the same men to preach not onely in their owne, but forreine and straunge contries. And our English Protestant publishers of Matthew of Westminster, incline to
thinke

thinke fo of diuers sent into Fraunce by S.
Clement. (*Matth. Weftm. an. 94.*) amonge
whome there are numbred S. Nicasius, and
Taurinus; for where the Monke of Weftminfter faith, they were fent by S. Clement,
ad locandum in Gallijs nouæ fidei fundamen-
tum, to place the foundation of the faith in
Gallia : thefe proteftants giue a larger circuite, and fay plainely , *doctores mittuntur*
verfus occidentem, that S. Clement fent thofe
doctors, *S. Denis, Nicasius, Taurinus, Tro-*
phinus , Paulus , Saturninus, Aftremonius,
Martialis, Gratianus , Iulianus , Lucianus,
Firminus , Photinus into the Weft , where
Britanie is . *Proteftant Marg. annotat. in*
Matth. Weftm. fupr. an. 94. and very ftraung
it fhould be if S. Clement as before hauing
fo great charge giuen vnto him by S. Peter
as well of Britanie , as Gallia , and by his
owne words and promife was to fend Bifhops inro this our Britanie , fhould bee fo
mindfull of Fraunce fo nere vnto vs, to fend
fo many as we fee , thither , and forget S.
Peter, himfelfe, and Britanie fo much, as to
fend none vnto it at all.

7. That S. Clement , and confequently
thofe holy preifts and Bifhops which were

consecrated , and sent by him into these
parts, were sacrificinge and massinge preistes, is manifest before,& his owne works
ar so euident in this behalfe, that if S. Clement was not a massing preist, and Bishop,
and consecrated such , there neither is , or
euer was any massinge preist in the world.
For hee setteth downe at large the whole
order of that holy sacrifice, as it is now offered , and celebrated by Roman Catholicks , prouinge that vnbloody sacrifice to
bee the moste holie bodie , and blood of
Christ,so naming it,as also holy Oblation,
Masse , and other such titles as the present
Roman church doth. (*Clem. l. 6. constitut.*
cap. 23. l 2. cap. 6. 20. epistol. 2. l. 7. constitut.
Apostol. cap. 43. l. 8. cap. 35. l. 10. Recognit.
epist. 2. can. Apost. 3. 4. 5. 72.) hee remem-
breth also the consecrated Altars,whereon
it was offered, altare cloathes, and veales,
for the altare , lights thereuppon , church
vessels of gold, and siluer chalices , cruets,
pales, incensinge , holy vestures by the Bishops, and preists at that time, the signinge
with the Crosse, naminge of holy martyrs,
and their memories, the preface to the Masse, and canon thereof, wherein was offered
the

the fame facrifice, Chrift himfelfe inftituted. Prayers and facrifice for the deade, the
ghofpell and epiftle reade at Maffe, the pax
or holy falutation, and with other ceremonies the preifts benediction at the ende of
the holy facrifice , how the Catechumens
not baptifed were not permitted to be prefent at the facrifice , but difmiffed before,
and in no materiall thinge differeth from
the prefent miffale vfed in the church of
Rome. *epift. 2. l. 8. constit. cap. 16. 17. l. 2.*
constit. cap. 23. 61. 63. l. 8. cap. 17. l. 6. cap.
30. l. 8. cap. 18. 47. 48. l. 2. cap. 63. l. 8. cap.
15. l. 2. cap. 61. 62.

8. And it would bee a very vnlearned
obiection , in this cafe for any man to fay,
that S. Clements workes haue beene corrupted: for euident it is before, that all his
predeceffors in the fee of Rome, all the A-
poftles, Euangelifts, and their difciples in
all places, taught , and practifed this holy
doctrine, and facrifice of Maffe, fo that except S. Clement fhould be fingular againft
them all, in this point, which is manifeft-
lie vntrue before, his bookes could not bee
corrupted, or corrected in this refpect; and
if they had beene altered therin , they had

R 4   beene

beene corrected to the common receaued truth , and not corrupted with errors . Secondly no man that saith S.Clements workes to haue beene corrupted , as Ruffinus and others, doe say they were corrupted in any such matter,but by the Eunomian hereticks, thrustinge in some things , sauouringe of their heresie,into his books. (*Ruffin. Apolog.pro Origene.*) and Ruffinus and all those men were teachers, practisers and defenders of holy Masse. (*Ruffin.histor.eccl. l. 1. cap. 22.*) Thirdly our protestants which graunt the church to haue beene free from error longe after the first 400. yeares of Christ , before which Ruffinus liued, and these bookes were corrupted as hee with others testifieth , may not bee allowed by their owne Religion , to say these sacrificinge and massinge doctrines were errors, but truthes of those vnspotted times . And so it is not possible that exceptinge some thinge tendings to the Eunomians heresie foisted into his works by them, any thinge els about these matters should be thrust in; for Ruffinus who, as before was a patron, and practiser of Masse , and so teacheth it to haue beene the vniuersall doctrine , and

practise

practife of the church of God, witneffeth, that whatfoeuer was corrupted in S. Clements works, hee himfelfe beeing, *Apoftolicus vir, immo pene Apoftolus, an Apoftolick man, and almoft an Apoftle. Were fuch things as the ecclefiaftical rule doth not receaue; quæ ecclefiaftica regula omnino non recipit. Ruffin. Apolog. fupr.* therefore the holy facrifice of Maffe, and maffinge preifthood, beeing fo authentically allowed by the ecclefiaftical rule, both then, before, and after, could be none of thofe things, which were corrupted, or inferted into S. Clements works.

9. And to make this matter more fure, wee haue many and renowned Authors of that, and following times, faying clearely, that S. Clement did compofe, and publifh to the world, a forme of Maffe, which continued in fucceedinge ages, and fuch without any materiall chaunge, or difference, as the whole church of Chrift now vfeth. Amonge thefe is S. Proclus Patriarch of Conftantinople, fucceffor to S. Chrifoftom that great maffing prelate, who in his book of the facred Maffe, *de traditione diuinæ Liturgiæ*, writeth in this maner. (*Proclus Patriarch. Conftantinopol. tract. de traditione diuinæ*

diuina Liturgiæ.) *multi diuini Pastores, qui*
Apostolis successerunt , ac Ecclesiæ Doctores,
sacrorum diuinæ Liturgiæ mysteriorum ratio-
nem explicantes , scriptis mandatam Ecclesiæ
tradiderunt, in quibus primi & clarissimi sunt
S. Clemens , summi illius Apostolorum disci-
pulus & successor, qui sacrosancta illa myste-
ria, à Sanctis Apostolis sibi reuelata, in lucem
edidit. Many diuine Pastors, which succeeded
the Apostles, and Doctors of the church , ex-
poundinge the order of the holy misteries , of
the diuine Liturgie Masse , committed it to
writing, and deliuered it to the church, among
whome the principall and most renowned were
S. Clement , the disciple and successor of that
cheifest of the Apostles , which did publish to
light , those holy misteries reuealed vnto him
by the Apostles. Where wee see, that S. Clement did not onely write the order of Masse , but is recompted in the first place, as
one of the cheifest, that performed this holie worke.

10. The others which he there nameth
ar S. Iames the Apostle, first Bishop of Hierusalem , S. Basile the great, and S. Iohn
Chrisostome , this mans *spirituall Father,*
Pater noster Ioannes, cui aurea lingua cogno-
men

men dedit. Who as hee saith did shorten the Apostles Masse, takinge some things from it, becaufe for the length it did not so well pleafe some men, declined from that great zeale of the Apostles, and their time: for as he writeth in the same place, the holy Apostles were exceedingly deuoted to this most holy sacrifice, as a thinge most necessary, and principall in their function: *postquam Seruator noster in cælum assumptus est, Apostoli priusquam per omnem terram dispergerentur, conspirantibus animis cum multam consolationem in mystico illo Dominici corporis sacrificio positam inuenissent, fusissimè, & longa oratione Liturgiam decantabant. Hæc enim diuina sacra vna cum dicendi ratione coniuncta, cæteris rebus anteponenda censebant, atque maiori & alacriori rerum diuinarum, & sacrificij sacrosancti studio & desiderio flagrabant, & illud obnixe amplectebantur.* After our Sauiour was assumpted vnto heauen, the Apostles before they were dispersed through all the earth, assemblinge together, with agreeivge mindes, applied themselues to pray all the day: and when they had found much consolation placed in that mysticall sacrifice of our Lords body, they did singe Liturgie (Masse most largely

gely with longe prayer. For they did thinke these diuine sacrifices ioyned with preachinge to bee preferred before all other thinges, and were incensed with a greater and more chearfull affection and desire of diuine things, and the holy sacrifice, and did embrace it, with all their power. Hitherto this auncient Saint, and Patriarch.

11. Of Ruffinus I haue spoken before, onely I add here, that he beeing commonlie take to be the interpreter of many these works of S. Clement, where the holy sacrifice of Masse, and massinge preisthood ar so euidently approued, and acknowledging S. Clements works had bene in some things corrupted, euer taketh these for the true writings, and doctrine of S. Clement, and far from being corruptions, or insertions by others. The holy learned and auncient Bishop Nicholaus Methonensis. *Episc. l. de vero Christi corpore in Eucharistia.* hauinge shewed, how S. Iames said Masse at Hierusalem, S. Peter and S. Paule at Antioch, S. Marke at Alexandria, S. Iohn and S. Andrew in Asia, and Europe, concludeth with an eminency for S. Clements Masse. *Omnesque vniuersa Ecclesia vbicum-*

que

que sint, per eam quam Sanctus Clemens con-
scripsit Liturgiā tradiderunt. And all the Bishops haue deliuered to the whole church,
whersoeuer dispersed, the Liturgie or Masse accordinge to that order which S. Clement wrote. And to put vs out of al doubt,
hee meaneth this of the holy sacrifice of
Chrifts body and blood in the Masse, that
that his booke is instituted, *de vero Christi*
corpore in Eucharistia, of the true body of
Christ in the Eucharist, Marcus Ephesius
and Bessarion write the very same, of S.
Clements Masse, citinge diuers testimonies, from thence for the reall presence, of
Christ in that most holy sacrifice, and diuers others deliuer the like. *Marcus Ephes.*
l. de corpore & sanguine Christi Bessarion l.
de Sacramento Eucharist. M. S. Gallic. an-
tiq. pr. or que nous sommes. an Dom. 81. in S.
Clement.

12. Whereby is euidently proued that S.
Clement did not only write a forme of the
Masse, & practise, as a sacrificing preist that
holy sacrifice but this was so renowned,
that it was published by the Bishops, & receaued in all churches. And amonge these
in this our Britanie, except the Brittish ātiquities

quities themselues written before the vnion
of the Chriſtian Britans with the diſciples
of S. Gregory, and the conuerted Saxons in
this contrie do deceaue vs, which our Engliſh Proteſtãts generally extolling the credit of thoſe monuments, and the Chriſtian
Britans Religion, may not affirme. This antiquitie ſo auncient as I haue related, and
purpoſely entreatinge of the firſt order of
ſaying Maſſe, eſpecially in Fraunce, and
this kingdome of Britanie, comprehending
England and Scotland, is in that reſpect
though with a later hand writinge thus in-
tituled : *prima inſtitutio & varietas eccleſia-
ſtici ſeruitij, præcipue in Britannia & Gallia:*
The firſt inſtitution and varietie of the eccleſiaſticall ſeruice eſpecially in Britanie &
Fraunce. And it termeth it, *curſum,* the
courſe or order of the publick Liturgie, or
Maſſe thereby expreſſed. *Bed. in Martyrolog. 4. cal. Ianuar. Beatus Trophinus Epiſcopus Arelatenſis, & Sanctus Photinus Martyr,& Epiſcopus Lugdunenſis, diſcipulus Sancti Petri Apoſtoli, curſum Romanum in Gallijs
tradiderunt. Inde poſtea relatione beati Pho-
tini Martyris cum quadraginta & octo Martyribus retruſi in ergaſtalum, ad beatum Cle-*
                                        mentem

mentem quartum loci successorem beati Petri Apostoli deportauerunt. Trophinus Bishop of Arles, and S. Photin Martyr and Bishop of Lions, disciple of S. Peter Apostle, deliuered the Roman order in Fraunce. Then afterward the relation of S. Photin Martyr imprisoned together with 48. Martyrs, it was carryed to S. Clement, the fourth in succession to S. Peter, the Apostle. Where wee plainely see, that the church of Rome had then a publick order & forme of Masse and this was published throughout France by S. Trophinus, from whose fountaine as I haue shewed before, both from Catholicks, and Protestants, all the churches of Fraunce did receaue instruction. *Zosimus Pap. epist. To. 1. Concil. Petr. Cluniacens. Magdeb. centur. 2. pag. 2. col. 6. Martyrolog. Rom. die* 29. *Decemb.*

13. And this Masse after the death of S. Peter, Linus, and Cletus, was approued by S. Clement, and as it seemeth by an auncient Manuscript french history, hee added the epistle and ghospell which all were not written in S. Peters time. For thus it testifieth with others. *S. Clement Pope ordeyneth that in the solemnitie of the Masse, the epistle*
and

and ghospell should bee reade. (*M. S. French*
historie an. Do. 81. *cap.* 2.) and immediatlie
addeth, how then hee sent many preachers
and holy Bishops into Fraunce, and these
parts, which could bringe with them no
other Liturgie, or Masse, then that which
their Master S. Clement had so published,
and approued, both by his authoritie, and
practise before. And if the Masse of S. Marke
was not the same with Saint Peters, as some
thinke, yet sure wee are, seeing hee was an
Enangelist, S. Peters scholler and wrote his
ghospell, *ex ore Petri*, from S. Peters mouth,
as S. Hierome witnesseth, and by his approbation. (*Hieron. in Catal. script. in S.*
Marco.) that his Masse could not bee different from his Masters, in any materiall
thinge, and seeinge S. Peter approued his
ghospell, hee did not, and would not dis-
proue or disallowe his Masse. And yet this
old Brittish antiquitie is witnes, that the
Masse which the old Christian Scots, did
vse in his time, and was accompted very
holy, was practised by S. Marke, and from
him continued to the time of this Author,
by continuall tradition, from one to another.

14. *Ipsum*

14. *Ipsum cursum qui dicitur presenti tempore Scottorum, Beatus Marcus decantauit & post ipsum Gregorius Nazianzenus, quem Hieronymus suum Magistrum esse affirmat, & beatus Basilius frater ipsius S. Gregorij, Antonius, Paulus, Macharius vel Ioannes, & Malchus secundum ordinem Patrum decantauerunt. Inde postea beatissimus Cassianus, & post ipsum beatus Honoratus, & Sanctus Cæsarius Episcopus qui fuit in Arelata, & beatus Porcarius Abbas qui in ipso monasterio fuit, ipsum cursum decantauerunt, qui beatum Lupum, & beatum Germanum Monachos in eorum monasterio habuerunt, & ipsi sub norma regulæ ipsum cursum ibidem decantauerunt. Et postea Episcopatus. cathedram adepti in Britannijs & Scottijs prædicauerunt. Quæ vita beati Germani Episcopi Antisiodorensis, & vita beati Lupi affirmat. Qui beatum Patricium literas sacras docuerunt, atque enutrierunt. Et ipsum Episcopum in Scottijs ac Britannijs posuerunt, qui vixit annos centum quinquaginta & tres, & ipsum cursum ibidem decantauit: & post ipsum beatus Vuandilocus senex, & beatus Gomogillus, qui habuerunt in eorum monasterio Monachos circiter tria millia. Inde beatus Vuandilocus in predicationis ministerium à*

S

beato

beato Gomogillo missus est , & beatus Colum-
banus partibus Galliarum, & ibidem ipsum cur-
sum decantauerunt. That order which at this
time is called the order of Scots, S. Marke
did singe , and after him Gregory Nazian-
zen , whome Hierome affirmeth to haue
beene his Master, and S. Basil brother of
the said S. Gregory, Antonius, Paulus, Macharius or Iohn, and Malchus, accordinge
to the order of the Fathers did singe it. And
after that most blessed Cassian , and after
him S. Honoratus, and S. Cæsarius Bishop,
that was in Arles, and S. Porcarius Abbot,
which was in the same monasterie , did
singe that order, who had monkes in their
monastery S. Lupus and S Germanus, and
they three vnder rule did singe the same order: and after made Bishops preached in
Britanie , and Scotlande , which thinges
the life of S. German Bishop of Antisiodor,
and the life of S. Lupus doth affirme, who
taught S. Patricke holy learning, & brought
him vp , and placed him Bishop in Scotland, and Britanie, who liued an hundred
fifty and three yeares , and songe there the
same order. And after him Vuandilocus an
old man, and S. Gomogillus , who had in
their

their monastery about three thousand monkes. After S. Vuandilocus was sent to preach
by S. Gomogillus, as also S. Columbanus
to the parts of Fraunce, and there they did
singe the same order.

15. Hitherto the wordes of this so auncient, and approued Manuscript Brittish
antiquitie. So that whether soeuer, or to
whomsoeuer we turne our selues to enquire
of these thinges, whether Hebrues, Gre-
cians, or Latines, Apostles, Euangelists,
or their Disciples, & with vs at home, Bri-
tons, or Saxons, Catholicks or Protestants,
it is clearely and plainely confessed, that
generally in this first Apostolicke age,
and hundred yeares of Christ, which must
needes bee allowed for a rule, square, and
direction to all succeedinge times, and po-
sterities. The holy sacrificing preisthood of
the present Greeke and Latine church, and
all Christian nations, whether these late
nouelties, haue not entered, sacrificinge
massinge preists, and the moste holy sacrifice of Masse, were our Sauiour Christ Iesus his sacred ordinances and institutions,
and so vsed, practised, and with all honor
performed by the whole number of the

S 2　　　　　Apc.

Apostles, without exception, their disciples, and successors in all places, & among
the rest, to the great glory thereof, in this
our nation of great Britanie. And all this
without any materiall chaunge, or alteration in that sacrifice, the principall act, and
office of truely cōsecrated preists, & preisthood, as is before related, and our cheife
protestantes haue before confessed of the
moste contradicted and questionable thinges, a sacrifice instituted by Christ himselfe, conteyning an oblation of his moste
blessed body, and blood, both for the liuing
and faithfull departed, propitiatory for sinnes, with a memory of the holy Saints in
heauen, of which lesser instance hath bene
giuen, because few Saints of the new testament were then at the first deceased this
life, and entered into glory, yet the churches then dedicated to diuers of them, and
inuocation & praier then made vnto them,
as before appeareth, maketh it an vndoubted truth.

16. To which I only add for this kingdome of our Britanie from those antiquities, both printed, and Manuscripts, which
our protestants most allowe, and approue,
that

that S. Ioseph of Aramathia , and his holy
company, besides their buildinge a church,
in honor of the blessed Virgin Mary , did
expressely serue her , and pray vnto her:
*duodecim prædicti in eodem loco, Deo & beatæ
Virgini deuota exhibentes obsequia , vigilijs,
ieiunijs, & orationibus vacantes, eiusdem Virginis Dei, genitricis auxilio in necessitatibus
suis refocillabantur.* The twelue holy men
spoken of before, S. Ioseph and his companions , yeeldinge deuout seruices to God,
and the blessed Virgin, attendinge to wat-
chings, fastings, and prayers, were in their
necessities releiued by the helpe of the same
Virgin, Mother of God. (*Antiquitat. Glast.
apud Capgrau. in Catalog. in S. Ioseph ab Ara-
math. & S. Patricio. antiq. M. S. tabulis af-
fixa in ead· Eccles. Glaston. and others.*) So
that whomsoeuer S. Peter, S. Paul, S. Ioseph,
or any other man will truly and seriouf-
lie allowe, or in his owne singular conceipt
or phantasie imagin, to haue beene the first
preacher, & teacher of the Christian faith,
and Religion, in Britanie, or what or whose
order and forme of Masse , and Liturgie,
they will say was then here vsed and practised, they must needs by all authorities, &

war-

warranted iudgements acknowledge, that
the holy preists here in that time were sacrificinge massinge preists, their externall
Liturgie and sacrifice, the sacrifice of Masse, wherein Chrilts holy body and blood
were consecrated, and offered both for the
liuinge, and faithfull departed, the Saints
were remembred, and prayed vnto, and
no materiall difference betweene that, and
the present Masse, of either the Greeke or
Latine church. And so I end this first age
and hundred yeares of Christ.

THE SECOND AGE OR HVN-
DRED YEARES OF CHRIST.

THE XV. CHAPTER.

Wherein demonstration is made, both by pro-
testants and other antiquaries, that sacri-
ficinge massinge preists, and Bishops, and
sacrifice of Masse, continued and were hono-
red in this kingdome of Britanie from the
beginninge of this hundred yeares, vntill
Kinge Lucius time, when it was wholly con-
uerted to that faith.

VV E are now come to the beginninge of the second age, or cen-
tury

tury of yeares of Chrift , when by all accompts in hiſtorie, Kinge Coillus , that
was bred vp at Rome , was Kinge in Britanie , and S. Anacletus Pope of Rome.
When many of our before remembred maſſinge and ſacrificinge Brittiſh preiſts , as
namely *S. Manſuetus* , *S. Beatus*, his holy
companion before by ſome named *Acha-*
tes, and *S. Timotheus* were liuinge . And
though I doe not find any particularly named, whome S. Anacletus ſent hither , of
the holy preiſtly maſſinge order, yet to followe euen the opinion, and direction of
Engliſh Proteſtant antiquaries, in this buſines, wee muſt needs graunt, that hee had
a care of this contry as wel as others in this
kind, for they teſtiſie of this Pope; *Ab ipſo*
Domino primatum Romanæ Eccleſiæ ſuper om-
nes Eccleſias, vniuerſumque Chriſtiani nomi-
ne populum conceſſum eſſe aſſeruit . (*Robert.*
Barns l. de vit. Pontiſic. Roman. in Anaclet.
Ormerod. pict. Pap. pag. 78.) *Pope Anacletus*
affirmed , that ſupremacy was graunted from
our Lord himſelfe , to the church of Rome, ouer
all churches , and all Chriſtian people. Becauſe,
ſaith hee, Chriſt ſaid to S. Peter , who liued
and died at Rome, thou art Peter , or a rocke,

and

and vppon this *rocke I will builde my church.*
Quia, inquit, Petro agenti & morienti Romæ
dixit, tu es Petrus & super hanc petram ædi-
ficabo Ecclesiam meam. By which reason a-
monge others, diuers other learned English
Protestant writers, with publicke priuilege
and allowance, doe proue vnto vs first con-
fessinge with this holy Pope, that Christ
made S. Peter the supreame and cheife go-
uernour of his church : secondly that this
supreamacy was necessary and to continue
for euer in his church: and thirdly because
S. Peter dyinge Bishop of Rome, and at
Rome, and there onely possibly to haue his
laste and immediate successor, and so constituted by himselfe as is euident in S. Clement before, it euidently followeth by the
reason of this holy Pope, and protestants,
that euen by Christ himselfe this supreamacy ouer all churches and Christians, was
graunted to the church of Rome. Whereuppon these protestants testifie in his life,
that hee ordeyned diuers lawes bindinge
the whole church, and still obserued. *Rob.*
Barnes in Anacleto.

2. And if we may beleeue the first Protestant Archbishop of Canterbury, and in
the

the whole world also, Matthew Parker, hee
telleth vs how in particular his iurisdiction
extended into this kingdome of Britanie,
and that the diuision and constitution of
Archbishops sees with vs, was by Pope
Anacletus his ordination: *Ex Anacleto hu-*
ius insulæ diuisionem. (*Matth. Parker anti-*
quitat. Brit. pag 24.) And that he was a sacrificinge massinge preist, it must needs
be graunted, both by his owne, and our
protestant testimonies also of him; for
hee himselfe is witnesse, that hee was
made preist by the great sacrificinge and
massinge Apostle S. Peter: *à Sancto Petro*
Apostolorum Principe, presbyter ordinatus.
(*Anacletus epist. 3. To. 1. concil.*) and our
protestants do plainely confesse of this holie Pope: *Sacerdotem sacrificaturum, ministros*
vestibus sacris indutos, seu testes & custodes
sibi adhibere ordinauit. Episcopos vero, & plu-
res ministros sibi in sacris faciendis adiungat:
& quod Sacerdote maior ac dignior sit. (*Ro-*
bert. Barnes l. de vit. Pontif. Roman in Ana-
cleto.) Pope Anacletus ordeined, that when
a preist was to offer sacrifice, hee should
take vnto him as witnesses and keepers,
ministers in holy vestiments. And that a
Bishop

Bishop should ioyne vnto him more ministers, when he said Masse : And that hee is
greater , and more worthie then a preist.
The authoritie from whence they cite this,
is much more plaine, where the very order
wee still vse in solemne Masses is expressed.
But the protestant words manifestly proue
that the sacrifice of Masse and sacrificinge
vestures, were vsed frō the daies of the A-
postles. Therfore this holy Pope exercising
supreamacy , and enactinge lawes for the
whole church in Britanie or wheresoeuer,
as these protestāts there doe testifie, it must
needs bee confessed, that the preists which
in his time either for Britanie, or any other
nation , were consecrated immediatlie by
himselfe,or mediatly by his authority,were
as himselfe was,sacrificinge massinge preistes , and the deacons also for which hee
made decrees , by the testimony of these
men. (*Robert.Barnes Sup. in Anaclet.Matth.
Parker. antiquitat. Britan. pag. 24.*) were
also as they teach , such as serued at the altare and sacrifice of Masse, as Master Foxe
speakinge of the very deacons ordeined by
Pope Anacletus proueth in these termes.
therefore serued the office of the deacons , as
wee

wee reade, to lay the offerings of the people vp-
pon the altare, to bee hallowed, and when
the misteries, be consecrated, to distribute the
cupp of the sacred blood of the Lord, to the
faithfull people. (*Foxe Tom. 2. in Q. Mary.*
Ambros. l. de omnib. diuin. offic.)

3. And much part of the aboade, and residency of this holy Pope, as also of his predecessors and successors as appeareth before, and will bee more manifest hereafter,
was in that knowne massinge and sacrificinge house, of our noble contriwoman S.
Claudia, or her children. And the order of
Masse which hee vsed, was the same which
was practised by S. Peter the Apostle, and
by him deliuered to the church, as these
protestants haue before with other Authors
confessed. (*Matth. Parker antiquitat. Brit.*
pag. 47. cap. 17.) and such was the condition of his next successor *S. Euaristus,* vsing
the same order of saying Masse, with S. Peter, and both claiminge, and exercisinge
supreamacie ouer all churches, as these protestants assure vs. (*Parker supr. Barn. in vit.*
Pontif. in Euaristo. Io. Funoc. commentar. l.
5. an. 105. Ed. Grimston.) and Nennius the
auncient Brittish writer, who as these protestants

testants say, wrote a thousand yeares since, doth expressely affirme, in his Manuscript history, that hee delt with the Kinge himselfe of this our Britanie about the conuersion thereof, probably before Kinge Lucius was borne: *Missa legatione à Papa Romano Euaristo.* And many were conuerted by this his meanes. (*booke of estates pag.* 435. *Bal. l. de scriptor. cent. 1. in Nennio Banchor. Nennius histor. M.S.*) therefore this Pope being knowne to bee a massinge Pope, the preists which were (by Nénius) set hither by him, must needs bee massing preists, as all others here, at, and before that mission were.

4. Next is Pope Alexander, a man, by our protestants allowance, *studio euangelizandi & miraculis celebris, interfectus martyr obijt:* renowned for his zeale in preachinge the ghospell, and miracle, and dyinge a martyr. (*Whitguift. answ. to the admonit. pag.* 97. 98. *Rob. Barnes l. de vit. Pontific. Rom. in Alexandro* 1. *Bal. act. Rom. Pontific. in eodem.*) this Pope as Albertus Krantzius writeth, sent preachers, and preists into this our Britanie. (*Albert. Krantz. Metropol. l.* 1. *cap.* 6.) therefore to know of our protestáts whether they were massing preistes,

stes, we must enquire, and learne of them,
what he was in this respect that sent them,
because hee would not , not could send o-
thers then hee himselfe was, for such a busines. That hee was a sacrificinge massinge
preist , and Pope these protestants thus af-
sure vs, by the lawes and decrees which as
they thus testifie , hee made and published
for the church . (*Robert: Barn. in vit. Pont.
in Aleaandro 1. Io. Funccius l. 5. commentar.
in Alexand. 1. an. 111.*) *In Euchariſtiæ sacrificio aquam vino admiſceri voluit. Ad Euchariſtiæ oblationem azimum panem non fermen-
tatum, ſumendum eſſe præcepit. Vno die vnam
tantum Miſſam à ſingulis ſacrificijs fieri debere, decreto ſanciuit. Peccata ſacrificio (de Euchariſtia loquens) deleri ait: Ideo paſſionem in
Miſſa recitandam inſtituit. Rationem effectus
huius ſacrificij , hoc eſt, quod peccata expiet,
adiecit, dicens: Quia corpore & ſanguine Chriſti in ſacrificijs nihil maius eſt.* Hee tooke order that in the sacrifice of Eucharist, water
shoulde bee mingled with wine. He commaunded, that vnleuened and not leuened
breade should bee vsed for the sacrifice of
the Eucharist. Hee made a decree, that no
sacrificing preist should say more then one
Maſſe

Masse in one day. Speakinge of the Eucharist he saith, that sinnes ar blotted out with
sacrifice: therefore hee ordeyned that the
passion should bee recited at Masse. He added the reason of this effecte of this sacrifice to purge sinnes, sayinge: because in sacrifice nothinge is greater, then the body
and blood of Christ.

5. These protestants add further of this
massinge Pope, in this busines (*Rob. Barns*
supr. in Alex. 1.) *In Missa pridie quam pate-*
retur, vsque ad hæc verba. Hoc est corpus
meum addidit, ad memoriam passionis Christi
inculcandam He added in the Masse, the day
before hee suffered, vnto these words, this
is my body, to impresse in our memories
the passion of Christ. Where we see it euidently confessed by these protestants themselues, that this primatiue holy Pope Alexander that liued (to speake in a Protestant
Archbishops words, *anno* 111. *in the yeare*
of Christ one hundred and eleuen) *and was a*
godly Bishop. (*Ioh. Whitguift answ. to the*
admonit. sect. 1. 2. *pag.* 97. 98. *and def. of the*
answ. pag. 594.) and by the German historian before sent preists into this kingdome,
was as farr engaged in the misteries of holie

lie Maſſe, as any Roman maſſinge preiſt is
at this preſent, acknowledging it to be the
greateſt of al ſacrifices, the body and blood
of Chriſt, a ſacrifice expiatinge and propitiatory for ſinnes. And what matter was to
bee vſed and conſecrated, and how preiſts
were to behaue themſelues in this moſt holie ſacrifice. And it appeareth euen by theſe
mens teſtimonies, that the preiſts of that
time are ſo far from not ſayinge Maſſe, that
they did not onely daily offer this moſt holie ſacrifice of Chriſts body and blood for
ſinnes, but they ſaid Maſſe more often then
once a day, diuers Maſſes in one day, vntill it was forbidden as before by this holy
Pope, *That one preiſt, ſhould ſay but one Maſ-*
ſe a day . Vno die vnam tantam Miſſam à ſin-
gulis ſacrificijs fieri debere, decreto ſanciuit.

6. This Pope was as all Chriſtians then,
far from beinge a parlamentary proteſtant
of England to puniſh ſayinge or hearinge
of Maſſe daily with a yearely penaltie of
foure and twenty thouſands, three hundreds & twenty pounds & twenty markes,
an hũdred markes for euery Maſſe, or make
holy ſacrificing maſſinge preiſts to be trai-
tors, and their entertayners fellons, when
by

by these protestants (*Rob. Barnes sup. in Ale-*
xandro 1. *.) this holy Pope excommunicated*
those that resisted the Popes Legats, and for-
bad preists and cleargie men to bee conuented
before a lay tribunall. Legatis Apostolicis ob-
sistentes, decreto excommunicauit. Clericum
ad plebeium tribunal pertrahere prohibuit. And
yet hee was so holy and renowned a man,
as besides that which protestāts haue testified of him before, an other writeth (*Edw.*
Grimston. in the estate of the church of Rome.
pag. 435. in Alex. 1.) *Alexander a Roman, a*
man of so holy a life, as many Roman Senators
receaued the Christian Religion by reason of
his great pietie. So wee may be assured that
all Christiās thē were of his opiniō in these
things, as they before him were: for none
of these things which these protestāts here
say, hee decreed, were new, or inuented
or added by him, but confirmed in their
first institution and integritie, as I haue
proued from these protestants and others
before, that the mixture of water with wine
was an apostolicall tradition. *Couel against*
Burg. pag. 122.) which S. Alexander himselfe confirmeth, when hee saith of it. (*Cy-*
prian. epistol. 63. *Alexand.* 1. *epistol.* r.) *à pa-*
tribus

tribus accepimus, & ipsa ratio docet. We haue
so receaued it from our predecessors, and
reason it selfe so teacheth, and therefore
commaundeth, *vt panis tantum, & vinum
aqua permixtum in sacrificio offerantur*, that
onely breade and wine mixed with water,
bee offered in the sacrifice, and S. Cyprian
plainely saith it was, *Dominica traditio*, a
tradition of Christ himselfe, by his owne
order and example. And hee with others
so expoundeth Salomon in the Prouerbs to
prophesie therof, as I haue declared at large
before. *Prouerb. c. 9. Cyprian: epist. 63. ad Ce-
cilium.*

7. The eminency of this sacrifice, aboue
all others, how it conteyneth the body and
blood of Christ, and is satisfactory for sinnes, as S. Alexander by these protestants
teacheth, they haue often told vs before,
that it was soe esteemed from the first institution thereof by Christ. That which
hee saith, how it ought to bee solemnized
with vnleuened breade, was also, as the
protestants, besides the generall practise of
the Latine church, assure vs, the ordinance
of Christ himselfe, and the lawe it selfe, as
a Protestant Archbishop with others thus

T   expoun-

expoũdeth this confirmatory decree of this holy Pope. (*Ioh. Whitguift answ. to the admonit. sect. 1. 2. pag. 98. and def. of the answ. pag 594.*) *Alexander was a good and godly Bishop, it is reported in some writers, that hee appointed vnleuened breade to bee vsed in the Eucharist, because that Christ himselfe vsed the same accordinge to the lawe written Exod. 12. Deuteron. 16.* The wordes: *pridie quàm pateretur*, the day before Christ suffered, vnto the words, *hoc est corpus meum*, this is my body ; were not newly added by Pope Alexander, but declared by him to bee the institution of Christ himselfe, and so of necessitie to bee vsed. For these hee testifieth thereof. (*Alexand. 1. epist. 1. ad omnes Orthodox. Tom. 2. concil. de conse. diß. 2. nihil in Sac.*) *Ipsa veritas nos instruxit &c. Christ Iesus truth it selfe hath instructed vs to offer the chalice and breade in the Sacrament, when hee saith: Iesus tooke breade, and bleßed it, and gaue to his disciples, sayinge: Take and eate for this is my body, which shall bee giuen for you, likewise after hee had supped, hee tooke the chalice, and gaue to his disciples, sayinge : Take and drinke you all of it, for this is the chalice of my blood, which shall*

bee

bee shed for you, for remission of sinnes. For offences and sinnes are blotted out with these sacrifices offered vnto our Lord. And therfore his passion is to bee remembred in these, by the which wee are redeemed, and often to bee recited, and these to bee offered vnto our Lord. With such sacrifices our Lord will bee delighted and pacified, and forgiue great sinnes. For in sacrifices nothinge canbee greater then the body, and blood of Christ. Nor any oblation better then this, but this excelleth all. Which is to be offered to our Lord with a pure conscience, and to bee receaued with a pure minde, and to bee reuerenced of all men. And as it is better then all others, so it ought more to bee worshipped and reuerenced. Quæ pura conscientia Domino offerenda est, & pura mente sumenda, atque ab omnibus veneranda. Et sicut potior est cæteris, ita potius excoli & venerari debet.

8. This was the opinion of this holy Pope, and all good Christians vnder his charge, in that prime age of Christianitie, and hereby wee perfectly knowe, that S. Alexander did not add any new thinge to the holy sacrifice of Masse, but only proposed the ordinance and institution of Christ

him.

himſelfe, to bee followed and obſerued, as
is euident in that I haue cited from him,
wherby it appeareth, that what he wrote in
that matter , *ipſa veritas nos inſtruxit*, that
Chriſt the infallible truth , did teache and
ſo inſtruct and inſtitute, as euidently is proued by comparinge thoſe wordes , which
theſe proteſtants ſay S. Alexander added in
the Maſſe, to the inſtitution of Chriſt , as
it is deliuered in holy ſcriptures by the E-
uangeliſts and S. Paule. The words ſuppo-
ſed to bee added bee theſe: *Qui pridie quàm*
pateretur: who (Chriſt) *the day before his*
paſſion tooke breade into his holy and venera-
ble hands, and lifting vp his eyes towards hea-
uen to thee, God his Father omnipotent , gi-
uinge thanks vnto thee, bleſſed it , brake and
gaue to his diſciples, ſaying, take and eate you
all of this . For this is my body. All vnto the
laſt wordes , *for this is my body .* They ſay
were S. Alexanders addition . But S. Paul,
as hee is tranſlated by our proteſtants, hath
the ſame from Chriſts inſtitution , in this
maner. (1. *Corinth. cap.* 11. *verſ.* 23. 24. 25.
26.) *I haue receaued of the Lord that which*
alſo I deliuered vnto you, that the Lord Ieſus
the ſame night in which he was betraied tooke
bread,

bread, and when hee had giuen thankes, hee brake it, and saide, take, eate, this is my body, which is broken for you: doe this in remembrance of mee. After the same maner also hee tooke the cup, when hee had supped, sayinge, this cup is the new testament in my blood, this doe yee as oft as yee drinke it, in remembrance of mee. For as often as yee eate this bread, and drinke this cup, yee doe shew the Lords death till hee come. Wherfore vvhosoeuer shall eate this bread, and drinke this cup of the Lord vnvvorthily, shall be guilty of the bodie, and blood of the Lord. The like haue the Euangelists, S. Matthew, Marke, and Luke from the wordes and institution of Christ himselfe. *Matth. cap.* 26. *Marc. cap.* 14. *Luc. cap.* 22.

9. And it plainely appeareth by that is said, that without these wordes, or their equiualent, it is vnpossible to obserue the institution and commaundement of Christ in this behalfe. And therfore our most learned, holy, and auncient contriman S. Albinus, or Alcuinus, Remigius Antisiodorensis, and others after them, confidently and truely say. (*Albin. Flac. Alcuin. l. de diuin. officijs cap. de celebratione Missæ. Remigius*

gius

*gius Antissiodor. in exposit. Missæ. Hoc quod
sequitur, qui pridie quàm pateretur, vsque in
memoriam facietis: Apostoli &c.* This which
followeth, who the day before hee suffered,
vnto those wordes, you shall doe it in my
commemoration, the Apostles had in vse
after the ascension of our Lord. Therefore,
that the church might celebrate a continuall memory of her redeemer, our Lord
deliuered it to his Apostles, and the Apostles generally to the whole church in these
wordes, without which, no tonge, no Re-
gion, no citie, that is, no part of the church
can consecrate this Sacrament. Which the
Apostle doth make manifest, sayinge: for
I haue receaued of our Lord, which I haue
also deliuered vnto you, that our Lord Iesus the night when he was betrayed, tooke
breade, and the rest. Therfore by the power
and wordes of Christ, this breade and this
chalice was consecrated from the beginninge, is euer consecrated and shall be consecrated. For he speakinge his words by his
preists, doth by his heauenly blessing, make
his holy body and blood.

10. S. Ambrose relateth this in the same
maner in these wordes. *Ambros. l. 4. de Sa-
cramentis*

cramentis cap. 5. vis ſcire quia verbis cæleſti-
bus conſecratur &c . Wilt thou knowe that
conſecration is done by heauenly wordes?
receaue what the wordes bee . The preiſt
doth ſay: make vnto vs, ſaith he, this oblation ratified, reaſonable, acceptable: which
is the figure of the body, and blood, of our
Lord Ieſus Chriſt. Who the day before hee
ſuffered did take breade in his holy hands,
and looked to heauen , to thee ô holy Father, omnipotent euerlaſtinge God, giuing
thanks: bleſſed it , brake it , and beeinge
broken gaue to his diſciples, ſayinge, take
and eate you all of this: for this is my bodie, which ſhal be broken for many. Likewiſe alſo hee tooke the cup after hee had
ſupped, the day before hee ſuffered, looked
to heauen to thee ô holy Father eternall
God, giuinge thankes: bleſſed it, gaue it to
his Apoſtles , and diſciples , ſayinge take
you, and drinke you all of it: for this is my
blood . Behold all thoſe wordes are the E-
uangeliſts, vntill thoſe , take and drinke,
either body or blood . After they bee the
words of Chriſt : take drinke you all of it:
For this is my blood. Conſider euery thing,
who the day before ſaith hee that hee ſuffe-

red,

red, hee tooke breade in his holy hands, before it is consecrated it is breade, but after the words of Christ come vnto it, it is the bodie of Christ.

11. The like hee hath in other places, so haue other auncient and holy Fathers, and so plainely that our protestants themselues doe freely graunt. (*Foxe Tom. 2. act. and Monum. in Queene Mary.*) that it was so practised, and deliuered by the Apostles themselues, and that it was further the expresse commaundement of Christ to vse those or their equiualents words: *verba institutionis cænæ recitata omnino videntur. Nam Paulus eã non frustra 1. Cor. 11. repetit & quidem annexum mandatum hoc facite in mei commemorationem, postulat vt historia illa de institutione & passione Christi recolatur, vt Paulus 1. Cor. 10.* The words of the institution of the supper doubtles, were recited in the Apostles time, for Paul doth not in vaine repeate them, in his first Epistle, and eleuenth chapter, to the Corinthiens, and certes the commaundement of Christ, do this in commemoration of mee, doth require, that the history of the institution, and passion of Christ, bee related, as

Paul

Paul witnesseth 1. Cor. 10. (*Magdeburgen-
tentur. 1. l. 2. cap. 6. col. 500. c. Ritus circa
cænam Domini.*) Therefore by all consents,
this holy Pope exercisinge supreame spirituall iurisdiction in all places, and beeinge
so famous a massinge Pope, and still retay-
ninge the Masse of the Apostles, and by
some (as before) sendinge preists into this
our Britanie, neither these which he is sup-
posed to haue sent hither, or those others
which stil after this suruiued of this natiō,
were or could bee any others then sacrificinge massinge preists: neither our Christian Brittans at Rome so neare vnto him,
bee others then hearers or sayers of holie
Masse.

12. Successor to S. Alexander was S. Sixtus the first of that name, who as these protestants tell vs, was Pope ten yeares, three
moneths and 21. dayes, succeedinge his
blessed predecessor as well in this opinion,
and practise of sacrificinge preisthood, and
holy Masse, as in the papall dignitie, for as
these men say. (*Robert. Barnes in vit. Pontt-
fic. Rom. in Sixton. Io. Func. l. 5. commentar.
in Sixto 1. an. 121.*) *sacra vasa ne quis præter sacros ministros attingerent, præcepit.
Quod*

Quod corporale appellant, ex lineo panno fieri iussit. Missam non nisi in altari celebrandam esse, constituit. Hee commaunded that none but sacred ministers should handle the sacred vessels, that which they call the corporall hee commaunded to be made of linnen cloath. He ordeyned that Masse should not be celebrated, but vpon an altare. And so wee are assured by these enemies to holy Masse, and sacrificinge preisthood, that he in all places maintained both, for hee was so absolute for the Popes supreamacy euen by these witnesses, that, *hee gaue power to all ecclesiasticall ministers to appeale from their Bishop to the Pope of Rome. Ab Episcopo ad Romanum Pontificem appellandi ius dedit ecclesiasticis ministris.*

13. Successor to S. Sixtus was Telesphorus, both in dignitie and doctrine also by the warrant of these protestats, for by them hee was so deuoted a defendor, and teacher of sacrificinge preisthood, and holy Masse that, *hee decreed euery preist should say three Masses vpon Christ-Masse day, and an other dayes they shoulde not say Masse before the third hower of the day.* Hee commaunded that the songe of the Angels glory to God on high,
should

should bee *sunge* at *Masse*. Yet say two Protestant Bishops, and one theire primate: *there is nothing conteyned in gloria in excelsis, but the same is taken out of the scriptures, and to bee vsed of all true Christians . Telesphorus who added it, Was a good Bishop, a man notable for learninge, and Pietie ; eruditione ac Pietate vir insignius, and the church of Rome as yet pure in doctrine.* Rob. Barn. supr. *in Telesphor.* Func. l. 5. comment. an. 129. Stowe and Howes histor. *in Helius Adrian.* Cartwright adm. Whitguift answ. to. admonit. pag. 101. & dcf. pag. 602. Bal. l. 1. de act. Pontif. Rom. in Telesphor.

14. S. Higinius succeedinge, succeeded also by thefe protestants, as well in exercising spirituall supreamacy ouer all Bishops, decreeinge, *that no Metropolitane shoulde condemne any Bishop of his Prouince*, without the aduise of the other Bishops. And for sacrificinge preisthood, and Masse, hee honored them so much, that liuinge in the time of the Emperor Antonius Pius, a fauourer of Christians, he decreed that Christian churches should be dedicated, *with solemne rite of sacrifice of Masse . Cum solemni ceremoniarum & sacrificiorum ritu dedicanda esse.*

esse. (*Io. Funcc. l. 5. commentar. an. 141. Rob. Barn. in Higin. supr.*) and by an other protestant: *Templa dedicare cum solemni ceremonia & sacrificio iussit.* In this Popes time, as many of our protestant antiquaries with others from antiquities tell vs, we had manie godlie Christian preachers, and preists in Britanie, which by so many testimonies before without any exception must needes be sacrificing massing preists, and by many authorities conuerted many to that holy faith, and sacrificinge massinge Religion of Christ in this kingdome. (*Annal. Burton. an. 140. or 141. Harrison descript. of Britanie Io. Caius l. 1. antiq. Cantabrig. Theater of great Britanie l. 6. Harris Theat. Tom. 2.*) and no meruaile whē so many Authors write, that in one towne of Cambridge there were thē nyne such learned Christiās of that only place; a schole of learninge, at, and diuers hundreds of yeares before that time, as the antiquities and antiquaries of that vniuersitie informe vs. And no man can doubt of many such preists being here then, if he duely consider the difficulties of a generall conuersion of so large, and Idolatrous sauage nation, as this at that time

was

was, and how all agree, it was wholly conuerted long before the death of Kinge Lucius, who by Matthew of Westminster,
commended by our protestants for an ex-
act calculator of times, and others, beeinge
borne in the 115. yeare of Christ, was at
the death of this Pope, holdinge the papa-
cie but 4. yeares, 3. moneths, and a very
fewe dayes, 35. yeares of age, and had bene
Kinge 25. yeares, his Father Coillus dying,
when hee was but 10. yeares olde, and yet
by all antiquities, in all his life euen before
his owne conuersion, a great frend and fauourer of Christians, and this his kingedome a refuge, and receptacle of them, that
were in those times persecuted for Christian Religion. *Matthew of West. Anno gratiæ* 115. *Ioh. Bal. l. de script. in Matth. Westm.
Reb. Bar. sup. in Higinio. Matth. Westm. an.
150. Matth. Westm. an. gratiæ* 124.

15. And to omit forreine examples be-
yonde number in this case, when the Saxons of this nation, were conuerted by the
disciples of Gregory, though S. Augustine
was a very miraculous man, and his companions many and holy learned men, and
industrious in that sacred worke, & found

many

many worthie and renowned Bishops here
with their cleargies that assisted them with
al their power in the conuersion of this nation, as those glorious Bishops S. Molocus
that ioyned with, *S. Bonifacius*, sent from
Italy with many good mē, *cum piorum catu,*
S. Iue, S. Kentegern, S. Asaph, S. Lethardus stiled the precursor, *and vvay maker to*
S. Augustine, præcursor & ianitor venturi
Augustini, with others, and had all the fur-
therance the holy Queene S. Bertha, and
her husband Kinge Ethelbert the most potent in this Iland reigninge from the vttermost coasts of kent vnto Humber, and by
the vertues of S. Bertha and S. Lethardus
by many arguments, a Christian in iudgement and affection before S. Augustines
cominge hither. *Hect. Boeth. hist. l. 9. fol.*
178. Holish. hist. of Engl. l. 5. c. 29. pag. 112.
Capgrau. in S. Iuone M. S. in vit. eius & in
S. Asaph.& Kentegern.Godvvin. Catal. Bal.
centur. 1. de script. Capgrau. in S. Lethard.
Matth. Parker. antiq. in S. Augustin. Stowe
histor. in Kinge Ethelb. Holinsh. histor. of
Engl. Theater of great Brit. in K. Ethelbert.
Bed. l. 1. histor. & l. 2.

16. Yett S. Augustine and fiue other
Arch-

Archbishops of Canterbury after him S.
Laurence, S. Mellitus, S, Iustus, S. Honorius, and S. Adeodatus, were deade, and
aboue foure score yeares passed, after the
cominge of S. Augustine into England, before this kingdome wholly submitted it self
to the true discipline of holy church, in the
time, and by the labours of that our moste
learned Archbishop, S. Theodor. *Godvvin.*
Catal. in Theodor. Matth. Parker in eodem
Capgrau. & M.S. in vit.S.Theodori. Therfore seeing wee haue so ample warrant in
antiquities, as the olde chronicle of Landaffe, ascribed to S.Telian, S. Bede, the
old English Chronicle, named Beatus, Co-
celin, and others that the faith of Christ
was preached in Britanie in the time of
Kinge Lucius in the 156. yeare of Christ,
and very many conuerted by preists sent
from the Pope of Rome, which was not
aboue three yeares after the death of this
Pope S. Higinius, & in the papacy of Pope
Pius the first, we may not with iudgement
thinke, but these preists or diuers of them
that had wonne so many to Christ in that
time, were sent in the dayes of this massing
Pope S. Higinius, and his sacrificinge predecessors

deceſſors which beſides that is already ſaid
in this matter, will more appeare in the
next Pope S. Pius the firſt. *Chronicon Lan-*
daf. apud Io. Caium l. 1. antiq. Cantabrig. pag.
107. Beda l. 1. hiſtor. cap. 4. Chronicle Bru-
tus an. 156. Gocelin. in vita S. Auguſtini cap.
31. Stovve hiſtor. in Kinge Lucius Io. Ca-
ius ſupr.

17. This holy Pope by all accompts gouerned the church of Chriſt at Rome, whē
by ſo many auncient authorities the preiſts
ſent from thence, had ſo increaſed and propagated the Chriſtian faith in this kingedome, who the better to bee mindefull of
this nation, as his predeceſſors, by that a-
monge other motiues, were, liued and
conuerſed moſte, and more then with
any of any other contrie, or nation, with
our Chriſtian Britans, that were then at
Rome, in ſo much that we haue allowance
both from Catholicks & Proteſtants, that
a great part of their cheife reſidency was in
the houſe of S. Claudia, our noble Chriſtian contriwoman, and with ſuch free-
dome and libertie to commaund therein,
that diuers proteſtants, beſides all Catholicke antiquities aſſure vs, this holy Pope
by

by the graunt & donation of her holy children did cōſecrate it for the firſt Chriſtian
church in Rome . (*Robert. Barnes in vita*
Pontif. Rom. in Pio I.) *Thermas nouati tem-*
plo dedicauit, Pope Pius the firſt dedicated the
houſe of Nouatus (ſonne of S. Claudia) *for*
a church. An other thus writeth of him, in
this matter . *Hee conſecrated the firſt temple*
of Rome, vvhich vvas dedicated to S. Puden-
tiana, the Temples of Chriſtians hauing bene
in former times in hidden and obſcure caues.
Edvv. Grimſton booke of eſt. in the church of
Rome. pag. 436.) the Catholicke antiquities that teſtifie this, are to many too be cited. (*Act.& vit. S. Pudentianæ & Breu. Rom.*
die 19. Maij. Martyrol. Rom. 19. Maij. Baron.
annot. in eod. Rom. Martyrol. die 20. Iunij.)
but they all agree , that the Popes of Rome
were ordinarily intertayned in this houſe
of our Chriſtian Britans , and eſpeciallie
this holy Pope Pius ſaid Maſſe there , *and*
vvas there releiued by S. Pudentiana, daugh-
ter to our Brittish Ladie Claudia , and the
Christians came thither vſually to heare Maſ-
ſe, vvhen Antoninus the Emperor had forbid-
den Christians to haue Maſſe publickly. Quòd
ab Antonino Imperatore ſancitum erat , ne

Chri-

Christiani publicè sacrificia facerent: Pius Pon-
tifex in ædibus Pudentianæ cum Christianis
sacra celebrabat.

18. And to manifest farther vnto vs,
what a massinge Pope this S. Pius was, and
how in all probable iudgement, that holy
doctrine amonge others, was propagated
here in Britanie, these antiquities tell vs,
there was in that Brittish house, *ninty sixe*
Christian men, nonaginta sex homines Chri-
stiani. (*Pius Pap. 1. epist.*) and the like hee
writeth of the house of Euprepia, where
hee also liued, and said Masse, *vbi nunc cum*
pauperibus commorantes, Missas agimus. And
hee was so zelous herein, and to haue Masse
said with all attention, & deuotion, that he
decreed as these protestants testifie, to
write in their owne words: *Sacerdotibus ne-*
gligentius Missæ sacra facientibus pænas sta-
tuit. (*Robert. Barnes in vit. Pontific. Rom. in*
Pio 1. Grimston in Pius 1. Io. Func. commen-
tar. in Chronolog. l. 5. in Pio 1. an. 145.) He
ordeyned punishments for preists that said
Masse negligently. That if any by impru-
dency shoulde shedd any of the blood of
Christ, vppon the ground, hee shoulde doe
penance fourtie dayes. If vppon the altare,

3.

3. dayes. That if vpon the linen cloath vnder the chalice 4. dayes. If vpon the other
linen cloathe 9. dayes. That hee should lick
vp the blood of Chriſt, that was ſhedd, or
if that could not be, either pare it, or waſhe
it away, and ſo pared or waſhed, either to
bee burnt, or kept reſerued in the ſacrarie.
Vt ſi quis per imprudentiam de ſanguine Chri-
ſti effunderet in terram, pænitentiam ageret
dies 40. Si ſuper altare, dies 3. Si ſuper linte-
um ſubſtratum calici, 4. dies. Si ſuper aliud
linteum, dies 9. Sanguinem Chriſti effuſum
lambere, vel ſi id fieri non poſsit, aut radere,
aut eluere: & raſum aut lotum, vel comburi,
vel in ſacrarium repoſitum ſeruari.

19. Therefore this Pope beeinge in all
mens iudgements, Catholicks and Proteſtants. (*Ioh. Bal. l. 1. act. Pontif. Rom. in*
Pio 1.) an holy Saint, and martyr, and to
vſe a Proteſtant Biſhops words, *one that did*
many vvorks of true pietie in the feild of the
Chriſtian church, multa veræ pietatis opera,
in agro Chriſtianæ Eccleſiæ feciſſe perhibetur,
was ſo wel acquainted with our Chriſtian
Britans, and both claymed and exerciſed
ſupreame ſpirituall iuriſdiction ouer all places, and parſons in matters of Religion by

theſe

these proteſtants (*Robert. Barnes in vit. Pÿ*
1.) *Quæ ad Religionem ſpectant, à ſuæ dioce-*
ſeos ſynodis audienda eſſe ſtatuit : ſalua tamen
Pontificia authoritate, of all natious this our
Britanic muſt needs then bee an honorer of
ſacrificinge preiſts, and holy Maſſe, in this
time, and euer after, vnto the generall conuerſion of it in the time of S. Eleutherius,
betweene whome and this Saint Pius there
were but two Popes, S. Anicetus and S.
Sother, both which were not Popes many
yeares by theſe proteſtāts, not 18. yeares by
any of their accompts. *Robert. Barn. in Pio*
1. Anicet. & Sother. Io. Balæus in act. Pon-
tif. in eiſdem Edvv. Grimſt. in the ſame Popes.
Foxe Tom. 1.

20. And theſe Popes were ſo far from
croſſinge with this, and others their predeceſſors in theſe points of ſupreamacy, ſacrificinge preiſts, and ſacrifice of Maſſe, that
by the confeſſion of theſe proteſtants, they
made decrees, which confirmed them all,
makinge lawes bindinge all Archbiſhops,
Primates, and Metropolitans, and ſhewing
they were ſubiect to the Pope of Rome, and
preſcribed rules for all preiſts ſayinge Maſſe, and ſhauing their crownes, as they now
vſe

vſe in the Roman church, at this day, *Ar-chiepiſcopum à ſuo Epiſcopo, aut ceram primate, aut Romano Pontifice accuſandum eſſe. Archie-piſcopos non Primates, ſed Metropolitanos ap-pellandos eſſe dixit, niſi iſta prærogatiua à Ro-mano Pontifice concederetur. Capitis verticem ſpherula inſtar radendum Sacerdotibus, præ-cepit. Ne Sacerdos celebraret, niſi vt minimum duo adeſſent, ordinauit, ne Monacha pallam contrectaret, neuè thus in aceram poneret, ſta-tuit.* So wee are ſure, theſe two holy Popes, Saints and Martyrs, were alſo ſacrificinge Popes, and all preiſts at that time vnder them, whether in Britanie or els where, beeinge ſubiect and obedient vnto them, were maſſinge preiſts. And ſo wee are now come with a continuall deduction of theſe ſacred doctrines and practiſes, both in the church of this our Britanie, and others vn-till the time of Pope and Saint Eleutherius, when and by whoſe happy meanés hiſto-rians commonly tell vs, this kingedome was generally conuerted to the faith of Chriſt.

THE

THE XVI. CHAPTER.

Wherin is proued by teſtimonies of proteſtants,
and others, that this kingdome in the time
of Kinge Lucius, was conuerted by maſsing
Preiſts, and Bishops, and the holy ſacrifice
of Maſſe, and such maſsinge preiſts and Bi-
shops, continued here in honor, all this age.

IN this happy generall conuerſion of this
kingdome, no man of what Religion
ſoeuer, can without prophane and irreli-
gious boldnes, and impudentnes affirme in
iudgement, that ſo wiſe and vertuous a
Kinge, his Nobles, ſo many learned Druides, and others, eſpecially moued to Chriſtian Religion by the patience, pietie, and
vertue of the glorious Martyrs, and Saints
of thoſe dayes by all antiquities, Maſſe ſayinge or Maſſe hearinge Chriſtians, would
write ſuch ſuppliant letters, and ſend Am-
baſſadors ſo longe a iorney, as from hence
to Rome, to bee conuerted to any other Religion of Chriſt, but that ſacrificinge and
maſſinge profeſſion, by the miracles and
ſanctity of whoſe profeſſors, they were ſo
moued

moued and conuinced in iudgement, it was the only truth. Neither would or could Pope Eleutherius an holy & learned Saint, and succeffor onely to facrificinge maffing Popes, and preifts, recommend vnto King Lucius, and this kingdome, any other then maffinge preifts, and Religion, or the learned meffengers of Kinge Lucius, as our proteftants ftile them. (*Io. Bal.centur. 1.de fcriptor. in Eluan. & Meduuin. Math.Parker. antiq. Brit. Godwin. Conuerf. of Britanie.*) confent to any other, or fo many renowned both preifts and Biſhops, as were ftill remayninge in, or of this nation knowne maffinge preifts, and biſhops, ioyne with the Legats of Pope Eleutherius, in teaching and preachinge any other doctrine, or Religion.

2. Such were our renowned contrimen S. Manfuetus, yet liuinge except the Annals of Treuers, or the fame name deceaue vs, confecrated preift by S. Peter, and now remoued from Toul to Treuers, for the ecclefiafticall Annals of that archiepifcopall fea tell vs. (*Petr. Merffæus Annal. Archiep. Treueren. 7.*) that S. Manfuetus (I reade of no other of that name but our holy contryman

V 4 man

man in that time) *was Archbishop of Treuers
in the yeare of Christ* 160. *Mansuetus , qui
huic nomini & vocationi suæ vita proba, anno
Domini* 160. *optimè respondit .* And S. Marcellus or Marcellinus our glorious contryman, who before his departure out of Britanie had moued Kinge Lucius to the faith
of Christ , and after of the Tungers , and
Archbishop also of Treuers returninge hither with the Popes Legats, was so renowned an instrument in the conuersion of this
kingdome , that the Annals of the place
where hee was Archbishop say, that by the
preachinge of this Saint , the third Bishop
of Tungers Kinge Lucius was baptised.
(*Annal-Treuer. in S. Marcello.*) S. *Marcellus , alijs Marcellinus fuit Tungorum tertius
Episcopus,& huius prædicatione Rex Angliæ,
id est Lucius, baptizatus est.* The catalogue
of the Bishops of Tunger giueth him greater honor, tellinge vs, *that by his preaching
hee conuerted Lucius Prince of Britanie with
the whole nation to the faith of Christ .* Lu-
*cium Britanniæ Principem cum tota gente, sua
prædicatione ad Christum conuertit. (Catalog.
Episcop. Tungrens. in S. Marcello.)* And yet
I haue shewed before, that these were massinge

singe preists and Bishops, as their predecessors in those places, S. Valerius, Eucharius, Maternus and others were.

3. The same I say of S. Tymotheus, our holy contryman, by his Mother S. Claudia beeinge a knowne massinge preist, and one of the owners of that his, and his brother Nouatus and Sisters house in Rome, so notoriously dedicated to bee the first publick massinge church there : for this holy massinge preist came hither in this time, and was so great a worker in the conuersion of this his contrie, that the histories of Treuers themselues, which giue such honor as before to their Archbishop S. Marcellus in this busines, yet freely also acknowledge that Kinge Lucius, *was brought to the Religion of Christ by S. Timothie*, whome they call S. Paules disciple, perhaps because S. Paul maketh so honorable a memory of his parents, S. Pudens, and Claudia (2 *Timoth.*4.) & likely did baptize this S. Timothie, and therby called his disciple though a very child, when S. Paul was martyred. (*Martyrolog. Rom. die* 20. *Iunij Baron. annot-ib. Sur. Tom.* 3. *die* 12. *Iunij.*) and the other S. Timothie his scholler dead

longe

longe before . *S. Lucius Britanniæ Rex S.*
Timothei Apostoli Pauli discipuli eruditione
ad Religionem Christi inductus est . (*Petr.*
Merßaus & Annal. Archiep. & eccl. Treuer.
in S. Marcello.) If wee reflect vppon the
Saints that were sent cheife Legats hither,
from Rome , *S. Fugatius*, and *Damianus*,
the principall of them in all antiquities, as
wee must needs to giue them their due,that
bee chosen and selected mē, they must needes be learned vertuous,and of mature age,
and iudgment to be imploied in so weigh-
tie a busines,and as all histories testifie they
were , and so must needes bee consecrated
massinge preists, beeing sacred by those remembred sacrificinge Popes,which neither
did , nor could consecrate any other , nor
they bringe any other doctrine in this or
any other points of Religion,but what they
had receaued from those holy Popes.

4. And to this, besides so many generall
Arguments , S. Gildas the moste auncient
and renowned Brittish Author is a particular witnes,if it could please our protestants
to publish it to the worlde , except that renowned Abbot Doctor Fecknham did a-
buse his auditory in the first parlament of
Queene

Queene Elizabeth in his publicke oration,
which no indifferent man will thinke, hee
did or durst to doe, for feare of open shame
and confusion, if hee should haue aduou-
ched an vntruth in that assemblie. And yet
speaking principally of the sacrifice of Masse, then to bee condemned by that parlament, citeth Gildas in the prœme of his
history, testifyinge that the same Religion,
and church seruice, the sacrifice of Masse which
was then to bee abrogated was brought hither,
and settled here in the Latine tonge by the Le-
gats of Pope Eleutherius. (*Abbot Fecknham*
orat. in parlam. 2. of Queene Elizabeth.) and
all our cheife protestant antiquaries and historians of England, as their Bishops, Parker, Bale, Godwine, with others Gosteline,
Powell, Foxe, Fulke, Middleton, Stowe,
Holinshed & others confidently affirming,
that the Christian Brittans neuer chaunged in any materiall thinge, that holy Religion which they receaued in the time of the
Apostles, but constantly continued in the
same, vntill the cominge of S. Augustine
hither, from S. Gregory the great Pope of
Rome, and after. *Parker antiquitat. Britan.*
pag. 6. 45. 46. Balæus l. 2. de act. Pontif. Rom.

in Gregor. 1. *l. de scriptor. cent.* 1. *in August.*
Dronotho. Godwin. conuers. of Brit. Powel. an-
not. in l. 2. *Giraldi Camb. de Itiner. Cambr.*
cap. 1. *Foxe act. pag.* 463. *edit. an.* 1576. *Fulke*
answ. to a count Cath. pag. 40. *Middelt. pa-*
pistom. pag. 202 *Stow histor. in S. Augustine*
and Kinge Ethelbert. Holinsh. histor. of Engl.
cap. 21. *pag.* 102.

5. But as I haue proued before by these
protestants and otherwise, the Britans by
that Apostolicke man receaued the doctrine, profession, and practise of sacrificinge
preisthood, preists, and sacrifice of Masse,
and continued them vnto this time; soe I
will demonstrate by them and all antiquities hereafter, in euery age, that they kept
and obserued the same inuiolablie to those
dayes, and after without interruption. And
yet this is but a needles probation; for being
so inuincibly proued before, that they receaued these holy doctrines and professions
from the Apostles, and from them to these
daies, if they had departed from them now,
or after, they should bee apparantly guiltie
of error in departinge from those truthes,
which the Apostles, and all from them to
these dayes continued. And if wee looke
into

into the catalogues of holy writers, in this
time, whose works bee preserued to posteritie, wee shall see, that the holy sacrifice
of Masse, and massinge preists, were generally in al places in as great vse and honour
as at this day. The moste renowned writers
of this time whose bookes bee extant now,
were S. Iustine, S. Irenæus, and Tertullian, all they doe plainelie testifie, that the
sacrifice of Masse, offeringe vp the sacred
body, and blood of Christ, was the generally vsed, & knowne sacrifice of the Christians in this time, *in omni loco*, in euerie
place, saith S. Iustine. (*Iustin. Dialog. cum
Tryphone.*) *Ecclesia in vniuerso mundo offert
Deo.* The church doth offer it in all the
world, saith S. Irenæus. (*Irenæus aduers. Hæres. lib. 4. cap. 32.*) therefore the church of
Britanie must needs offer it; and I haue proued by our Brittish antiquities before, that
Rome, Fraunce, and Britanie in these daies
of Eleutherius, and Irenæus which went
to Rome in the papacy of S. Eleutherius,
vsed one and the same order of Masse. And
Tertullian that notorious massing Author,
declaring how Christiā Religion was then
dilated in the worlde, and the sacrifice of

Masse

Maſſe was the common ſacrifice thereof, expreſſely nameth this our Britanie to haue receaued the Chriſtian faith, and to agree with other Chriſtian nations therin. (*Tertullian. de cultu Faminar. cap. 11. l. ad Scapul. cap. 2. l. de orat. cap. 14. l. de vel-Virg. cap. 9. l. contra Iudæos.*) & S. Iohn Chriſoſtome ſpeaking of this conuerſion of our Britans, witneſſeth manifeſtly, and our proteſtants acknowledge it for truth, that the Brittiſh churches then founded, which were many had altars, for their preiſts, erected in them. (*Chriſoſtom. ſerm. de Pemtecoſt. proteſt. Theater of great Britanie l. 6. §. 12.*) which as is confeſſed before by theſe proteſtants, neither were, nor could in Chriſtian Religion bee ordeyned but for maſſinge preiſts, and the ſacrifice of Maſſe, as wee finde in the moſte auncient churches of this nation; as S. Ioſephs dedicated to our Lady at Glaſtéburie. (*Antiquit. Glaſton. Capgrau. in S. Patricio M. S. antiq. in Lucio.*) S. Martins at Canterbury, and the olde church at Wincheſter, where as we read there were Chriſtian altares, ſo alſo that the ſacrifice of Maſſe was from their firſt foundation offered on them. (*Bed. hiſt. l. 1. cap. 27. Galſr. Monum.*)

Monum. l. 11. *histor. cap.* 4. *Stowe histor. in Constantine sonne of Cador. &c.*) so of S. Peters church in Cornhill in London and others. And S. Damianus and Phaganus the cheife Legats of S. Eleutherius, bearing so great deuotion to the massing church builded by S. Ioseph at Glastenbury, that they themselues continued, and dwelled there some time, and settled twelue of their company to continue there duringe their liues, must needs bee massinge preists, as all had here euer beene from the Apostles time: in which faith and Religion this holy Pope, as our protestants with al antiquities assure vs, confirmed the kingdome of Britanie: *Eleutherius vt bonus paterfamilias effecit, vt confirmatis & consolidatis Britannis in suscepta prius ab Apostolis doctrina, totum illud regnum, in eius fidei verba iuraret. Ioh. Bal. l. 1. de act. Pontif. Rom. in Eleutherio.*

6. So that by this Protestant Bishop, and his and other authorities, those doctrines of sacrificinge preists and Masse which from the Apostles dayes, as I haue aboundantly proued, had without discontinuance euer continued here in diuers particular places and parsons, were now generally by this

holy

holy Pope, and his massinge Legats, established and confirmed in this kingedome: *confirmatis, & consolidatis*, and this Pope highly commeded for that his general confirmation, *vt bonus paterfamilias*. And by their first Archbishop with others before, and as I haue proued by continuall deduction, the order and forme of Masse which S. Peter deliuered to the church, was still continued after this time, without any materiall chaunge, alteration, addition, or diminution. Neither doth any Protestant Author challenge S. Eleutherius, of any innouation in Religion, but the contrary: how hee condemned all innouators therein as Tatianus and the Seuerians, makinge a decree against them, and the knowne Religion of Christ, his sacrificinge Religion, as before is proued was much increased by him. *Sub hoc Pontifice cæpit Ecclesia esse secusior, ob id Christianorum Religio plurimum aucta est.* And yet no chaunge at all therin. (*Bal. & Robert. Barnes in vita Eleutherij. Eleutherius epist- decretal. ad prouincias Gall. To. 1. conc. Io. Bal. act. Pont. Rom.l. 1. in Eleutherio. Rob. Barn. in vit Pontif. Rom. in eodem.*) therefore all those Bishops, & preists
which

which by all writers hee confecrated, muft needs bee maffinge Bifhops, and preifts, as all thofe three Archbifhops, & 28. Bifhops, which he confecrated, or confirmed for this kingdome renowned in hiftories , and all the preifts of this our Britanie vnder them, muft needes bee maffing Archbifhops, Bifhops, and preifts . Whofe fucceffion here continued vnto the conuerfion of the Saxons , and after by all hiftories , and vntill both thofe peoples vnited themfelues , as well in this maffinge and facrificinge doctrine, which both the Britans, and Saxons had euer obferued from their firft conuerfions, as in al other points of Chriftian Religion. The names of many of them I haue remembred in other places.

7. And concerninge the fupreame fpirituall power , which this holy Pope both claimed, and exercifed, both in this kingedome , to fettle thefe facred points of Religion here, and in other nations, thefe proteftants affure vs , it was as great and ample, as euer any his fucceffors did , or now doe challenge in fuch affaires . Thefe men tell vs. (*Rob. Barnes in vit. Eleutherij. proteſt. annot. Mag. in Matth. Weſtm.an.* 188.)

X   hee

hee condemned hereticks, and made decrees against them; he made lawes binding
all cleargie men, & in the cases of Bishops,
reserued iudgement to the see of Rome, *vt*
nihil nisi apud Pontificem definiretur. In his
epistle to Kinge Lucius, so recommended
by our protestants, hee prescribeth what
lawes hee was to vse. Hee appointeth the
limits and bounds of Britanie, as these
men witnes in the lawes of Kinge Edward the Confessor. His Legats disposed of
all spirituall things here, in that time, and
he by his papal authoritie confirmed them.
And so they continued vntil heresie and in-
fidelity in the Pagan Saxons time did ouerthrowe them, as all histories and antiquities, Brittish, or Saxon, Catholicks or protestants, as their Bishops, Parker, Bale and
Godwine, with Cambden, Powell, Holinshed, Stowe, and others cited in other places are witnesses. Therefore it will bee but
a superogated worke, to proceede further
to followinge ages, yet for a generall and
compleate content to all, I wil though with
more breuitie, speake also of them, and here
end this second age, or hundred of yeares,
Pope Eleutherius dyinge in the later ende
thereof,

thereof, and Kinge Lucius not longe after
in the beginninge of the next age, and Pope
and S. Victor, the immediate fuccessor of S.
Eleutherius both endinge this, and giuing
entrance to the next enfuinge age, and centenary of the yeares of Chrift by his papall
regiment.

THE THIRD AGE, OR HVN-
DRED YEARES OF CHRIST.

THE XVII. CHAPTER.

How notwithstandinge the manifold tumults,
and perfecution of Chriftian Religion, in
this kingdome of Britanie, in this third
hundred yeares, yet the holy facrifice of
Maſſe, facrificinge and maſſinge preifts, and
Bishops ftil here continued, without any to-
tall difcontinuance.

K Inge Lucius dyinge, as Matthew of
Weftminifter with others writeth, in
the yeare of Chrift 201. the firft of this third
hundred yeare, without heire; This our
kingdome by that meanes in the beginning
of this age was pitifully vexed with warrs,
and

and tumults; & towards the later end therof lamentably tormented, and afflicted (as
the whole Christian worlde almoste then
was) with the moste cruell and barbarous
persecution of Diocletian, in which among
other miseries, all monuments of Christian
Religion, so neare as he could, were ruined
and destroyed ; whereby it came to passe,
that little memory of ecclesiasticall things
then, in this nation is left to posteritie, yet
sufficient is to be found, that together with
the Popes supreamacy in such affaires , the
holy sacrificinge preisthood , the sacrifice
of Masse, and diuers renowned sacrificinge
Bishops and preists , here still continued
without discontinuance, in al this age, notwithstandinge so huge an army of moste
sauage , and cruell enemies still fightinge
against them. *Matth.* We*stm. an. gratiæ* 201.
Bed. l. 1. *histor. c.* 4. 6. *Parker. antiquit. Bri-*
tan. Godwin. conuersf. of Britanic. Stowe histor.
in K. Lucius. Theater of great Brit. l. 6. *Foxe*
Tom. 1. *Holinsh. histor. of Engl. Galfr. Mo-*
num. hist. Britan. l. 5. *cap.* 1. 2. 3. 4. 5 6, 7.
Ponticus Viran· Brit. histor. l. 5. *Gildas l. de*
excid. & conquest. Britan. cap. 7. 8.

2. For First our cheife protestants haue
told

told vs before, that S. Peters Maſſe continued in vſe in the church without any
chaunge, vnto the time of Pope and S. Zepherine, which was next ſucceſſor to S.
Victor, therefore by their allowance, wee
haue the ſacrifice of Maſſe, a maſſinge
preiſthood, and preiſts to offer that holie
ſacrifice all his time. Therefore when wee
finde by many antiquities and hiſtorians,
aſwell Catholicks as Proteſtants, that hee
ſent many learned preiſts and preachers
into this kingedome, eſpecially the more
northren parts thereof, which wee now cal
Scotland, wee muſt needes if wee had noe
other argument, conclude, that they were
ſacrificinge, and maſſinge preiſts, becauſe
they receaued both their conſecration, and
iuriſdiction from ſoe knowne a maſſinge
preiſt, and Pope his authoritie. Yet to make
this matter more euident, and ſhew the ſupreame ſpirituall power which hee vſed e-
uen in this, beſides that which he both claimed and exerciſed in excommunicatinge
the church of Aſia for their not due obſeruation of Eaſter, hee confirmed the order
and inſtitution of his predeceſſor S. Eleutherius, in ſubiectinge all the churches, and

X 3 Chri-

Christians of that part of Britany now termed Scotlád, to the Archbishop of Yorke,
a massing preist & Prelate, as I haue shewed before, these parts and countries then
beeing temporally ruled by diuers temporall Kings, or Princes, and at difference or
enmity at that time one with an other. And
to make this Religió more permanent with
that rude nation, *the Scots themselues then
began to study diuinitie.* (*Hector Boeth.
Scot. histor. l. 6. fol. 89. pag. 2.*) *beeing therin
instructed by those preists which Pope Victor
sent thither euen to the vttermost part therof
to propagate Christian Religion. Incepere &
nostri tum primum, sacras colere literas, Sacerdotibus praeceptoribus, quos Victor Pontifex
Maximus, ad Christi dogma propalandum in
extremam miserat Albionem.* Which was in
the yeare of Christ 203. *Humanae salutis tertius supra ducentesimum.* And euer continued in the same as theire historians contend, vnto these dayes of heresie, *nostri qua
fide & pietate instituti semel fuerunt hactenus erroribus aspernatis, perseucrant.* Which
was written in the yeare of Christ 1526.
*Anno salutis Christianae sexto & vigesimo su-
pra, millesimum quingentesimum.*

3. So longe and longer these massinge preists & sacrifice of Masse continued there with honor, by their writers, and our English Protestants affirme as mnch in these termes. (*Edw. Grimston. in the est. of the K. of great Britanie pag.* 20. *cap.* 17.) *Scotland receaued the Christian faith in the time of Pope Victor the first, in the yeare* 203. *and idolatry did quite cease, vnder Kinge Craknite, who died in the yeare* 313. *Celestine the first sent Palladius thither to roote out the Pelagian heresie, which began to encrease there vnder Eugenius the seconde, who died in the yeare* 460. *since this time the realme continued longe in the profession of the Romish church, vntill these later dayes,* the daies of Kinge Iames, our present soueraigne, as hee there expresseth. Therefore seeing the profession of the Romane church, which frō. the beginning by these authorities, and testimonies, both Catholicke and Protestant, euer continued there, was the profession of the sacrifice of Masse, and massinge preists, such was the profession euer vntill now in those parts. Againe this part of this Iland was subiected both by Pope Eleutherius, and Victor, to the Archbishop of Yorke a massing Prelate,

late,

late, either S. Theodosius or S. Sampson,
therefore the preistes subiect to that see,
must needs bee massinge preists. (*Harrison
description of Britanie in K. Lucius. Godwin
Catalog. in Yorke pag.* 555. *edit. an.* 1515.)
and both S. Gildas, S. Bede and all antiquities assure vs, that this Religion was preserued in peace, and quiet here, vnto the persecution of Diocletian. *Gild. l. de excid. Britan. cap.* 7. *Bed. histor. eccl. l.* 1. *cap.* 4. *antiq.
Winton. apud Godw. Catal. in Winchester.* 1.)
and the Annals of Scotland tell vs expres-
selie, of the altars chalices, patens, and all
vessels, instruments, and ornaments vsed
in the holy sacrifice of Masse, to haue bene
in honorable, and publicke vse in this time
in that contry. (*Hector Boeth. Scot. histor.
l.* 6. *fol.* 102.

4. And if we leaue Britanie and returne
againe to Rome, and the Pope there, S. Zepherine, these protestants assure vs, *he was,
rei diuinæ magis quam humanæ intetus, a man
more giuen to diuine then humaine affaires,* a
Protestant Bishops words: and yet they ab-
solutly teache, hee claimed and exercised
supreame spirituall iurisdiction, and made
decrees, concerninge the holy sacrifice of
Masse,

Maſſe, of what mater, the chalice and pa-
ten, in, and on which the body and blood
of Chriſt ſhould be conſecrated, in that ſacrifice, were to bee made, and how preiſts
ought to bee preſent when the Biſhop celebrated the ſacrifice of Maſſe, *cum Epiſcopus
celebraret Miſſæ ſacra iuſsit omnes presbyteros
adeſſe.* (*Bal. in act. Pontif. Rom. l.* 1. *in Ze-
pherino. Edw. Grimſton pag.* 436. *in Zepherin.
Rob. Barnes in vit. Pontif. Rom. in Zepherin. alij. Sacer*) and by the ſentence of their
firſt Proteſtant Archbiſhop, hee was ſo far
from doing any diſhonor to this holy ſacrifice of Maſſe, that, *ad pulchriorem materiam
formamque mutare voluit.* The chaunge hee
made, was for the more honor therof. *Math.
Parker antiquitat. Britan. pag.* 47. *Magdeb.
cent.* 1. *cap.* 5. *col.* 146.) beeing nothing but
that I cited before of cauſing the ſacrificing
inſtruments to be made of a better matter,
making no other chaunge at al therin. And
within few yeares after, the next Pope but
one, Vrbanus the firſt, as theſe proteſtants
aſſure vs made a lawe, that euē in the poo-
rer churches the ſacrificinge veſſels ſhould
either bee of gold, ſiluer, or tinne. *Ne vaſa
ſacra vitrea, ſed aut aurea, aut argentea,*
aut

aut stannea in inopioribus Ecclesijs essent, legem tulit. (*Rob. Barnes in Vrban. 1. Edw. Grimston. estate of the church of Rome in Vrban. 1. pag. 436. Magdeb. cent. 1. cap. 6. col. 146.*) and that Pope Fabian an holy Saint, and miraculously chosen to the papall dignitie, made a decree about the sacrifice of Masse, what preists were to bee allowed to say Masse. And they put it out of all question, that the most renowned other Fathers of this age, as Tertullian S. Ciprian, with others taught and maintained this doctrine of the sacrifice of Masse. *Magdeburg. cent. 1. cap. 4. col. 83. titul. de Eucharist. & sacrificio.* so they write of Pope Stephen, Fælix & Sixtus in this age, whom they acknowledge for holy Saints, and open maintayners and practisers of this blessed sacrifice, shewinge how in their time, the whole canon was secretly read, as is now observed. *Sixtus, dum Sacerdos canonem ante celebrationem sub silentio legeret, vt in populo Sanctus triplicatum caneretur, instituit.* And neither bringe any Pope, or Father to the contrary, or any Pope altered any thinge in this holy sacrifice, which they doe or can dislike.

5. **And**

5. And concerning communion it selfe in one onely kinde, by the laitie, and such as saide not Masse, now vsed in the Latine church, with much dislike of many protestants, these protestants themselues confesse vnto vs. (*Magdeburgen. cent. 3. cap. 6. de ritib. circa canam col.* 149) that it was the custome of the church of Rome, of Italy, and with other Bishops for the communicants, to receaue onely vnder the forme of bread. And some of our English Protestants as Master Parkins. (*Parkinsus l. demonstr. probl. m. pag.* 155) giueth many instances and examples of such communicating. And amonge others bringeth S. Ciprian to bee a witnes hereof, writinge in this time, as also the Protestants of Germany doe, teachinge this custome in those churches of Rome, Italy, and others to haue bene more auncient then this time: and moste certaine it is, that both S. Ciprian, and Tertullian before him, testifie it was also soe vsed in Afrike to communicate onely vnder the forme of blood. (*Ciprian. l. de laps. & l. de spectacul. Tertullia. l. 2. ad Vxorem. cap* 5) S. Irenæus proueth the same of the age before; and both S. Chrisostome, or whosoeuer author

thor

thor of the *opus imperfectū ſuper Matthæum,*
S. Auguſtine, Iſichius, S. Bede, Theophi-
lact, and others doe ſo expound, that act &
example of Chriſt at Emaus, in S. Lukes
Ghoſpell, after his reſurrection, thus by our
proteſtants tranſlation: *hee tooke bread, and
bleſſed it, and brake, and gaue to them.* (*Homil.* 16. *operis imperfect. ſupr. Matth. Auguſt.
conſenſ. Euang. l.* 3. *c.* 25. *Iſych. l.* 2. *in Leuit. c.* 9. *Bed. & Theop. in c.* 24. *Luc. cap.* 24.
v. 30.) the ſame expoſition is made of breakinge of breade, in the 2. and 20. chapter
of the acts of the Apoſtles, by the auncient
author, of that vnperfect worke, and our
learned coutrimen, *Ionas Aurelianenſis,* and
S. Bede, and the Syriake text readeth, *in
fractione Euchariſtiæ,* in breakinge the Euchariſt. And Iohn Caluine himſelfe doth ſo
plainely expounde the later place of the 20.
chapter. *Actor. cap.* 2. *v.* 42. *cap.* 20. *v.* 7. *Homil.* 17. *operis imperfecti. Beda ad cap.* 20. *act.
Ionas Aurelianen. l.* 3. *de Imaginib. text. Sy-
riac. Caluin. in act.* 20.

6. And to make all ſure, the parlament
ſtatute of three Proteſtant Princes, Kinge
Edward 6. Queene Elizabeth, and Kinge
Iames. (*Statut. parlam. an.* 1. *Edw.* 6. *an.* 1.
Elizab.

Elizab, and an. 1. *Iacobi Abridg. of stat. titul.*
seruice and Sacram.) doth warrant vs , that
in the primatiue church, communion was
often vsed in one only kinde. And the three
first Euangelists S. Matthew , Marke and
Luke ar ample witnesses, that the words of
Christ, *drinke you all of this* (the ground of
protestants in this contention) were onely
present with him , and by him at that time
made preists by all antiquities. (*Matth. cap.*
26. *v.* 20. *Marc. cap.* 14. *ver.* 17. 18. *Luc. c.* 22.
v. 14.) and so the words and commaunde-
ment could not possibly bee generall , for
that cause , and if they had beene generall , all the whole Christian worlde, in all
ages Catholicks from the beginninge, and
protestants since their new cominge , had
beene, and ar guiltie of transgressinge that
institution and commaundement . Therfore seeing wee cannot finde any innouation in these misteries , in this time , let vs
seeke out some more massing preists of this
nation , in this tempestuous season . For
such we finde particularly at Rome S. Mel-
lanius as the Romane Martyrologe with o-
thers nameth him, but by the auncient Manuscript history of his life and Capgraue,

S.

S. Mellon. He beeing a noble Britane, and
going hence to Rome to pay the tribute of
his contry and ſerue the Emperor, was conuerted to the faith of Chriſt, by the maſſing
Pope S. Stephen , and by him takinge firſt
all inferior orders , was made a maſſinge
preiſt . *Quem præfatus Papa ſibi adhærentem
per omnes Eccleſiæ gradus vſque ad Sacerdotium promouit.* (*Martyrolog. Rom. die* 22. *Octob. Baron. ib. Vincent. l.* 11. *c.* 74. *Petr. de
natal. l.* 9. *c.* 93. *Demochar. contr. Caluin. M.
S. antiq. de vita S. Mellonis. Ioh. Capgrau. in
catal. in S. Mellone Epiſcopo.*) and was ſo
deuout a ſayer of Maſſe, that among other
times, as hee was ſayinge Maſſe an Aꝛgell
openly appeared both to the holy Pope, and
him , at the right hand of the altare , and
Maſſe beeing ended deſigned him to goe to
Rouen in Normandy , where hee was the
ſecond Biſhop , next to S. Nicaſius , as the
Annals of that church are witneſſe , and
continued there a maſſinge preiſt, and Biſhop ſent from that maſſinge Pope , vntill
about the yeare of Chriſt 180 which being
before the beginninge of the perſecution of
Diocletian , wee had then here in Britanie
great numbers of maſſinge preiſts, and Biſhops,

fhops , as I haue proued before by our beft
antiquities.

7. And though for that time wee are in
a great defect and want of monuments, yet
wee haue warrant enough , that both in,
and after that perfecution , wee had both
maffinge preifts and Bifhops to continue
our hierarchicall fucceffion for the prefent
time of the perfecution in this part of Britanie, where the Romans ruled, & the perfecution by that oportunitie and power ra-
ged, wee muft not looke into our churches
and altars deftroyed for publick vfe of thefe
holy points of Religion; for as our beft and
mofte auncient author , S. Gildas writeth,
the Chriftians that remained, did hide them-
felues, in woods, and deferts and hidden caues.
Qui fuperfuerant filuis ac defertis abditifque
fpeluncis fe occultauere. (*Gildas l. de excid. &*
conq. Biitan. cap, 8.) S. Bede and others after both Catholicks and proteftants haue
the like. (*Bed. hiftor. Eccl. Angl. l. 1. cap. 8.*
Matth. Weftm. in Dioclet. Theater of Brit. 16.
Stowe Holinsh. hiftor. of Eng.) but if wee
goe into the Northern parts , beyond the
Romans wall and bounds, where the Chriftian Britans and Scots vnder King Crathlint

lint that renowned glory of that nation
then reigned, we shal finde both Maffe, and
maffinge preifts of this our part of Britanie
flying thither in honor, and offeringe publicklie the mofte holy facrifice of Maffe,
with great reuerence and folemnitie : *fuch*
were the holy mafsinge preist and Bishop S.
Amphibalus, Modocus, Prifcus, Calanus, Fer-
ranus, Ambianus, and very many others, a-
lijque permulti, preachinge the doctrine of
Chrift in all the Scottifh contries , *Christi*
feruatoris doctrinam omnes per Scotorum re-
giones concionando multis pijfque fudoribus fe-
minantes. Hector. Boeth. Scot. hiftor.i. 6.fol.
102. Veremund.apud eund.ib. Holinsh.hiftor.
of Scotland in K. Crathlint.

8. And among thefe holy doctrines, that
of holy Maffe, facrificing preifts, & preifthood were fo honorable , and renowned,
that this religious Kinge Crathlint did
build a cathedrall church, for that our perfecuted maffinge Bifhop , and preifts , en-
dowinge it with great guifts, and al things
neceffary for the honorable and reuerent
fayinge of Maffe, *as chalices, patens, Cand-*
lesticks, and other fuch thinges, requifite for
the vfe of facrifice, made of filuer and gold, and
an

an altare inclosed with copper and brasse . Sed & Crathlinius Rex , sacra Antistitis ædem muneribus ornauit amplisimis , calicibus , patenis, candelabris , alijsque similibus , ad sacrorum vsum commodis , ex argento auroque fabrefactis, altarique cupro, & ære clauso. And that these and many others flyinge thither, in this time were of this part of Britanie, where the English inhabite, it is plaine by these histories: so that it is moste manifest, that all this third age or hundred yeeres of Christ, the holy sacrifice of Masse, massing preists, & preisthood, stil cõtinued in al this kingdome of great Britanie, although not in such splendor , and glory , by reason of the great afflictions , and miseries of those dayes: as in better times, I will make mention of diuers our massinge preists, and Bishops, that escaped death, and suruiued after this persecution, in the next age, and so end with this.

Y

THE

THE FOVRTH AGE, OR HVN-
DRED YEARES OF CHRIST.

THE XVIII. CHAPTER.

How the holy sacrifice of Masse, sacrificing and massinge preisthood, preists and Bishops continued in this kingdome of great Britanie in al this age, without any interruption or discontinuance.

IN the beginninge of this age, and fourth hundred yeare, the state of the church of Christ was little different, either in Britanie, or any other nation, from that wherin it was in the later end of the former, for as our histories tell vs, the persecution begun by Diocletian did not cease, although not in such extremitie of rigour, vntill Cōstantine the great our contriman had bene Emperor some yeares, in the seuenth yeare of his Empire by Matthew of Westminster, Florentius Wigorniensis, and others: *capta semel persecutio, vsque ad septimū annum Constantini seruere non cessauit.* (*Matth. Westm. an. gratiæ* 304. *Florent. Wigorn. an.* 299. *al.* 321.) neither doe our Scottish writers, *Ve-*

re-

remundus, Hector Boethius, and others differ herein, for they are witnesses, that manie holy Christians of this southern part of Britanie, in the time of Constantius, fledd to the Picts, and Scots, for succour, and were there religiously entertained by King Crathlint. (*Veremund. apud Hect. Boeth. l.6. Scotor. hist. fol.* 102. *pag.* 1·) *Constantius Diocletiani more in Britannia Christianæ Religioni fuerit insidiatus. Vnde magnus piorum numerus persequêtium sæuitiam declinare cupiens, ad Scotos & Pictos côcessit. Hos Crathlintos Rex, ad se confugientes beneuolo affectu suscepit.* And the Romane histories agree with this, teachinge, that in the beginning of the Empire of Constantine, & vntill he had the vision of the Crosse, and was admonished to seeke and send for S. Siluester, then Pope, to baptize him, the persecution still continued, and S. Siluester hid himself in the mountaine Soracte, which an English Protestant Bishop with the Italian writers thus relateth. (*Io. Bal. l. 1. de act. Rom. Pont. in Siluestro.*) *At postquam soboles Helenæ sanctissima, Cæsar Constantinus, apud diuos hominesque fauorem nactus, in excelso vidit crucis æreformam. Tunc redijt tandem*

Y 2   *Romam,*

2. Yet notwithstanding this secret profession and practise of Christian Religion, in this time wee haue certaine testimonies of the continuance of these holy doctrines of the sacrifice of Masse, sacrificing preists, and preisthood, in this our Britanie in those dayes. For our Scottish historians before alleaged, giue euidence, that those massinge preists which I haue named before, did liue awhile after this time, and that in the isle Mona, there was a sacrificinge Bishop, and preists that said Masse, with such ritche ornaments and instruments for that time as I haue described, and that this massinge Bishops name was Amphibalus Bishop of Soder, beeing a Britane, liued, and died there an old man, longe after the death of S. Amphibalus our martir. *Amphibalus Brito vir insigni pietate, primus Antistes ibi creatus, Christi dogma per Scotorum Pictorumque Regiones propalando, multa contra Gentilium Religionem dicendo, scribendoque gloriosum & Christiano viro plane dignum, multa senectute viuendo fessus, falicemque sortitus est finem. (Boeth. & Veremund. sup. l. 6. histor. Scot.*

Scot.) where besides the time not agreeing, and the old age wherein this S. Amphibalus liued and died a glorious confessor, but no Martyr, the contry whence hee was a Britan, *Amphibalus Brito*, proue it was an other different Saint, from the Martyr Amphibalus, of whome we doe not reade that hee was a Bishop, nor a Britan, but coming hither from other places of persecution, as the writers of his life are witnesses. *Vir quidam meritis & doctrina clarus nomine Amphibalus, transiens in Britanniam verolamina Domino ducente peruenit.* (*M.S. antiq & Author vitæ S. Albani antiquus in vit. S. Albani Ioh. Capgrauius & alij in vit S. Albani.*) which he also himselfe doth witnes in this words to S. Alban. *My Lord Iesus Christ the sonne of the liuinge God, hath preserued mee from daungers, and for the saluation of many, sent mee into this nation. Dominus meus Iesus Christus filius Dei viui securum inter discrimina me custodiuit: & pro multorum salute ad istam me misit prouinciam.*

3. And we had at this time here in Britanie, liuinge after the persecution of Diocletian, many others both Bishops, and preists, that exercised and offered the sacri-

fice

fice of Maffe, amonge which S. Taurinus
was Archbifhop of Yorke, except our proteftant antiquaries, and others ar deceaued:
not that Taurinus which was in, or before
the dayes of Kinge Lucius, but another
more late, and liuinge in this time, placed
Archbifhop there in the time of Conftantius Chlorus, who came hither as Matthew
of Weftminfter writeth, in the yeare of
Chrift 302. (*Matth. Weftm.an. gratiæ* 302.)
and by the confent of the fame Conftantius, or more, as a Proteftant Bifhop and
antiquary from antiquities thus deliuereth.
(*Godwin. Catal. of Bifhops in Yorke* 1. *pag.*
555.) *it is reported that Conftantius Chlorus*
appointed Taurinus Bifhop of Eureux to bee
Archbifhop there, at Yorke. Which is al-
mofte or fully 200. yeares after the other
Taurinus was fent into Fraunce by S. Clement, both by Catholicks and Proteftants.
And by all writers S. Reftitutus was at this
time or foone after Archbifhop of London:
for in the yeare of Chrift 326. hee was of
fuch renowne and honor, that he was cho-
fen the onely Bifhop of this Britanie, to be
prefent at the great councell of Bifhops, at
Arles in Fraunce, to which hee thus fub-
                                        fcribed

scribed for this our Britanie : *Ex Prouincia Britanniæ ciuitate Londinensi Restitus Episcopus. Martyrol. Rom. die* 11. *Augusti Vsuard. eod. die. Vincent. in spec. l.* 11. *c.* 78. 79. *Petr. in catal. l.* 4. *cap.* 50. *Matth. Westm. an.* 94. *protest. annot. marg. in eund. Tom.* 1. *concil. in Arelat. conc. Io. Bal. l. de scrip. cent.* 1. *in Restit. Godwin Catal. in London in Restitutus Matth. Parker antiq. Brit.*

4. And a friuolous exception it is , for Stowe with all others so to confesse, and after to add: *Hee writeth not himselfe Archbishop, and therefore maketh that matter of Archbishops doubtfull, or rather ouerthroweth that opinion.* (*Stowe histor. in Kinge Lucius.*) For it is euident by the subscriptions of that councell, that many of the greatest Archbishops in this part of the world were present, and subscribed there : yet not anie one of thē subscribed by the name of Archbishop, so it was in other councels. And as a Protestant Bishop and antiquary assureth vs, in these words. (*Godwin supr.*) hee *subscribed to the decrees of the same coūcel, which hee brought ouer with him.* In which it is decreed , that none but sacrificinge consecrated preistes, might offer the sacrifice of

Y 4 Masse.

Masse. (*Concil. Arelat.can.*15.) And among
so many Bishops, and preists, as were present there, Claudianus and Auitus the Legats of that renowned massinge preist and Pope S. Siluester by protestants confession, were present and subscribed to this councell. Therefore this our Archbishop, then the primate of all Britanie, must needs bee a massinge preist, as also all preists and Bishops vnder him. Of our third Archiepiscopall see at Caerlegion I doe not finde the name of any Archbishop, before *Tremounus vrbis legionum Archiepiscopus*, Archbishop there in the time of *Aurelius Ambrosius*. (*Galfrid. Monum. histor. l. 8. cap.* 10.) though wee know, that many were there before this time. And yet the memories of all our Bishops that escaped aliue from this persecution, are not perished. For besides those I haue recompted, we are assured both by Catholicke and Protestant antiquaries, that the Bishop of Winchester called Constance, was now liuinge, and dedicated there a church newly reedified to the honour of S. Amphibalus the Martyr, in the yeare of Christ 310. within 21. yeares after it was destroyed in the persecution. Because

it

it is a memorable hiſtory, and not onely
warranted by an old Manuſcript, but publiſhed and approued by a new Proteſtant
Biſhop, I will relate it in theſe his owne
words. *Manuſcript. antiq. Godwin. Catal. of
Biſh. in Winch. pag. 207.*

*This church as the ſame Author, olde Ma-
nuſcript, ſaith, was hallowed and dedicated
vnto the honour of our Sauiour, October 29.
189.by Faganus & Damianus Biſhops, about
the ſpace of 100.yeare the church of Chriſt had
then peace in this land, viz. vntill the reigne
of Diocleſian, who endeauouringe to roote out
Chriſtian Religion, not onely killed the profeſſors of the ſame, but pulled downe all churches and Temples, any where conſecrated vnto
the exerciſe thereof. Amongeſt the reſt this of
Wincheſter at that time went to wracke, the
buildings thereof beeinge ruinated, and made
euen with the grounde, and the Monkes and
all the officers belonginge vnto it, either ſlaine
or enforced to flie for the preſent time, and yet
afterward to denie Chriſt.This happened anno
289. not longe after the death of this cruell
Tyrant, to witt, the yeare 309. The church
aforeſaid was againe reedified, and that with
ſuch wonderful forwardnes, and zeale, as with-*

in

in one yeare and thirtie dayes , both it and all the edifices belonginge vnto it , as chambers and other buildings for the Monkes, were quite finished in very seemely and conuenient maner. The 15. *day of Marche following, it vvas againe hallovved and dedicated vnto the honor, and memory of Amphibalus, that had suffered death for Christ, in the late persecution, by Constance Bishop , as my author saith , of Winchester, at the request of Deodatus, Abbot of this nevv erected monastery* . The like or greater expedition was vsed in buildinge , and dedicatinge a church to S. Alban of great coste & sumptuousnes, where hee suffered Martyrdome , and yet as Matthew of Westminster writeth, it was finished or builded within ten yeares of his death and martyrdome . *Fabricata decem scilicet annis post passionem eius elapsis.* S. Bede saith as soone as the persecution ceased , a church of wonderfull worke was builded there vnto his honor. *Vbi postea redeūte temporum Christianorum serenitate Ecclesia est miri operis, atque eius Martyrio condigna extructa* . So our histories testifie of S. Iulius and Aaron in particular. *Bed. histor. Eccl. l.* 1. *cap.* 7. *Matth. Westm. an. gratiæ* 313. *Io.*

Cap.

Capgrau. in S. Albano.

6. And to make it manifest vnto vs, that there were many Bishops left here after this persecution, to consecrate and dedicate so many new builded, founded and consecrated churches, as were presently (after the persecution ended) erected in this kingedome, and to execute other episcopall fun-ctions, the best and moste auncient histories wee haue, as S. Gildas, S. Bede with others testifie, that, *bilustro necdum ad integrum expleto*, before ten yeares of persecution were ended (S. Gildas words) *the Chri-stiãs euery vvhere renevv their churches pulled dovvn to the ground, found, build & finish churches of their holy Martyrs, and celebrate their festiuities. Bilustro supradicti turbinis necdum ad integrum expleto, emercescentibus-que nece suorum Authorum nefarijs decretis, lætis luminibus omnes Christi Tyrones reno-uant Ecclesias, ad solum vsque destructas, ba-silicas Sanctorum Martyrum fundant, con-struunt, perficiunt, ac velut victricia signa pas̄sim propalant, dies festos celebrant.* And that wee may be assured, that among these holy Christian exercises, the holy sacrifice of Masse was offered, by their sacrificinge

and

and maffinge preifts, it immediatly followeth in thefe renowned antiquities : *facra mundo corde oreque conficiunt* . They celebrate theire facrifice with a pure hart and mouth . And our antiquaries both Catholicks and Proteftants affure vs , there were altars for facrifice in thefe churches. S. Gildas calleth the altars, *altaria facrofancta*, facred altars, whereon the heauenly facrifice is offered and laied. *Sacrificij cælestis fedem.* And that all the preiftes , of thefe Brittifh churches, were facrificing or maffing preiftes at the altars : *Sacerdotes facrificantes inter altaria stantes. Gild. l. de excid. S touu histor. in Constantine 2. Galf. Mon. histor. Brit. l. 11. cap. 4. Matth. Westm. an. gratiæ 543.*

7. And if we wil appeale to other churches and iudges in this time , whether to our Kinge and Emperor now a Chriftian, or to the Popes of Rome, yet Saints and holie men by the licence of our proteftants, or to generall councels the firft being celebrated in this time, or to the renowned Fathers that liued and wrote in this age , wee fhall finde thefe holy doctrines and exercifes of the facrifice of Maffe, facrificinge, & maffinge preifts, and preifthood, to haue beene

In

in greateſt honor, as well in all other Chriſtian nations, as in this kingdome. For Cõſtantine our Kinge, Emperor, and contryman, we cannot better learne what minde, and Religion hee was of, in theſe matters, then from S. Silueſter then Pope, and his Maſter and Father in Chriſtian Religion, who inſtructed him therein: and from the firſt generall councell of Nice, wherin, and wherto hee was preſent and conſented. And to make all ſure, and walke with the paſſe of proteſtants in this trauaile, wee are told by theſe men, that this maſſinge Pope, declared and decreed, in what ſacred attire, both the preiſts which offered, and the deacons which ſerued, and miniſtred in the ſacrifice of Maſſe, ſhould bee inueſted. (*Rob. Barnes l. de vit. Pontif. Roman. in Silueſtro.*) and to ſpeake in a proteſtant Biſhops wordes; *Huius Silueſtri permulta feruntur inſtituta, de chriſmate conſecrando, pueris confirmandis, templis ornandis, altaribus tegendis, miſſatoribus conſtituendis, vngendis, veſtiendis, hoſtijs adorandis, ſeruandis, ſacrificijs, ceremonijs alijſque ritibus.* Very many inſtitutions are aſcribed to this Silueſter, of conſecratinge chriſme, confirminge children,

dren,

dren, adorninge churches, coueringe altars, makinge massinge preifts, anointinge and veftinge them, adoringe and referuing the confecrated hoftes, of facrifices, ceremonies, and other rites. By which no man can doubt, but S. Siluefter was a maffing preift, and Pope, & this renowned Emperor conuerted by him, a reuerencer of holy Maffe and facrificinge preifthood.

8. which truth and doctrine for this age is more confirmed, by the great generall councell of Nice, where Conftantine prefent affented, and S. Siluefter alfo prefent by his Legats, Victor and Vincentius fubfcribinge, approued: in which it is plainely declared, that none but confecrated maffinge preifts haue power to offer that holie facrifice. (*Concil. Nicen. 1. can. 14. & per al. tranflat. can. 18.*) and to carry our proteftants confents with vs herein, the prefent proteftant Archbifhop of Canterbury, director of Mafter Frauncis Mafon, together with this his directed fecretary, warrant vs herin fufficiently in thefe words. *The Nicen councell in that canon which Caluine and all other receaue, faith plainely, that the Lambe of God offered vnbloodily, is laide vpon the holy table.*

table. Fran. Mason in pref. of his booke of confecrat. & pag. 243.) therfore this holy councell being by all iudgements generall, hauinge befides the confent of the Pope, and Emperor, the allowance and fubfcription of 318. Bifhops, and immediatly in thofe dayes, as our proteftants. (*Theater of great Britanie l. 6.*) with others affure vs, receaued here in Britanie, and at this prefent by our proteftant parlaments of higheft authoritie, and to bee embraced of all. (*Statut. in parl. an. 1. Elizab. & an. 1. Iacob.*) we muft needes fay, that the facrifice of Maffe and maffinge preifthood then was, & now ought by all men to bee honored, and approued in this kingdome. And if wee will enquire of the other holy and learned Fathers which liued in this age, and were not of that number 318. prefent in the Nicen councell, we fhall finde they were al without any exception, both of the Greeke, and Latine church, facrificinge, and maffinge preifts, their number is too great to bee related, therefore I will exemplifie onely in thofe, which all accompt renowned, as S. Bafile, S. Epiphanius, and S. Chrifoftome in the greeke church, all which as our pro-

testants

testants confesse, were not onely massinge
preists, but did write and set forth a publick
forme of Masse; which are yet extant, and
in noe materiall thinge different from that
of the present Latine church, and by the
confession of these protestants. (*Edw. Sands
Relat. of Relig. cap. 53. or 54. Middleton Papistom. pag. 51. Morton Apol. part. 2. pag. 81.*)
still vsed in the churches of Greece, which
also vse the present Romane Masse of S.
Gregory translated into Greeke, as they testifie of the Greeke church in these termes.
*Their liturgies bee the same that in the olde
time, namely S. Basils, S. Chrisostomes and S.
Gregories translated without any beding them
to that chaunge of laguage, which their tonge
hath suffered. Edwine Sands sup.*

9. And if wee come nearer, vnto the
Romane and Latine church, wee shall
finde S. Ambrose in Italy, so renowned for
this, that to speake in protestants wordes.
(*Foxe act. and Mon. Tom. 1. & Tom. 2. pag.
131.*) *vntill about the yeare of our Lord 780.
the Liturgie of S. Ambrose was more vsed in
the Italian churches then S. Gregories. Pope
Adrian the first was hee, vvhom vve declared
in the former part of this treatise, to ratifie*
                                                    and

*and confirme the order of S. Gregories Masse,
aboue the order of S. Ambrose Masse.* Where
wee see this twice approued by one great
protestant; which an other, a Bishop among
them, thus confirmeth · (*Ioannes Bal. act.
Pont. Rom. l. 3. in Hadriano 1.*) *Hadrianus
primas missarum ritus à magno Gregorio edi-
tos, occidentalibus Ecclesijs imperauit.* Pope
Hadrian the first, commaunded that order
of Masse which was published by Pope
Gregory the greate, to bee vsed by the western churches. Yet, to vse the words of an
other protestant Author. (*Edvv. Grimston.
in Pope Adrian 1.*) *this Pope Hadrian vvas
one of the moste famous of all his predecessors,
in bountie, learning, and sanctitie of life.* And
hee could not bee the worse, for so recom-
mending the Masse of S. Gregory. (*Bal. act.
Pont. Rom. l. 2. in Gregor. Magno.*) *the most
excellent of all the Romane Popes, both for
learning, and life. Gregorius Magnus omnium
Pontificum Romanorum doctrina & vita pra-
stantissimus.* As the laste cited, protestant
Bishop. (*Bal. supr. in Greg. Magno.* writeth,
and stileth him iustly with the title of honor therefore commonly and duely giuen
vnto him, *Gregory the great.* That the Masse

vsually

vſually called the Maſſe of S. Gregory, becauſe hee was the laſte Pope that added to
the old Maſſe, yet not foure lines, and not
eſſentiall in any thinge, nor doth not in any
leaſte point, now queſtioned, differ from
the olde Maſſe, continued ſince the Apoſtles time, as theſe our proteſtants ſhall ſuf-
ficientlie teſtifie in due place, and order
hereafter.

10. Or if we will come nearer home, into
Fraunce, wee ſhall finde there by the euidence of the brittiſh old Manuſcript I haue
cited before, that S. Cæſarius Archbiſhop
of Arles, the greateſt in that kingedome
then in preeminence, and power, and S.
Porcarius Abbot there, by whome S. German, and S. Lupus which were ſent Legats
into Britanie to ſettle the ſtate of our then
diſturbed church, by S. Cæleſtine Pope,
were brought vp, and inſtructed, did vſe
S. Markes Maſſe. (*M. S. antiq. Britan. in S.
Cæſario Arl. & Porcar.*) at which time alſo
S. Kebius our noble contryman of Corn-
wal, was many yeares ſcholler to S. Hilary,
that renowned ſacrificinge preiſt, and Biſhop of Poictiers in Fraunce, which was ſo
far engaged for the honor of this holy ſacrifice

crifice of Masse, and sacrificing preisthood,
that he boldly and roundly wrote to Constantius the Arrian Emperor, that his soul-
diers and himself in offering violence vnto
these, had sinned as greatly as the Iewes did
in puttinge Zachary to death. *Mediolanen-*
sem pijssimā plebem tu furore terroris tui tur-
basti, Tribuni tui adierunt Sanctæ Sanctorum,
viam sibi omni per populum crudelitate panden-
tes, protraxerunt de altario Sacerdotes. Le-
uius te putas, sceleste, Iudæorum impietate
peccasse? effuderunt quidem illi Zachariæ san-
guinem, sed quantum in te, concorporatus
Christo, à Christo discedisti. (*Hilar. l. 3. ad*
Constantium Imperatorem.) and yet that our
worthie contriman liued 50. yeares with
this massinge Bishop. (*M. S. antiq. in vit.*
S. Keb. Io. Capgrau. in eod.) and by him
made a massinge preist, and Bishop, returned into, and liued so and died a miraculous Saint in his owne contry in this kingdome. *Apud Hillar-pictanēsem Episcopum per*
quinquaginta annos manens Sanctus Kebius,
cæcos illuminauit, leprosos mundauit, paraliti-
cos, mutos, & dæmoniachos sanauit, & gradu
Episcopali ab Hillario accepto, admonitus est ab
Angelo in suam patriam remeare.

11. And

11. And that all the Bishops of Britanie, beinge many at that time , together with their preists, vnder iurisdictions, were massinge and sacrificinge preists , and in this holy sacrifice aswell as other matters in Religion consenting with the Popes of Rome, the Fathers of the councell of Nice , and Sardice , where wee had diuers brittish Bishops present, and with the sacrificing Catholicke Bishops and preists of Fraunce, namely S. Hilary the great glory of that nation, and S. Athanasius, that most renowned massing Prelate, who as Zonoras writeth, was here in Britanie, we haue a world of witnesses: and great S. Chrisostome, S. Hilary , S. Athanasius , Constantine our Kinge, and Emperor, S Hierome, Theodoret, Socrates, Sulpitius Seuerus, Glycas, Zonoras, as appeareth in my marginall citation of them, and other later writers, not only Catholicks, but Protestats also in their great Theater of Britanie, Stowe, Howes, Hollinshed with others. *Chrisost. in Homil. quod Christ. sit Deus. Hilar. l. de Sined. Athanas. epist. ad Costant. 2. Hieron. epist. ad Euagr. Theodoret. l. 4. hist. cap. 3. Socrat. l. 2. c. 16. Sulpit. Seuer. l. 2. sacra histor. Glyc. part. 4. Annal.*

nal. Zonor. To. 3. c. 2. Theater of great Britanie. l. 6. Stowe and Howes histor. in Lucius. Holinsh. hist. of Engl. Godw. Conuers. of Brit.

12. And such plentie, and great numbers of these massinge preists, and Bishops wee had here in this our Britanie, at that time, that as I am warranted both by forreine and domesticall writers, leauinge our Archbishops, and Bishops sees furnished, we had diuers british Bishops, besides with their preists and cleargie, sent from hence for Armorica, or little Britanie in Fraunce, as the holy massinge Bishops, and Martyrs, sent and martyred with S. Vrsula, and the other 11000. Virgins, and Martyrs of Britanie, *S. Michael, Iacobus, Columbanus, Iwanus, Elutherius, Lothorius and Mauritius. Episcop. Gen. in vit. S. Vrsul. Matth. Westm. an. 391. Io. Capgrau. Catal. in S. Vrsula. M. S. antiq. ibid. Harris in Theatr. To. 4. in S. Vrsula. antiquitat. Ecclesiæ Coloticen. & al.* al which with all other Bishops and preists of this kingdome cōsented with the whole Christian world, as is shewed before in the doctrine of holy Masse, sacrificinge preists, and preisthood, which our protestants will more demonstrate vnto vs, by the publick-

Z 3

lie

lie taught and receaued Religion of Britanie in this time : for they produce vnto vs, an old auncient sermon, written in the latine tonge, and translated into the saxon language by Aelfricus in the yeare 996. and to write in protestants words, *this sermon was vsuall to bee read in the church here in England in the yeare 366.* (Iohn Foxe *Act· Monum. pag.* 1142.) which must needs bee a moste excellent testimonie for this age & time. And yet amonge many other thinges tendinge to the same purpose, thus we finde by our protestants translation therof. *In the olde lawe faithfull men offered to God diuers sacrifices, that had foresignification of Christs body, which for our sinnes hee himselfe to his heauenly Father hath since offered to sacrifice. Certainely this housell which wee doe now halow at Gods altare, is a remembrance of Christs body, which he offered for vs, and of his blood, which hee shed for vs : So hee himselfe commaunded, doe this in my remembrance . Once suffered Christ by himselfe, but yet neuerthelesse his sufferinge is daily renevved at this supper, through mistery of the holy housel.* And againe: *In that holy housel, there is one thing in it seene, and an other vnderstoode. That*

vvhich

vvhich is there seene hath bodily shape: and that vvee doe there vnderstand, hath ghostly might. The housell is dealed into sondry parts, chevved betvveene teeth, and sent into the belly: hovvbeit neuerthelesse after ghostlie might, it is all in euery part. Many reeeaue that holy body, and yet notvvithstandinge, it is so all in euery part, after ghostly mistery.

13. And shewing how the Paschal Lambe was a figure of this holy sacrifice of Christ, the Lambe of Innocency, and God, which taketh away the sins of the worlde, as in holy Masse wee so pray vnto Christ there present, vnder that denomination, they teach it was the vse and custome of our Christians in Britanie in that time, to doe the same, the very words of that olde brittish publicke homely by our protestants translation bee thus: *That innocent Lambe vvhich the olde Israelites did then kill, had signification after ghostly vnderstandinge, of Christs sufferinge, vvho vnguiltie shedd his blood for our redemption. Hereof singe Gods seruants at euery Masse, Agnus Dei qui tollis peccata mundi, miserere nobis:* That is in our speache: Thou Lambe of God, that takest away the sinnes of the worlde, haue

Z 4   mer-

mercie vpon vs . Where wee fee plainelie
acknowledged , by this fo auncient antiquitie , in this fourth hundred yeare , and
the proteftants themfelues , fo tranflatinge
and propofinge it , that generally in that
time, the holy facrifice of Maffe was offered by the Bifhops , and preifts of Britanie
in all places,and all the feruants of God did
then acknowledge, & profeffe,that Chrift
the true Lambe of God that taketh away
the finnes of the world was therin offered,
and there prefent, prayed vnto by all Gods
feruants. Which is as much as any maffing
preift, Bifhop, or Pope holdeth, teacheth,
or practifeth at this time concerning thefe
things.

14. And becaufe in this age this our
kingedome had by agreement both of auncient and late writers , and by proteftants
themfelues. (*Bal. l. de fcriptor. in Palladio &*
Niniano.) a greate dependance of Rome,
both in temporall and fpiritual affaires,and
many of our cheifeft cleargie men , as S.
Teruanus, and S. Ninianus thofe two glorious Northrē Bifhops, had both their education, inftruction, ordination, and iurifdiction from thence , as many others had
[at

at this time , and the Bishops of Rome are so much charged by our protestant writers for adding vnto the holy sacrifice of Masse, I will only vse these mens authority, which say they will set downe what euerie Pope did add, *Quid aly Pontifices addiderint , suo loco in Pontificijs actis dicetur.* And they are so farr from not performinge their promise in this , that they rather relate more then lesse added by these holy Popes, as will bee made euident by theire owne testimonies hereafter. Yet for more ample satisfaction let vs followe them in this point. Of S. Siluester I haue spoke before, next to him succeeded S. Marke, who as these men say, was Pope in the time of Constantine the great, *Constantino Imperante in Pontificatu sedit,* which time was an holy time in Religion, by our Kings iudgement , and so this Pope not likely to make any publick lawe vnholie. Therefore these protestants onely say of him , that hee ordeyned the creede of the Nicen councell to bee said or sunge at Masse. (*Rob. Barnes in act. Pont. Rom. in Marc. 1. Io. Bal. in vit. Pont. in eod. Edw. Grimston. in Marc.*) but this Nicen creed is holy in all iudgements, and was receaued, and vsed in

Bri-

Britanie here, in that time, as I haue proued, & it is receaued by the protestant parlament of England, subscribed and sworne
vnto by all the protestant Bishops and ministers of England, allowed in the articles
of their Religion, and practised in theire
churches. (*Parlam. an. 1. Eliz. K. Iames can.
articles of Relig. articl. Creed. commun. booke
&c.*) and therefore doth a protestant antiquarie iustly say of that holy creed, & time,
in the yeare of Christ, 330. *At this time the
Nicen creed was commaunded to bee sunge or
said, in all Christian churches.* (*Stowe hist.
Rom. ad an. 330.*) therefore none but Arrian
Hereticks euer did, or will impugne it.

15. The next Pope which these mē finde,
to haue added any thinge to this holy sacrifice, was holy Damasus, an acknowledged
good Bishop, and as they teache, hee onely
added the Confiteor, Confession, vsed in
the beginninge of Masse, in which there is
nothinge, which protestants disallowe, but
confession and prayer to Saints there remembred. (*Io. Whitguift. ansvv. to the admonit. pag. 78. and def. of ansvv. pag. 489.
Bal.in vit. in Damaso. Barnes in eodem. Grimston. in Damasus.*) which as I haue proued
before

before was vſed in the church of God, and
in this Realme of Britanie in the Apoſtles
dayes. And to paſſe ouer ſo many examples,
and teſtimonies, of other Chriſtian people,
and places, in the ſecond age our Apoſtles
S. Damianus and Fugatius praied to S. Mi-
chaell the Archangell, and other Angels,
& dedicated a church or chappell to them,
the ruines yet ſtandinge neare Glaſtenbu-
rie. (*antiquit. Glaſton M. S. Gapgrau. in Ca-*
tal. & alij.) diuers churches beſides with
their allowance were founded and dedicated to S. Peter, S. Martin, and other Saints.
In the third age S. Amphibalus at his Mar-
tirdome publickly prayed to S. Alban Martyred a little before, ſo did other holy Brittiſh Chriſtians to him and other Martyrs
and Saints of Britanie at that time. (*tabul.*
M. S. in Eccleſ. S. Petri in Cornhill. Stowe
hiſtor. in K. Lucius Caius antiq. Cantabrig.
Harris l. 2. Holinſh. hiſt. of Engl. M. S. an-
tiq. in Lucio M. S. antiq. in S. Amphibal. Cap-
grau. in eod. & S. Alban. legend. antiq. &
alij.) in the beginninge of this fourth age,
I haue ſhewed before, what generall buildinge, and dedicatinge of churches there
was, to our Martyrs, that had ſuffered a little

tle before , and solemnizinge their festiuities, and consequently prayer and inuocation vnto them . And all this longe before
S. Damasus was Pope, being scarcely borne
at that time . Therefore many our protestants of England confesse, that prayer and
inuocation of Saints and Angels, was publicklie vsed in the primatiue church , euen
in the sacrifice of Masse. And some of them
make it an article of our creede: for to speak
in their wordes . *If wee deny it , wee shall
peraduenture depriue ourselues of a great part
of their Angels ministery , and dissolue that
communion of Saints , which vvee professe to
beleeue as an article of Gods truthe. Couel examin. pag.* 295. 178. *Parkins problem. pag.* 89.
93. *Ormerod. Pict. Pap. pag.* 26. 27. *Middlet.
papistom. pag.* 129. *Morton. Apolog. part.* 1.
pag. 227. 228. *Couel ag. Burges pag.* 89. 90.

16. Wherefore I may boldly conclude
of this holy Pope , in this matter , in these
words of a Protestant Archbishop: *Damasus vvas a good Bishop, and therefore no good
thinge by him appointed , to bee disallovved.
(Io. Whitg. ansvv. to the admonit. pag.* 78.
sect. 2.3. *and def. of ansvv. pag.* 489. of Pope
Siricius they say , hee commaunded that
                                        Masses

Masses should bee said in places consecrated by the Bishops: *Missas in loco ab Episcopo sacrato celebrandas esse.* (*Rob. Barnes l. de vit. Pont. Rom. in Ciricio.*) but this was onely a ceremoniall decree, and to Gods more honor, as I haue shewed in our old Britans by their dedication of churches, and our protestants in England after their ceremonies obserue it to this day. What a protestant Bishop meaneth, when hee writeth of this Pope, *Missæ memorias adiunxit.* Hee adioyned memories to the Masse. (*Io. Bal. l. 1. de act. Pontif. Rom. in Siricio.*) I know not, if hee meaneth memories of Saints, to pray vnto them, or memories of other faithfull departed, to pray for them (as one of them hee must needs vnderstand) I haue proued before, they were both vsed from the Apostles time, and so cannot bee said to bee any additiō of Pope Siricius in this time. These protestants do not mention any other Pope in this age, to haue added, or altered any thinge, in this holy sacrifice: Therefore by their good leaue I doe here end this fourth hundred of yeares.

THE

THE FIFTHE AGE, OR HVN-
DRED YEARES OF CHRIST.

THE XIX. CHAPTER.

Wherein is manifestly proued, that all this fift
age, the sacrifice of Masse, massing preists
and Bishops did continue in honor in
this our Britanie.

THe first Pope which offereth himselfe
in this next and fifth hundred of yeares , to speake as a late protestant writer
doth, *was Innocent of Albania , or Scotland.*
(*Edw. Grimst. est. of the church of Rome Pope
41. pag. 44. an. D. 402.*) and commonly it
is written of him, both by protestants and
others. (*Rob. Barnes in vit. Innocentij & Io.
Bal. in eodem.*) that by contrie hee was *Al-
banus,* or of Albania, the old common and
receaued knowne name of Scotland. And
if hee was of this our Albania, it might be
occasion that the Scots and Britans of this
kingdome did more frequent Rome at this,
then other times . But whether hee was of
Northren Albania, that is in the east, or of
Alba

Alba in Italy, or whencesoeuer, sure wee
are, that many of this nation which proued holy preifts, and Bifhops alfo, had their
education, and inftruction in Religion, at
Rome in thefe dayes, by the maffing and facrificinge preifts, and Popes in that place.
Such were S. Teruanus made Archbifhop
of the Picts, by S. Paladius the Popes Legate
in Scotland, about the yeare of Chrift 432.
as our Scottifh writers teftifie. And that he
was inftructed in the faith at Rome, I gather from the fame Authors, affirming that
S. Paladius baptized him, beeing an Infant.
Teruanum Infantem luſtrico lauerat fonte Pal-
dius. (*Hector Boeth. l. 7. hiſtor. foli* 133. *Poſ-*
feuin. in appar. To. 2. pag. 452.) which muft
needs bee at Rome from whence S. Palladius was fent into this kingdome, in or a-
bout the yeare of Chrift 431. & died foone
after his cominge hither. And fo hauinge
for his Mafter and Tutor in Religion, that
maffinge preift, and Bifhop, and the Pope
alfo then being the like, this man could not
bee inftructed there in any other Religion,
different from that. And in the fame age,
before this, S. Ninian who was alfo brought
vp, and inftructed by the maffinge Popes,
and

and their disciples at Rome, was sent from
thence, to teach the same and other holie
doctrines of Christian faith to the same
people, and was theire Bishop, as all antiquaries Catholicke and Protestant testifie.
(*Bed. hist. Angl. l. 3. c. 4. Bal. l. de scriptor.
cent. 1. in Ninian. Capgrau. in eod. Theat. of
great Brit. l. 6.*) whose successor S. Teruanus was, and about the same time as our
Scottish and other histories tell vs, S. Ser-
uanus was made Bishop of the Orchades
beinge instructed and consecrated by the
massinge Bishop Paladius, which that famous massinge Pope S. Celestine sent his
Legate into this nation, of whome herafter.
Hector Boeth. Scotor. histor. l. 7. fol. 133.

2. Besides these extraordinary, the ordinary Archbishops, and Bishops with their
whole cleargie perseuered in these holy doctrines, none to contradict them herin but
in other questions moued by Pelagian hereticks. And that S. Innocentius the first
Pope in this age vnder whome our remembred Bishops had theire education and instruction, was a massinge Pope, our protestants assure vs, testifyinge that hee confirmed the ceremonie of giuinge the Pax in
Masse.

Maſſe. *Vt pax in Miſſa daretur ordinauit.* The
like they teſtifie of Pope Sozimus, and Bonifacius, which were betweene S. Innocentius, and S. Celeſtine, that ſent ſo many
Biſhops into this kingdome, affirming how
they both maintayned ſacrificinge preiſthood, and holy Maſſe, with the ceremonies
thereof, and the ſupreamacy of the ſee of
Rome. (*Io. Bal. l. 2. de act. Pont. Rom. in Innocent. in Sozimo & Bonifacio. Robert. Barns
in vit. Pontif. in eiſdem.*) And for the ſacrifice of Maſſe, that it was, *Miſſa papiſtica, the
papiſticall,* or, *papiſts Maſſe,* ſuch as Catholicks of this time (whome they call papiſts,
and their Maſſe preiſts and Religion papiſticall) doe vſe. (*Bal. ſupr. lib. 2. in Cæleſtino.*)
before the dayes of Saint and Pope Celeſtine, who as they ſay added ſome thinges
to the papiſticall Maſſe, vſed before his pa-
pacie. *Papiſticæ Miſſæ inſeruit.* And yet this
ſacrificinge maſſinge and papiſticall Pope
was hee, by all antiquities, on whome Britanie in thoſe dayes did cheifly depend for
direction, and inſtruction in matters of Religion.

3. Therefore to make all peace, and attonement, wee may by the proceedings and
inſti-

institutions of this holy Pope, and our Master and Pedagogue in Christ, let vs learne of our protestants themselues, what were the things he added to the sacrifice of Masse, whether any matter essentiall, or that may be excepted against. They haue told vs, that before his additions, the Masse was papisticall, and concerninge his additions, *In initio sacrificij, vt psalmus, Iudica me Deus, & discerne causam meam & c. à sacrificaturo diceretur ordinauit: graduale in Missa ordinauit.* He ordeyned that the psalme, Iudge mee ô God & discerne my cause, should be said in the beginning of the sacrifice, by the preist that offereth the sacrifice: and he ordeyned the graduale should be said in Masse. (*Rob. Barn. l. de vit. Pontif. Rom. in Cælest. Magdeb. cent. 5. in Cælest.*) so write others of these protestats, amõg whom one a Bishop saith: *Cælestinus introitum, graduale, responsorium, tractum, & offertorium, vt propria inuenta, papisticæ Missæ inseruit.* Pope Celestine did put into the papisticall Masse, as inuentions of his own, the introite, graduale, responsorie, tract and offertory. (*Iohn Foxe Tom. 2. in Q. Mary. Cartwright admon. Whitg. answ. to the admonit. pag. 94. sect. 1. 2. Io. Bal. l. 2 act. Pontif.*

tif. Roman. in Cælestino.) which wordes of
his, *vt propria inuenta*, as his owne inuentions, are the euident forgery and inuention of this protestant, for all these thinges
are plaine wordes of holy scriptures in all
places, and so the inuentions of God himselfe, and not Pope Celestines; And if hee
meaneth that the placing them in the Masse was his inuention, which hee doth not
insinuate, why was it not lawfull for him
to vse the scriptures in Masse? otherwise no
prayer or part of Masse, or whatsoeuer liturgie or publicke office of any church
could bee lawfull, nothinge could be lawfull, for nothinge is more lawfull or warranted then the word of God and scripture.
Yet it was not S. Celestines inuention, to
place any one of these in the Masse, but they
were all vsed therin, before his time, euen
by the confession of these protestants themselues. For first concerning the introite, it is
one of the psalmes of Dauid the 42. by the
Latine accompt, and by the Hebrue 43. and
such kind of introite to the holy Masse, was
in vse longe before this Popes time, as our
protestants acknowledge, wherof one thus
confesseth. (*Io. Foxe To. 2. Act. and Mo-*

num. Q. Mary pag. 1401.) Chrisostome *in the eleuenth homely vpon the Ghospell of S. Matthew, saith, that in his time, and before his time, the vse was to singe whole psalmes till they were entered and assembled together:* And so belike Cælestinus borrowed this custome of of the Greekes, and brought it into the Latine church. Therfore by these men S. Cælestine was not the Author of this custome: yet if he had bene, no protestat or Christian will say, that sayinge or singinge holy psalmes, so warranted in scripture, is an vnlawfull, but a lawfull and godly exercise.

4. The same protestant Author maketh the graduale, response, and tract of as auncient standinge, when hee thus speaketh of the graduale and consequently of the others belonging vnto it. (*Foxe supr.*) *the graduale the people were went to singe when the Bishop was about to go vp to the pulpit, or some higher standinge, where the worde of God might be better & more sensibly heard at his mouth, readinge the epistle and the ghospell*. Which custome hee maketh as auncient, or more auncient, then the time of Pope Alexander, in the Empire of Traian. Touchinge the laste which is the offertorie, it is euident by

these

these proteſtants, and al teſtimonies before,
that it was, and of neceſſitie muſt needs be
vſed from the begininge, for where there is
Maſſe, ſacrifice, and oblation offered, there
muſt needes bee an offeringe or offertorie
thereof, otherwiſe it could not bee offered.
Foxe ſupr. Therefore this proteſtāt acknowledgeth it to haue bene vſed before the time
of S. Irenæus ſo neare the Apoſtles, and that
hee thus doth remember it. *Iren. l. 4. cap. 18.*
pro diuerſis ſacrificiorum ritibus ſimplex oblatio
panis & vini fidelibus ſufficiat. In ſtedd of diuers rites of ſacrifices in the oide lawe, one
oblation of breade and wine ſerueth. Therfore I will conclude with theſe words, of a
proteſtāt Archbiſhop. *Celeſtinus was a godly*
Biſhop, and the church of Rome at that time
had the ſubſtance of the Sacraments, according
to Gods word, neither was there any ſuperſti-
tion mixed with them. Iohn Whitg. def. of
the anſw. to the admonit. pag. 588.

5. And in this opinion are, and ought to
bee, all our Engliſh Proteſtant antiquaries,
and diuines, which generally hold, & teach,
that the Britans of this kingedome, inuiolablie kept the true faith and Religion of
Chriſt, in all things, vntill the cominge of

374 *An historie of the holy preisthood, and* S. Auguftine, and his companions from S. Gregory the great Pope of Rome, in the later end of the fixt hundred yeares: for moft certaine and vndoubted it is, by all antiquities, that this nation at this time of S. Celeftine, being infected with the Pelagian Hereticks, learned and fubtile in difputation, this holy Pope fent many holy Bifhops hither to confute that herefie, inftruct the ignorant, repaire the decaied difcipline of our church, and reforme many abufes growne by reafon of that herefie, and the Saxon Pagans, which then were entered into this Iland. Which Legates of this holy Pope, muft needs bee adiudged to bee of the fame faith, and Religion with him, that fent them, by his authoritie and direction to effect thofe holy labours. He fent the two holie Bifhops S. Germanus, & Lupus into this part of Britanie, S. Palladius into Scotland, S Patricke and Segetius into Ireland. I haue fpoken of S. Palladius before, how by his power from the fee of Rome, hee placed facrificing and maffinge preifts and Bifhops amonge the Scots, and Picts, in the north parts of this kingdome, of vnited great Britanie. *Profper, in Chronic. ad An.* 432. *Rob. Barnes*

Barnes l. de vit. Pontif. Rom. in Cælestino. Io.
Bal. l. 2. Act. Pontif. Rom. in eod. Bal. l. de
scriptor. Brit. cent. 1. in Leporio Agricola.

6. Also I haue shewed out of our aun-
cieut Brittish Manuscript & otherwise before, how both S. German and Lupus were
massinge preists, and Bishops, and obserued
the auncient forme of Masse composed by
S. Marke, therefore beeing sent by authoritie from that massinge Pope, S. Celestine,
they neither did, nor might vary and differ from the opinion, and practise of him,
that sent him, as S. Prosper who liued at
that time, and others write, to supply his
owne place and parson in ordering and re-
forminge the church of Britanie. *Papa Ce-*
lestinus Germanum Antissiodorensem Episco-
pum voce sua mittit, vt deturbatis hæreticis
Britannos ad Catholicam fidem dirigat. Hee
consecrated many massinge preists, and Bishops in this kingdome, among whom the
cheifest was, that massing Saint Dubritius
Archbishop, the cheife Doctor, Primate &
the Popes Legate. (*Prosper. in Chronic. An.*
D. 432. Io. Capgrau. in S. Dubritio. Matth.
Westm. Galfrid. Monument. hist. Brit. l. 9. cap.
12. Rob. Canal. l. 2. M. S. Gallic. antiq. M. S.
antiq.

376 *An historie of the holy preisthood, and antiq. & Io. Capgrau. in vita S. Dubrity.)* *Episcopos in pluribus locis Britanniæ consecrarunt: & dextralis partis Britanniæ beatum Dubritium summum Doctorem & Archiepiscopum statuerunt :* a protestant Bishop writeth : Dubritius was made Archbishop by Germanus and Lupus, and they appointed his see to bee at Landaffe. (*Godwin.Catalog. in S. Dauide.*) this holy Archbishop by the heauenly direction, did consecrate that notorious massinge preist S. Sampson Archbishop of Yorke, in whose consecration a miraculous vision appeared to confirme his callinge and Religion, and both S. Dubritius and others did see a piller of fier miraculously proceeding from his mouth as hee celebrated the holy Masse, and hee himselfe all his life had Angels ministring vnto him in that blessed sacrifice. *Angelus Domini beato Dubritio apparens, Sampsonem ordinari Episcopum præcepit. In cuius consecratione qui aderant, columbam celitus emissam immobiliter super eum stare videbant. Eodem die Sampsone celebrante, Dubritius cum Monachis duobus, columnam ignis de ore eius procedentem rutilare perspexit. Ille vero omni tempore vitæ suæ Angelos dum celebra-*

ret,

*ret , sibi afsistere , & in sacrificio ministrare
meruit* · (*M. S. antiquit. & Capgrau. in S.
Sampsone Episcopo.*) what massinge preistes and Archbishops the immediate successors of these two renowned Archbishops were, I shall lay downe herafter more
at large.

7. And such as these were, such also was
the Archbishop of London S. Vodinus, and
all Bishops and preists vnder him , and so
consequently in all Britanie at that time:
which aswel appeareth, by their owne historian, S. Gildas, venerable S. Bede, as also
Matthew of Westminster with others, who
speaking of the miserable, and generall per-
secutiō of the christian Britans, in al places
quasque Prouincias, amonge other cruelties
they tel vs, these infidels martyred the Brittish preists, as they were standing at the altars where they said Masse. *Sacerdotes iuxta
altaria trucidabāt.* (*Gild. de excid. & conquest.
Brit. Matth. Westm. an. gratiæ 462. Bed. l.
1. histor. Ecclef. cap. 15.*) therefore the preistes generally then, were altare, sacrificinge
and massinge preists, otherwise they could
not haue beene thus cruelly put to death, at
the altars, and places of saying Masse, in all

parts

all parts of this nation at that time. Neither could there possibly, at that time bee any other preists, but massinge preists, except they would turne hereticks (which we doe not reade) and leaue the doctrine and Religion of their both Archbishops, Bishops, and Masters in diuinitie, which in this time were by all testimonie both of Catholicks, and Protestants, either the onely or principall, S. Dubritius of whome I haue spoken before, S. Iltutus, and S. Gildas, all moste holy and miraculous men, and knowne massinge preists. For concerninge S. Iltutus he was (as a Protestant Bishop with Vicentius, and Antoninus confesseth) scholler to the renowned Popes Legate and massinge Bishop S. German, spoken of before, *Io. Bal.l.de script. Britan· cent.* 1. *in Ilchtuto alias Iltuto.* And to proue him a massinge preist, and all his schollers after him, that were preists, to haue bene massinge preists, Nennius our moste auncient (exceptinge Gildas) writer which wee haue left, testifieth in his Manuscript historie, that there was in a church which this massinge Saint Iltutus builded, a miraculous Altar, susteyned only without any propp, or foundation by the power

power of God, *altare quod nutu Dei fulcitur.* (*Nennius histor. M. S. in fine post nomina ciuitatum Britanniæ.*) and this miraculous altar so inuisibly susteyned, did remayne in Nennius time, *& manet vsque in hodiernam diem altare potestate Dei fulcitum.*

8. To proue S. Gildas to haue beene of this opinion, and practise, his historie, *de excidio Britanniæ,* often cited in this treatise, is full of altars, massinge and sacrificinge preists, and maketh their irreuent sayinge of Masse, and often neglect of celebrating that holy sacrifice, to haue beene one of the cheise causes of Gods indignation against them, and depriuinge them of this kingedome, and giuinge it to the Saxons theire professed enemies. And hee was one of the renowned scholiers of his massing Master, S. Iltutus, as S. Sampson the great massing Archbishop of Yorke, of whome I haue spoken before, and S. Dauid, that moste holy sacrificinge and miraculous Archbishop of Caerlegion, of whome hereafter, and S. Paulinus were: as both Catholicks and Protestants are witnesses. (*M. S. antiq. de vit S. Iltuti. Ioh. Capgrau. in Iltuto. Ioh. Bal. centur. 1. de scriptor. Brit. in eod.*) what

this

this Paulinus was , and whether hee that was sent hither with S. Augustine I dare not affirme, yet considering the longe time S· Iltutus liued, as many then did , and hee beeing liuinge as diuers write . (*Bal. supr.*) in the yeare of Christ 520. hee might haue in his olde age a scholler , that might liue longer then S. Paulinus death , that came with S. Augustine, and was Archbishop of Yorke: for many our holy Bishops as S. Kentegern, and S. Dauid liued longer, and we finde no other renowned Paulinus here in those times. And Nennius who saith expressely , that hee omitteth of purpose to speake of those that came with S. Augustine, and were not of this nation, yet maketh a most honorable memory of that Paulinus Archbishop of Yorke, saying that hee baptized 12000. at one time, and ceased not baptisinge fourtie dayes together. *Nennius in histor. M.S. prope finem·*

9. So that it is not vnprobable but this holy man S. Paulinus, was the scholer of S. Iltutus, and leauinge his contry (as manie did in that rage of the Saxons) wét to Rome and liued to come hither againe to accomplish so holy labours, as hee did with those other

other maffinge preiftes fent hither at that
time. Which hee might well performe , if
wee allowe him , to bee 20. yeares old , at
the death of his Mafter S. Iltutus , as before in the yeare 520. and as an other Proteftant Bifhop writeth . (*Godwin Catalog.*
Yorke 1. *pag.* 558.) to haue died in the yeare
644. which accompt maketh him but 124.
yeares old, two yeares yonger then his fellow fcholler S.Dauid by all antiquities makinge him 146. yeares of age at his death.
Post 146. *ætatis annum, vt omnes eius faten-*
tur historiæ,mortuus. In the yeare of his age,
147. *anno ætatis suæ centesimo quadragesimo*
*septimo.*And twenty one yeares yonger then
S. Kentegern by all hiftories, dyinge when
hee was one hundred eightie and fiue yeares old , *cum esset centum octaginta quinque*
*annorum.Ioh. Bal. centur.*1.*de scriptorib.Bri-*
tan· in Dauid Menenien. Ioh. Capgrau· Ca-
tal. in S. Dauid. M. S.antiq.in eod. S. Asaph.
in vita S. Kentegern. Capg. in eod. Io. Bal.
centur. 1. *de script. Brit. in Kentegern. Elg-*
nen. Godwin Catalog. in S. Asaph. and Probus the auncient writer of S. Patricks life,
dedicateth it to Paulinus,about that time S.
Paulinus was Archbifhop here, which argueth

gueth that Paulinus had some acquaintance
with, or reference to S. Patricke, otherwise
an Irish Author would not haue dedicated
his worke to one in England. Those scholes
were here of high authority approued both
by the Popes & Kings of Britanie, as Cam-
bridg teacheth. *Probus in vita S. Patricij inter opera S. Beda. Io. Caius l. antiquitat. Cam-
tab. pag. 147. 148.*

10. Now let vs come to S. Patricke, who
although he was cheifly sent by S. Celestine
to the inhabitants of Ireland and Scotland,
yet hee was a Britane borne, and by many
antiquities preached much, and by some
many yeares together before his death liuinge in this nation, died here. Therefore
wee may boldly apply him as a Master and
witnes in this busines. This man being sent
by the massinge Pope S. Celestine, was so
farr also a massinge preist, and Bishop, that
as the auncient writer of his life, not S. Bede
but Probus an Irish man more auncier then
S. Bedes time, witnesseth. (*l. 2. de vita S.
Patricij in fine.*) the inchaunters and magiciens of that contry, especially three which
he called Locri, Egled, and Mel, did tell to
the Kinge and nobles of that contry beinge
ido-

idolaters, diuers yeares before the cominge
of S. Patricke thither., that a certaine Prophet should come thither with a new Religion, that though it was hard and austere,
yet it should quite destroy theire auncient
worship, and there continue for euer. And
to speake in this auncient Authors wordes
of S. Patricks sayinge Masse in particular:
præcinebant quasi in modum cantici lirico modo
compositi ante aduentum Sancti viri duobus
aut tribus annis decantantes de eo. Hæc sunt
autem verba cantici secundum linguæ illius
Idioma in latinum conuersa, non tamen mani-
festa. Adueniet artis caput, cum suo ligno præ-
curuo capite : ex eo omnis domus erit capite
perforata : incantabit nephas ex sua mensa ex
anteriore parte domus suæ, respondebit ei sua
familia tota, fiat, fiat. Quod nostris verbis po-
test manifestius exprimi. Adueniet totius ar-
tis Magister cum signo crucis, & quod omne
cor hominum compungitur, & de altari Sacra-
mentorum conuertet animas ad Christum, &
omnis populus Christianorum respõdebit Amen.
Quãdo erunt hæc omnia regnum nostrum gen-
tile non stabit. Quod sic totum completum est.
They did singe before the cominge of the
Holy man S. Patricke a songe made lyrick-
wise

wife of him two or three yeares. And these
are the words of the song according to that
language turned into latine, but not manifest. The head of art will come, with his
staffe with a crooked head, with that al the
house shall bee bored in the heade: he shall
singe wickednes from his table from the
former part of his house, all his householde
shall answere, so bee it, so bee it. Which in
our words may be more manifestly expres-
fed. The Master of all art shall come with
the signe of the crosse, and all the harts of
men shall haue compunction, and from the
altare of Sacraments hee shall conuert soules to Christ, and all Christian people shall
answere *Amen*. When all these things shall
bee, then our heathen kingedome shall not
stand. All which was so fulfilled. *Io. Cap-*
grau. in Catalog. in S. Patricio.

11. Iohn Capgraue and others in S. Patricks life thus set downe this prediction of
S. Patricke, *adueniet homo cum suo ligno cuius*
mensa erit in oriente domus suæ, & populus e-
ius retrorsum, & ex sua mensa cantabit, &
familia respondebit ei Amen. Hic cum aduene-
rit, Deos nostros destruet templa subuertet, &
doctrina eius regnabit in seculū seculi. A man
shall

shall come with his staffe, whose table shall
be in the east part of his house, and the people behinde him , and hee shall singe from
his table , and the companie shall answere
vnto him Amen. He when he cometh shall
destroy our Gods, ouerthrowe our temples,
& his doctrine shall reigne for euer. Where
wee see an euident prediction, and foretel-
ling, how this great Apostle should be a sacrificinge massinge preist , his altar should
bee in the east part of the church, as altars
vsually are, and the people should answere
Amen. How deuout a sacrificinge massinge
man hee was, the historie of his life is witnes, and of many miracles to proue the sanctitie and holines, both of that sacrifice, and
the sacrificer; Amonge which a sorcerer o-
uerthrowinge his chalice when hee said
masse, the earth opened and swallowed him
vp. *Factum est alio die cum Patricius Missam*
celebraret quidam magus effudit calicem suam,
& statim terra aperiēs os suum deuorauit eum.
(M. S. antiq. in vit. S. Patric. Capgrau. in
cod.) and the altare on which hee vsuallie
said Masse, healed diseases and wrought o-
ther miracles. And this moste holy Saint
by all testimonies both of Catholicks, and

Pro-

(*Bal. l. de scriptor. Britan. in Pa-tric. Prob. in vita eius. Capgrau. & al. in eod.*) was fo great a promoter of the bleffed fa-crifice of Maffe, and facrificinge maffinge preifts, and Bifhops, that for the honor and propagation of them, to infift in the words of Nennius. (*Nennius M. S. hift. in S. Patri-cio.*) hee founded 345. *churches to that vfe. Hee confecrated fo many or more Bishops, en-dued with the spirit, of God, and ordered 3000. massinge preists. Ecclesias numero fundauit 345. ordinauit Episcopos trecentos quadragin-ta quinque aut amplius, in quibus spiritus Do-mini erat. Presbyteros autem vsque ad tria millia ordinauit.*

12. Therefore this maffing Archbifhop liuinge and rulinge in Ireland and Britanie vntill the yeare of Chrift 491. by a Prote-ftant Bifhop makinge his age 122. yeares, and longer by Capgraue, & others, faying hee was, *annis centum triginta*, an hundred and thirty yeares old, & by Probus an hun-dred thirtie two, and more, when hee died. (*Bal. centur. 1. de scriptor. Britan. in Patri-cio. Capgrau. Catal. in eod. M. S. in vita S. Patric. Probus in vit. eiusd.*) this kingdome of Britanie could not bee without Maffe, and

and many maſſinge preiſts, and Biſhops in
this age. And as the great recited number
of maſſinge preiſts and Biſhops, eſpecially
Biſhops, aboue 340. could not bee wholly
employed in theſe kingdomes, which neuer
had ſo many in ſo ſhort a time, we may be
bold to extend his miſſion of ſuch maſſinge
men, to a larger circuite, and ſay hee ſent
diuers of theſe his maſſinge diſciples, euen
into Armerica it ſelfe: for wee finde in the
aunciently written life of S. Brendan 1100.
yeares ſince. (*M. S. antiq. & Io. Capgrau. in
vit. S. Brendani.*) of whom one of the Ilands
of America ſtill beareth name, that in his
longe and tedious trauailes, hee founde in
thoſe parts, diuers maſſinge preiſtes, that
did vſually ſay Maſſe, and had moſt ſump-
tuous Altars of Chriſtal, who affirmed they
were diſciples to S. Patricke, and by him
directed thither. And were moſt holie and
miraculous men, and amonge other things
then propheſied to S. Brendan, how that
contrie ſhould bee deſcryed, and viſited a-
gaine by Chriſtians, to their great good &
comforte after many ages, as happily wee
finde it was: *Poſt multa annorum curricula
declarabitur iſta terra veſtris Succeſſoribus,*

Bb 2   *quando*

THE XX. CHAPTER.

Wherein is proued by protestants and others, that the church of Britanie and Rome, accorded in this age in these misteries : and how all the Popes beeing massinge preists and Popes, yet no one of them made any materiall alteration in this sacrifice.

THus hauinge shewed both by Catholicke, and Protestant authorities, that the holy sacrifice of Masse, massing preists, and preisthood generally , and inuiolablie continued in Britanie all this age, and hundred of yeares , because it is confessed this nation was still hitherto directed in Religion, by the see Apostolicke of Rome, and there want not protestāt aduersaries, which say the Popes there in this time also added, and altered diuers things, to, and in the sacrifice of Masse , wee will now proue by these

thefe proteftants them felues, that not ante
one Pope altered , or added any one materiall , or leafte effentiall thinge therein in
this age . The firft Pope after S. Celeftine
which thefe men accufe for addinge, or al-
teringe in this matter, is that mofte learned
and renowned Pope, S. Leo, againft whom
a Proteftant Bifhop thus exclaimeth . (*Bal.
l. 2. de Act. Pontif. Rom. in Leone 1. Robert.
Barns in vit. Pont. in cod.*) *Leo primus Thuf-
cus, in canone Miffæ, hoc fanctum facrificium,
immaculatam hoftiam, & hanc igitur oblationem, non fine magna Dei blafphemia addidit.*
Pope Leo the firft, a Tufchan by birth, did
add in the canon of the Maffe, not without
great blafphemie of God , *this holy facrifice
immaculate offeringe , and therefore this oblation* . To this I anfwere , and firft to the
pretended addition of the prayer. *Hanc igitur oblationem*: That as our renowned contryman S. Albinus with others , proueth.
(*Albin. Alcuin. l. de diuin offic. cap. de celebrat. Miffæ.*) this prayer, efpecially the firft
part which hee taxeth, is as auncient in the
Maffe, as the Apoftles time , and was vfed
both by S. Peter and others of that facred
order; *Miffam Petrus Antiochiæ dicitur cele-*
braffe,

braße , in qua tres tantum orationes in initio
fidei proferebantur, incipientes ab eo loco, vbi
dicitur; Hanc igitur oblationem. Therefore S.
Leo added nothinge in this prayer, beeing
for the firſt part vſed by the Apoſtles , and
others in their dayes , which is that , this
Proteſtant Biſhop excepteth againſt : and
for the later end thereof, which hee taxeth
not, was by this man himſelfe, and others,
both Catholicks, and Proteſtants , added
longe time after, and then, firſt by S. Gregorie the great and firſt Pope of that name.
Baleus l. 2. de Act. Pontfic. Rom. in Gregorio
1. Rob. Barnes in vit. Pontif. Rom. in eodem.
& alij communiter.

2. So that it is euident S. Leo neither
did , nor could add any part of this prayer,
to the ſacrifice of Maſſe as his owne addition or inuention, all that hee did, or poſſiblie could doe therin, was to take order that
the decree or cuſtom of the Apoſtles ſhould
be obſerued , which cannot be either great
or little blaſphemie of God , as this barbarous mouth affirmed , but honor vnto God
in that behalfe. To make all ſure, I will cite
the whole praier then vſed thus in Engliſh:
Therefore ô Lord wee beſeech thee, that thou
                                          wilt

wilt be pleased to accept this oblation of our ser-
uice, and all thy family through Christ our
Lord. The reſt being added by S. Gregory,
is thus: *and diſpoſe our dayes in peace, and com-*
maund wee may bee deliuered from euerlaſting
damnation, and numbred in the flocke of thy
electedſeruants. In which addition of S. Gregory there is not any one word, of matter
now in controuerſie, but al holy and allow-
able, by Proteſtant Religion. And in that
part, which I ſay with S. Albin or Alcuine,
was vſed by the Apoſtles, there is not one
word, except, *oblation*, which is, or can by
proteſtants bee called into controuerſie, by
them or any Chriſtiã; Therfore to anſwere
that & *hoc ſacrificium, immaculatam hoſtiam,*
together; If S. Leo added theſe wordes, to
the canon of the Maſſe, then the canon of
the Maſſe was before S. Leo his pretended
additions: and in other places of this canon
of which no proteſtant doth, or will produce any Author, beeing as is proued before apoſtolicall, this Liturgie of Maſſe is
called. *(in can. Miſſæ antiq.) donum, munus,*
ſanctum ſacrificium illibatum, oblatio benedicta,
adſcripta, rata, rationabilis, ſacrificium, hoſtia
pura, hoſtia ſancta, hoſtia immaculata. A preſent,

ſent, a guiſt, holy ſacrifice vnſpotted, an oblation bleſſed, adſcribed, ratified, reaſonable, a ſacrifice, a pure hoſte, an holy hoſte, an immaculate hoſte.

3. And this Proteſtant Biſhop himſelfe hath teſtified alſo, that the offertorie was vſed in S. Celeſtines time before : which is this in Engliſh : *O holy Father omnipotent eternall God, receue this immaculate ſacrifice, or oblation, which I thy vnworthie ſeruant doe offer vnto thee, my liuinge and true God, for my innumerable ſinnes, and offences, and negligences, and for all here preſent, as alſo for all faithfull Chriſtians both liuinge and deade, that it may bee to mee and them for ſaluation to eternal life. Suſcipe ſanctè Pater omnipotens æterne Deus, hãc immaculatam hoſtiam, quam ego indignus famulus tuus offero tibi Deó meo, viuo, & vero, pro innumerabilibus peccatis, & offenſionibus, & negligentijs meis, & pro omnibus circumſtantibus, ſed & pro omnibus fidelibus Chriſtianis, viuis atque defunctis : vt mihi & illis proficiat ad ſalutem, in vitam æternam Amẽ.* So likewiſe it was for the chalice : *offerimus tibi Domine calicem ſalutaris:* ô Lord wee offer vnto thee the chalice of ſaluation: And I haue proued in all ages before,

fore, from Chriſt, euen with the allowance of our proteſtants, that Maſſe was an holie ſacrifice, and all truely conſecrated preiſtes, did euer in all times and places ſtill offer that moſte holy ſacrifice, both for the
liuinge and faithfull departed, and that this
was ſo an vndoubted and generally receued cuſtome, & truth in the whole church,
that by our proteſtants graunt, it was iuſtly
condemned to bee hereſie, to deny it, and
this longe time before S. Leo was borne:
Therefore none of thoſe names could bee
by any poſſibility his inuentiõ in this kind.
Which this proteſtant accuſing Biſhop him
ſelfe to confound and contradict himſelfe,
teacheth in the ſame place, when hee ſaith
of S. Leo, *Miſſæ ſacrificium approbauit* . Hee
did approue the ſacrifice of Maſſe: therfore
Maſſe was termed and knowne to be ſo accepted a ſacrifice, before his time, and approbation. For a thinge approued, or to bee
approued, vnſeparably carrieth with it a
precedency to the approbation, that which
is, not cannot poſſibly bee approued, as a
thinge paſt or preſent, and euery ſuch allowance or approbation neceſſarily ſuppo-
ſeth the thinge, to bee ſo allowed or approued.

ued. And this will suffice for S. Leo.

4. After whome in this age the onely
Pope which is produced by these men to
haue added, or altered in the Masse, is Gelasius : of this Pope a protestant thus writeth. (*Robert. Barnes in vit. Pontif. in Gela-
sio.*) *præfationem Missæ, verè dignū & iustum
est, instituit.* But this is euidentlie vntrue,
as I haue proued before, for S. Ciprian, and
before him Tertullian informe vs, it was in
vse in the church before their times; and S.
Ciprian alleadgeth it is an apostolicall,
common, & known custome of the church.
(*Ciprian. l. de orat. Dominic.*) and Foxe the
protestant proueth. (*Io. Foxe Tom. 2. in Q.
Mary.*) that this could not bee any inuention of Gelasius, for that both the auncient
Greeke church before that time , and both
S. Ciprian, and S. Augustine so agree it was
in vse before. *Ciprian. sup. Aug. de vera Re-
ligione cap. 3.*) therefore followeth therein
the opinion of Thomas Waldensis , that it
could not bee the inuention of Pope Gelasius . And Pope Vigilius which liued not
longe after Gelasius , who writinge to the
Bishops of Germany and Fraunce, desirous
to know the order which the church of
Rome

Rome obserued in the prefaces of Masse, anſwereth in this maner. (*Vigilius epiſtola ad Epiſcopos Germaniæ & Gallia.*) *Inuenimus has nouem præfationes in ſacro catalogo tantumodo recipiendas, quas longa retro veritas in Romana Ecclesia hactenus ſeruauit.* Wee finde that theſe 9. prefaces are to bee receued in the holy catalogue, which truth hath longe time from former ages hitherto obſerued in the Roman church. And thus hee recopteth them: *one of Eaſter, an other of the Aſcenſion of our Lord, the third of Pentecoſte, the fourth of the natiuitie of our Lord, the fift of the apparition of our Lord, the ſixt of the Apoſtles, the ſeuenth of the holy Trinitie, the eight of the Croſſe, the ninth in Lent.* And thus concludeth: *has præfationes tenet & cuſtodit ſancta Romana Ecclesia, has tenendas vobis mandamus.* Theſe prefaces the holy Roman church obſerueth; theſe wee commaund to bee kept by you. And Houeden as our proteſtants haue publiſhed him, reciteth all theſe, out of the ſame authoritie to haue bene receued in England in a councel of our Biſhops manie hundred yeares ſince, ſetting downe the begininge of euery one of them, and addeth the tenth of the bleſſed Virgin, *decimam de beata*

5. And our English Protestants themselues by their highest parlamentary authoritie in such things with them, vse the same prefaces, except that of the ¡Apostles and blessed Virgine, in their publick church seruice, their communion booke. (*Protest. communionbooke titul. communion.*) and yet in that of the blessed Virgine which seemeth to haue beene added after the dayes of Pope Vigilius, there is no inuocation of her, nor any matter now questioned by protestants found in it. And concerninge that of the Apostles of matters questioned there is onely this clause, or petition vnto God, for preseruing his church: *vt gregem tuum Pastor æterne non deseras: sed per beatos Apostolos tuos continua protectione custodias, vt ijsdem Rectoribus gubernetur, quos operis tui Vicarios eidem contulisti præesse Pastores. That God the eternall Pastor will not forsake his flocke, but keepe by his blessed Apostles, with continuall protection, that it may bee gouerned by the same Rulers, whome Vicars of his worke, hee hath appointed Pastors to rule it.* Which is not a prayer immediatlie to the Apostles, but

but to God for the protection of his Apoftles, and fuch as our proteftants themfelues in their publick feruice, on S. Michael
his day, doe vfe for the protection of Angels, as is manifeft in their colle&t or prayer
of that feaft, being the old Catholick prayer word by word tranflated into Englifh.
And yet if there were any immediate prayer vnto the Apoftles, or any other Saints or
Angels, in any of thefe prefaces, I haue
proued before, that it was the receaued do-
&trine of Chrifts church, from the beginninge.

6. And if wee fhould allow vnto proteftants, that Pope Gelafius did add in the
prefaces, all that claufe, *verè dignum & iuf-*
tum eft : vnto, *per Chriftum Dominum no-*
ftrum. What is there in it, but holy, and al-
lowable, and ftill practifed by themfelues
in their church feruice. This it is: *verè dig-*
num & iuftum eft æquum & falutare nos tibi
femper & vbique gratias agere Domine fanĉte
Pater omnipotens æterne Deus, per Chriftum
Dominum noftrum, ô Lord holy Father omnipotent eternall God, verely it is a thinge
worthie and iuft, right and belonginge to
faluation, that wee alwayes and in all places

ces giue thanks to thee by Chriſt our Lord.
Are not all Chriſtians in all iudgements
bound to bee of this minde, and this being
a dutie ſo bindinge and belonginge vnto al
that beleeue in Chriſt, is it not the better,
the oftner, and more publickly it be acknowledged? or if it be good by proteſtants,
and in their publick practiſe, how can it be
ill in Catholicks, or could bee ſo in Pope
Gelaſius? And if hee had added, *Te igitur
clementiſsime Pater per Ieſum Chriſtũ filium
tuum Dominum noſtrum ſupplices rogamus ac
petimus*: Therefore ô moſte mercifull Father, wee aske and beſeeche thee, by Ieſus
Chriſt, thy ſonne our Lord. It is the ſame
reaſon, as before, this beinge a very Chriſtian, and holy prayer, by Proteſtant Religion, to aske all things of God in the name
of Chriſt as hee himſelfe ſaid: *whatſoeuer
you shall aske in my name, that will I doe.* (*Io.
c.* 14. *v.* 13.) *and whatſoeuer yee shall aske of
the Father in my name hee may giue it you.
Io. c. 15. v.* 26.

7. Whereby theſe men may ſee, that neither the primatiue church which vſed inuocation of Saints, nor the preſent church
of Rome inſiſtinge therein, did, or doe di-
miniſh

minish any honor , or dutie to Chriſt , by
honoringe them, which honor him, and are
honoured by him. Yet S. Remigius witneſſeth, this prayer, *Te igitur clementiſsime Pa-*
ter , to haue beene vſed from the Apoſtles.
(*Remig. in epiſt. 1. ad Timoth. cap.* 2.) Wheras ſome proteſtants write of Pope Gelaſius.
(*Balæus l. 2. de actis Pontif. Rom. in Gelaſio.*)
Gelaſius hymnos, prefationes, gradualia, collec-
tas & orationes præſcripſit: Pope Gelaſius did
preſcribe hymnes, prefaces, graduals, collects, and prayers : I haue proued by theſe
proteſtants , that all theſe were vſed in the
church, and laudably longe before: and by
the word *præſcripſit, hee did preſcribe*, what
hymnes, prefaces, graduals, and collects, or
prayers were to bee vſed, it is euident, theſe
were before, and he being Pope, and cheife,
preſcribed the order how they ſhould bee
vſed: which proueth, he rather tooke ſome
away , then added any , for amonge them
were before, *præſcripſit, he preſcribed*, which,
and no others ſhould bee vſed. And wheras
there is a controuerſie , by ſome , whether
this preſcription and orderinge theſe things
was by Pope Gelaſius , or one called Scholaſticus; Maſter Foxe the Proteſtant hiſto-
rian

rian decideth this queſtion. (*Io. Foxe in Q.*
Mary, pag. 1403.) teaching out of, *31 vetuſto*
quodam libro de officio Miſſæ, an old booke of
the office of Maſſe, that theſe were both
one, and Gelaſius, beinge Scholaſticus before, was made Pope: *Gelaſius Papa ex Scho-*
laſtico effectus in ordine 48) And thus much
of Gelaſius.

8. After whome, for an intermedler in
theſe affaires, our proteſtants propoſe Pope
Symmachus. (*Barnes in vit. Pontif. Rom. in*
Symmacho. Bal.l. 2. in eod.) who commaunded, *gloria in excelſis Deo,* to bee ſunge vppon ſondayes, and feaſts of Saints . *In Do-*
minico die & Sanctorum natalitijs , gloria in
excelſis canendum eſſe dixit ; or by an other,
præcepit. But if they meane the firſt part, of
this holy hymne , it was the ſonge of the
Angels, at the birthe of Chriſt, and recommended vnto vs in ſcripture, and by one of
theſe proteſtants, vſed at Maſſe by the commaundement of Saint, and Pope Teleſpho-
rus, who liued in the Apoſtles time : *gloria*
in excelſis Deo &c. in Miſſa canendum præce-
pit . (*Rob. Barnes in vit. Pontif. Rom. in Te-*
leſphoro. & S. Petro.) and if they meane the
whole canticle, as it is now vſed, their brother

ther Iohn Foxe, with others, thus testifieth. (*Iohn. Foxe supr. in Q. Mary.*) The hymne, *gloria in excelsis, which was sunge of the An-gels at the birth of our Sauiour, was augmen-ted by Hilarius Pictauiensis, with those words, that follow, singing it first in his owne church, which was an. 340. & afterward brought into other churches by Pope Symmachus.* And our histories testifie it was vsed here in Britanie by S. German in his time. And our English Protestants vse it, in their publicke church seruice, at this day, by publicke authoritie. *Engl. Protestant communion booke morninge prayer.*

9. That which a Protestant Bishop wri-teth of this Pope, that he reduced the Masse to forme, *Missam in formam redegit.* (*Bal. l. 2. Act. Pontif. Rom. in Symmacho.*) is his for-mall forgery, or foolery, confounded by many vndeniable instances graunted by protestants before, as the forme of Masse of S. Peter, S. Iames, S. Matthew, S. Marke, S. Clement, S. Basile, S. Chrisostome, and Popes of Rome longe before this time, as amonge other witnesses this Protestant Bi-shop himselfe testifieth of S. Innocentius, Syricius, S. Celestine, S. Leo and Gelasius.

C c   (*Bal.*

(*Bal. in Act. Pontif. Rom. in Innocent. Syric. Cælestino Leon. Gelas.*) therefore without euident contradiction, and wilfull errour, he cannot intend, or affirme, that Pope Symmachus did first bringe the Masse into order. Therefore of necessitie to keepe himselfe from these absurdities, he must vnderstand, that Pope Symmachus confirmed, or allowed of the forme of Masse, formerlie vsed in the church, which all Popes & good Christians euer did, and ought to doe

10. And here endeth the fift hundred yeare, at which time, and longe after, as with others, our protestants assure vs, that S. Dubritius that great massinge Prelate, and Archbishop primate here, & the Popes Legate, and great Master of diuinitie, together with S. Iltutus priuiledged in the same facultie by papall authoritie, and S. Gildas by whome all Britanie and other contries receaued instruction were liuinge, and consequently agreeing in all thinges with the church of Rome. (*Bal. cent. 1. in Dubritio Iltuto Gylda Albanio. Godwin. Catal. in S. Dauids. Capgrau. Catal. in Dubrit. Iltut. Gild.*) About which time also amonge diuers others those three great lights of our Brittish church

church knowne maſſinge preiſts, and Biſhops S. Dauid that ſucceeded S. Dubritius in his archiepiſcopall dignitie, S. Thelians and S. Patern, began to floriſh, and went that great Pilgrimage to Hieruſalem. (*M. S. antiq. Capgrau. Catal. in S. Dauid. S. Thelian. & S. Paterno & alÿ. M. S. S. Theliai apud Godwin. Catal. in Landaff. 2.*) and both in going and returninge through Italy and thoſe places, and ordinarily ſayinge Maſſe, muſt needs vſe that order and forme therof, they found to bee vſed at Rome, and all places receauinge direction from thence in ſuch affaires, and ſo here I end this age, and centenary of yeares.

THE SIXTH AGE, OR HVN-
DRED YEARES OF CHRIST.

THE XXI. CHAPTER.

Wherein being confeſſed by our proteſtant wri-
ters, that all the Popes of Rome vnto S.
Gregory were maſſinge preiſts, and Popes,
yet not any one of thē by theſe proteſtāts cō-
feſſion, made any the leaſt materiall chaun-
ge, or alteration in theſe miſteries.

Now wee are come to the ſixt age, or hundred of yeares, of Chriſt, wherin
liued

liued S. Gregory the great, Pope of Rome,
that sent S. Auguſtine and diuers other holie cleargie'men hither, which conuerted a
greater part of this nation, and kingdome,
called England; Wherefore ſeeing by confeſſion of our beſt learned proteſtants, the
Chriſtian Britans of this Iland, had from
their firſt conuerſion vnto Chriſt, and did
at the coming of S. Auguſtine from Rome,
continue in the ſame holy faith, and Religion, which they had learned, and receued
in the Apoſtles time, and hitherto we haue
not found any materiall difference in any
age between them, & the church of Rome
in theſe cheif queſtions I haue in hand; now
to make euidét demonſtration by theſe ad-
uerſaries to the holy Romane Religion, that
this church neuer altered any ſubſtantiall
matter, by their owne iudgement, at, before, or after, the cominge of S. Auguſtine
hither, I will firſt ſet downe all the pretended chaunges additiós or alteratiós, which
theſe proteſtants charge that holy church
withall, in theſe affaires, prouinge them to
bee of no moment, or eſſentiall; And after
ſhew how the Chriſtian Britans in this age
alſo, as in all the former, ſtill agreed in theſe
queſtions

queſtions with the church of Rome. And
wheras there was then ſome difference betweene the diſciples of S. Gregorie and the
Britãs here about the obſeruation of Eaſter,
and ſome other queſtions, rather ceremoniall, then ſubſtantiall in Religion, that the
church euen by the teſtimonie of our proteſtants, did hold the truth in theſe matters,
and ſuch Britans and Scots as held the contrary, were in confeſſed, and vnexcuſable
error.

2. The firſt alleaged chaunger or additioner of any thing in the holy ſacrifice of
Maſſe, which our proteſtants obiect among
the Popes of Rome, in this age, is Horſmida, who as theſe men write: *commaunded
that altars should not be erected, without the
aſſent of the Bishop. Ne altaria ſine Epiſcopi
aſſenſu erigerentur iuſsit.* (*Rob. Barnes in vit.
Pontif. Rom. in Horſmida. Bal. in Act. Pont.
in eod.*) but this was according to holy ſcriptures, to haue Superiors and commaunders
to bee obeyed: *remember them which haue
the rule ouer you. Obey them that haue the
rule ouer you, and ſubmit yourſelues.* (*Hebr.
cap* 13. *v.* 7. 17. and S. Ignatius liuinge in
the firſt hundred yeares, proueth noe ſuch

thinge

thinge ought to bee done without the Bishops assent . (*Ignat. epist. ad Smyrnenses.*)
and the puritan presbytery, and among our
English parlament Protestats no such matter in their Religion may bee done, without the allowance of theire Protestant Bishops. And these protestant obiectors themselues before confesse, that Pope Syricius
tooke order, that Masse should not bee said
but in places cosecrated by the Bishop. *Mis-*
sas in loco ab Episcopo sacrato celebrandas esse.
(*Rob. Barnes in vit. Syricij Papæ.*) which was
soone after the ceasinge of persecution by
the Emperors, that places might bee freely
dedicated to God, and hallowinge of altars
beloged properly euer to the episcopal dignitie. And our protestants ar witnesses, that
this was then practised and obserued in Britanie by S. Dauid, S. Dubritius and others,
too many to be recited. And in Kinge Lucius his time, when so many churches with
their altars were dedicated by our holy Bishops to God, S. Peter, and other Saints.
Godwin conuers. cap. 2. pag. 11. Holinsh. hist.
of Engl. Theat. of great Britanie. Capgrau.in
S. Patricio & alij.

3. From Horsmida, they lepp ouer Ioan-
nes

nes 1. Fælix 4. Bonifacius 2. Ioannes 2. Aga-
petus 1. Syluerius 1. vntil they come to Pope
Vigilius, who as these men say, decreed,
that Masse should bee said towardes the easte:
Instituit vt Missa celebretur versus orientem.
(*Io. Bal. l. 2. de Act. Pontif. Rom. in Vigilio.*)
or as an other protestant interpreteth it: *Vi-*
gilius instituted that preists being to say Mas-
se, should turne their face towardes the east.
(*Barnes in vit. Vigilij*) *Vigilius instituit, vt*
Missam celebraturi, faciem ad orientem verte-
rent. But this is onely a ceremony if he had
first inuented it: but S. Basile telleth vs it
was an apostolicall tradition, so to pray
towards the east. (*Basil. l. de Spiritu Sancto*
cap. 27) for speaking of such traditions from
the Apostles, not conteyned in scripture he
saith: *vt ad orientem versus precemur, quæ do-*
cuit scriptura? to pray with our faces towardes the east is a tradition, and not taught in
scripture. And this tradition and custome
of the primatiue Christians to pray, and say
Masse turning their faces towards the east,
was so common, publick, and well known
longe before this time (*Proclus supra in vi-*
ta S. Patricij. Holinsh. histor. of Ireland in
S. Patrick) that as I haue declared before,

C c 4 both

both Catholick and Protestant antiquaries
so assuring vs, it was giuen for a distinctiue
signe, by the deuils and magiciens of Ireland, to the then Pagan inhabitants therof,
before the cominge of S. Patrick thither, to
know him and his Christian disciples by,
that they should sett their Altar, say Masse,
and pray towards the east, as wee general-
lie see chauncels & high altars of Christian
churches are framed. Therefore wee may
be secure, that hitherto the church of Rome
and Britanie agreed in these misteries, nothinge added yet by any Pope, which the
Britans did not embrace. For better testimonie wherof we are told by the antiquaries of Cambridge, that Kinge Arthur in
his charter of priuiledge, to that schole, or
vniuersitie, bearinge date at London, in
the yeare of Christ 531. doth therin expresse, that hee giueth that confirmation with
the counsaile and assent of *all and euery Bi-*
shops, and nobles of his kingdome, and licence
of the see Apostilick of Rome. *Consilio & con-*
sensu omnium & singulorum Pontificum &
Principum istius regni, & licentia sedis Apo-
stolicæ. (*Io. Caius l. 1. antiquit. pag. 69. Diplo-*
ma Regis Arthuri 7. die Aprilis an. 531. Lon-
dini

dini apud Caium supr. pag 68. 69. 70.) therfore if the then Kinge of Britanie , and all
the Bishops , and Noble men thereof , by
which the rest were gouerned, did then so
firmly adhere to the Pope of Rome in matters of Religion, that they would not ioyne
in such an Act, without his licence, no man
will thinke, there was or then could be any
difference in Religion betweene them. And
to côfirme vs the more in this great vnion,
and amitie of Rome and Britanie , in such
affaires, at this time of Pope Vigilius , and
Kinge Arthur, our protestants Matthew of
Westminster telleth vs. (*Matth. Westm an.*
533. that this Religious Kinge committed
Walwan sonne to Loth his sisters sonne,
Who should haue inherited the kingedome of
Norwey to Pope Vigilius to bee brought vp,
when hee was but 12. *yeares of age , and that*
hee was knighted by him . Erat autem Wal-
wanus filius prædicti Loth, duodecim annorum
iuuenis, Vigilio Papæ traditus ad nutriendum,
à quo etiam & militiæ cingulum accepit. How
farr this Pope intermeddled in ordering the
prefaces in Masse, I haue said before, & these
protestants being silent therin, thereby rest
contented in that point.

4. The

4. The next additioner with these protestants, is the next Pope, Pelagius the first:
who as these men say, gaue allowance that
in time of Lent preists might say Masse at
the ninth hower of the day, which is three
of the clocke in the afternoone by our accompt. *In quadragesima presbytero licere sacra
facere hora nona pronuntiauit.* (*Rob. Barnes in
Pelag.* 1.) an other saith: *vt quadragesimali
tempore hora nona sacrificulis missare liceret.*
(*Bal. in Pelag.* 1.) but this was but a ceremony, and argued, how reuerent and deuout preists were, in that time, to this holy
sacrifice, that they did, and would fast so
longe to say Masse, so nere the time it was
instituted by Christ, and Christ was offered vpon the Crosse, this proueth, they were
not protestants in that time, which neither
reuerence Masse, nor fast so longe, or at all
in Lent. But they add of this Pope: *mortuo-
rum memorias approbauit, ac lucri gratia mis-
sis adiecit.* Hee approued the memories of
the dead, and for gaine added them to Masses. (*Bal. in Pelag.* 1.) but this Protestant Bishop is either very forgetfull, or maketh no
scruple to contradict himselfe, for he telleth
vs before in the life of Saint and Pope Siricius

cius lōge before S. Celestine sent S. German and the rest into these parts, *that this S. Syricius adioyned memories vnto Masses, and yet died a confessor in the yeare of our Lord 399.* *Syricius Missæ memorias adiunxit, & anno Domini 399. confessor occubuit.* (*Balæus. l. 2. de Act. Pontif. Rom. in Syricio.*) and Tertullian in his time setteth it downe for an Apostolicall tradition, to say Masse for the deade, and keepe their anniuersary daies, *oblationes pro defunctis, pro natalitys annua die facimus.* (*Tertul. l. de coron. milit. cap. 3.*) S. Ciprian S. Chrisostome and others haue the like. And our protestants haue confessed before, that it was an Apostolicall tradition to say Masse for the dead, and that Aerius was iustly condemned of heresie, and for an hereticke for his denyall thereof. And wee had here in Britanie many foundations to say Masse, and pray for Christian soules, and frends deceased, as we find in the charter of Kinge Arthur before recited, wherin among other motiues of that his confirmatorie priuiledge to the vniuersitie of Cambridge, hee saith expressely, that hee doth it, with the consent of all his Bishops, for the helpe of the soules of his antecessors

Kings

Pro amore cælestis patriæ, remedioque animarum Antecessorum meorum Britaniæ Regum.Charta Regis Arthuri apud Caium supr. antiq. Cantabr. l. 1.pag. 69.

5. After this Pope, vntill they come to S. Gregory, these protestants complaine of no additions, but onely in Pope Pelagius the second, which was the immediate pre-decessor to S. Gregory, and sent him, yet a priuate preist, his legate to Constanti-nople: of this Pope they write: *nouem præfationes ante canonem in Missa canendas dedit.* Hee gaue nyne prefaces to bee sunge before the canon in Masse. (*Bal. in Pelag. 2. l. 2. in Act. Pontif.* an other thus more particularly expresseth it: *Pelagius nouem præfationes Ec-clesiæ dedit ante canonem, in Missa canendas: in Natali, in Epiphania, in Quadragesima, de Cruce, de Resurrectione, de Ascensione, in Pē-tecoste, de Trinitate, de Apostolis.* (*Barnes in Pelag. 2. in vit. Pont.*) Pelagius gaue nyne prefaces to the church, to bee sunge before the canon in Masse, one in the natiuitie of Christ, an other in the Epiphanie, in Lent, of the Crosse, of the Resurrection, of the Ascension, at Whitsontyde, of the Trinitie, of the Apostles. I haue answered this before,

fore, in Pope Gelafius, to whome thefe proteftants before contradictinge them felues
afcribe the preface, how vaine this quarrell
is I haue there declared, and onely add here
from theire proteftant like publifhed Matthew of Weftminfter: *Anno gratiæ* 581.
Papa Pelagius decreuit nouem præfationes tā-
tum ad Miffas debere cantari , caffatis quoti-
dianis quæ dici folebant : In the yeare of grace 581. Pope Pelagius decreed that only nine
prefaces fhould bee funge at Maffe , omit-
tinge the daily prefaces which were wont
to bee faid . Where wee fee that this Pope
did not add any thinge in this bufines , but
rather deducted fome prefaces, though they
had beene vfed to bee faid before, for fo the
words, *dici folebant,* manifeftly proue , as I
wrote of Pope Vigilius before . All which
doe euidentlie teftifie, that the auncient receued cuftome of the church of Chrift was
longe before thefe dayes , to vfe thefe prefaces.

THE

THE XXII. CHAPTER.

Wherein euident demonstration is made, euen
by these protestants themselues, that nei-
ther S. Gregory the great, which sent S.
Augustine, with many other holy learned
men into England, did make any materiall
addition, or alteration in these misteries.
But the Religion which those his disciples
preached here, was in all points by all testi-
monies both of God and man, Britans them
selues, and Saxons, Catholicks and Prote-
stants, auncient and late writers, the true
Religion of Christ, and in all things wher-
in they differed from the Britans, more pure
then that which they then professed.

Now wee are come to the happy dayes
of S. Gregory the great, that sent so
many holy men, to preach Christian Religion to this English nation, and so called
our Apostle, in which it will bee more manifest, euen by these protestant accusers
themselues, that whatsoeuer differéce there
was, betweene the holy disciples which he
sent hither, and some Britans, the error in
euery

euery point was in thofe that oppofed a-
gainft the Roman miffion. And for S. Gregory himfelfe, one of the four holy Doctors
of the church of Chrift, he was by all teftimonies a great learned man, & holy Saint,
and fo honored both in the Greeke and Latine church, and the Maffe hee vfed as our
proteftants haue told vs. (*Edw. Sands relation of Relig. fupr.*) both was, and is receued and publickly vfed euen in the Greeke
church, beeing tranflated into Greeke: hee
is ftiled by all writers proteftants and Catholicks, Gregory the great, and commonlie named the Apoftle of the Englifh nation, in all publicke proteftant Kalenders
placed amonge the holy Saints, and by a
Proteftant Bifhop his greateft accufer, dignified, with thefe honorable termes. (*Bal. l.
2. de Act. Pontific. Rom. in Gregorio Magno.*)
*Gregorius Magnus omnium Pontificum feu vt
dictum eft Patriarcharum Romanorum, doctrina, & vita præftantifsimus: inuitus ac demum
coactus Pelagio prædicto fuccefsit, vir doctus
& bonus* Gregory the great the moft excellent both for learninge and life, of all the
Romane Popes or Patriarkes, did againft
his will, and at lafte therto compelled, fuc-
ceed

ceed Pelagius the second, hee was a learned and good man. Therefore it cannot bee either probable , or possible , that a man so learned, vertuous, and holy, that hee is thus dignified by so great enemies, both for learninge and pietie aboue all the Popes that euer were so learned, & knowne holy Saints, and so vnwillinge to take that greatest honor, and charge vpon him, would or could contrary both to so great learning, and pietie , which could not consist with any the least error in Religion in essentiall things, make any erroneous publick decree in such affaires. For in so doinge hee should haue beene so farr from that eminent learninge, and pietie , and beinge a glorious Saint in heauen, which both by protestants and Catholicks are generally held and written of him , that quite contrary hee should haue beene an vnlearned, wicked, and damned man. Which no tonge or mouth that hath learned to cōfesse Christ, dareth to affirme or vtter.

2. But to giue all contentment , I will examine all whatsoeuer in particular, they say this so holy learned Pope added, or altered in these misteries, as they pretend. This

Proteſtant Biſhop ſaith of him (*Bal.l.2.ſupr. in Gregor. Mag.*) *introitum in Miſſa ex aliquo pſalmo canere iuſſit*. Hee commaunded the introite in the Maſſe to bee ſunge out of ſome pſalme. They haue told vs before of more auncient times wherein the introite was vſed, before S. German, Lupus, Palladius & Patricius were ſent into theſe parts. But if S. Gregory did any ſuch thing, ſeeing it was *ex aliquo pſalmo*, out of the holy ſcripture, neither theſe men, nor any which will not diſallow of holy ſcripture, may reprehend it. And where this proteſtant accuſer further ſaith: *Nonies in Miſſa, Kyrie eleyſon canere iuſſit*. S. *Gregory commaunded that Lord haue mercy vpon vs, ſhould bee ſunge 9. times in Maſſe*. Hee is deceued, for that is ſonge but 6. times, and *Chriſt haue mercy vpon vs*, thriſe: And his friend Maſter Foxe. (*Io. Foxe in Q. Mary pag.* 1401.) will tell him, that this was the auncient cuſtome of the Greeke church longe before, frō which is was taken by S. Gregory, only that S. Gregory added, *Chriſt haue mercy vpon vs*. But howſoeuer is it not a moſte holy and warranted cuſtome, ſo to pray? our proteſtants theſelues obſerue it in their publick church

D d   ſer-

seruice. (*Com. booke tit. Litan. & alibi.*) and
commonlie preferr them before all other
prayers, both in their priuate, and publicke
writings.

3. Of S. Gregories addinge, *diesque no-*
stros in tua pace disponas, and dispose our dayes
in peace , and graunt wee bee deliuered from
eternall damnation, and numbred in the flock of
thy elect. I haue spoken before, & here only
I add, that S Bede, whome this Protestant
Bishop, (*Io. Bal. l. de scriptor. Britan. centur.*
1. in Beda Girwino.) doth equall or rather
preferr before S. Gregory, S. Augustine, S.
Hierome, and S. Chrisostome, those great
lights of Christs church, doth say, that these
wordes which S. Gregory added in the holie Masse, *are words ful of greatest perfection:*
Beatus Papa Gregorius in ipsa Missarum cele-
bratione, tria verba maxima perfectionis plena
superadiecit, diesque nostros in tua pace dispo-
nas, atque ab æterna damnatione nos eripi, &
in electorum tuorum iubeas grege numerari.
(*Beda Eccles. histor. l. 2. cap. 1.*) in which
place hee also commendeth him , for cau-
singe in the churches of S. Peter and S. Paul
at Rome, Masses to be said ouer their bodies.
Fecit inter alia beatus Papa Gregorius , vt in
Ecclesijs

Ecclesijs beatorum Apostolorum Petri & Pauli
super corpora eorū Missæ celebrarentur. Which
sacred bodies of those two glorious Apostles, this lewde protestant superintendent,
& therin as his phrase teacheth, a Vigilan-
tian hereticke, calleth the deade carcasses
of the Apostles, so as wee terme the deade
bodies of beastes, and therefore disliketh S.
Gregory for that institution : *super Aposto-*
lorum mortua cadauera Missas celebrari man-
dauit. (*Bal. l. 2. de Act. Pontif. Rom. in Gre-*
gor. Magno.) but though it doth not belonge
to this place, and my promise, yet to free S.
Gregory from all pretended error in any
matter, I wil shew in the next chapter, when
I come to speake of the brittish preists, and
Bishops of this age, that they were as farr
engaged in this doctrine of reuerēce to holie relicks, as either S. Gregory, or his disciples hee sent hither were, or the Catholicks of the present Roman church bee at
this time. The same I wil demonstrate concerning the doctrine of Indulgences, an o-
ther pretēded blott, which they would gla-
dly find out, to staine, and blemish the glory
of that great Doctor, Pope, and Saint.

4. And whereas this protestant Bishop

saith

saith of this holy Pope : *Hee admitted Mas-*
ses for the dead, Missas pro mortuis admisit, I
haue often shewed by these protestants, that
this was vsed from the beginninge. And
whereas hee obiecteth. (*Bal. supr. in Greg.*
Magno.) that S. Gregory first instituted
Candelmasse day, and palme sonday, with
solemnitie of procession, though these bee
but ceremoniall, yet he contradicteth himselfe, knowinge and acknowledginge, that
processions were longe before in vse, and
that Candelmasse day was kept with candels in the time of Pope Vigilius, and by his
approbation: *candelarū festum instituit.* (*Bal.*
in Vigilio l. 2. Act. Pontific. Rom.) whereas
this man saith in S. Augustine, S. Gregories
disciple, *that hee brought hither altars, vesti-*
ments, holy vessels, relicks, and bookes of cere-
monies, introduxit altaria, vestimenta, vasa
sacra, reliquias, & ceremoniarum codices. (*Bal.*
l. de scriptor. Britan. l. 1. in Augustino. Mo-
nocho.) I haue shewed already, that all these
were in vse with the Christiā Britans longe
before, and this protestant obiector among
others, so acknowledgeth in diuers, both
Scots, and Britans, in this Iland, and in the
life of S. Patrick he receueth as S. Patricks,
the

the epistle written in his name : *Patricius
scripsit ad Aualonios Inculas epistolam.* (*Bal.
centur.* 1. *Gild. l. de excid. Bed. l.* 1. *histor. Ecclef. Bal. centur.* 1. *in Brigida Lagin. Kentegern. Patric. Iona. Monacho & alijs.*)in which
hee proueth both S. Patricke, S. Pope Celestine, S. Pope Eleutherius, and his Legates
S. Damianus, and Fugatianus in Kinge Lucius time, and all the Britans in those times,
to haue beene as great Patrons, and practisers of these doctrines and customes, which
hee disliketh in S. Gregory & his disciples,
as any of them the was, or any learned Catholicke at this present is. Thus farr these
protestants exceptions against the doctrine
of S. Gregory, and his disciples, all turning
to theire glory, and confusion of the protestant accusers by their owne sentence.

5. To which I will add one thing more
from our holy contrimã S. Aldelmus scholler to S. Gregory as his words import, who
thus relateth an addition of S. Gregorie to
the canon of the Masse, which our protestants doe not remember in their oblations.
(*S. Adelmus i. de laudib. Virginitat cap.* 22.)
*mihi operæ pretium videtur, vt Sanctæ Aga-
thæ rumores castisima Virginis Luciæ præco-*
nia

nia subsequantur: Quas Præceptor & pedagogus noster Gregorius, in canone quotidiano, quando Missarum solemnia celevrantur copulasse cognoscitur, hoc modo in Catalogo Martyrum ponens: Fælicitate, Anastasia, Agatha, Lucia. It is a thinge worth labour, that after speach of S. Agatha(he speaketh of the praise of virginitie) *the praises of the moste chaste Virgin Lucia, should follow, which our Master and Instructor Gregory, is knowne to haue coupled in the daily canon, when the solemnities of Masse are celebrated, placing them thus in the Catalogue of Martyrs: Fælicitas, Anastasia, Agatha, Lucia.* But this rather maketh against protestant quarrels, in this kinde, for they contendinge against the doctrine of prayer to Saints, are taught here, that it was the auncient custome of Gods church to pray vnto them, euen in their publick Masses. (*can. Miss. §. nobis quoque peccatoribus.*) for S. Gregory did here onely add S. Agatha, and S. Lucia, vnto the others, which were in the canon before, *copulasse cognoscitur*, and bee very many in particular, as appeareth in that place, besides all the Apostles and holy Martyrs in generall, *cum tuis Sanctis Apostolis, & Martyribus:* and the words,

words, *in canone quotidiano*, in the daily canon of Maſſe, are an euident conuiction,
that the daily canon of Maſſe was vſed, and
this honor of Saints alſo therin before this
time: as wee ſee in all old Maſſes, Greeke,
Latine, or Syriake. And I haue before proued, that this holy doctrine was euer from
the beginning of Chriſtianity in this kingdome reuerently obſerued. Of the truth and
excellency of S. Gregories and S. Auguſti-
nes Religion planted amonge the Saxons, I
haue ſpoken ſufficiently in all things in my
eccleſiaſticall hiſtorie at large.

6. To proue it breiſly in this place more
ſound and perfect then the Religion of the
Chriſtian Britans, ſo dignified by our proteſtant writers, I firſt vſe them for witneſſes thereof. And firſt the preſent Proteſtant
Archbiſhop of Canterbury D. George Abbots, the director of Maſter Frauncis Maſon, and this his directed ſcribe thus write,
producinge the Brittiſh Biſhops themſelues
at that time ſo acknowledginge. (*George
Abbot and Franc. Maſon l. 2. of conſecrat. of
Biſh. cap. 4. pag. 59.*) *The brittiſh Biſhops confeſſed, that they vnderſtood that to be the true
way of righteouſnes, which Auguſtine had*
Dd 4   *prea-*

preached. Yea the faith which S. *Augustine*
brought, and that which the Britans had before, *must needs be one and the same in all ma-*
teriall and substantiall points. Wherefore wee
cannot excuse the Britans, for refusing to ioyne
with him in the conuersion of the Saxons. The
like haue, Stowe, Howes, Hollinshed and
other protestants. (*Stowe and Howes histor.*
in K. Ethelbert. Holinsh. hist. of Engl. l. 5. cap.
15. *pag.* 96. *pag.* 97. *an.* 581.) shewinge directly, that the Christian Britans at the coming of S Augustine, and his companions,
were farr inferiour vnto them, both in holines of life, and puritie of doctrine. Which
is testified with great lamentation by S. Gildas a Britane, S. Bede writer of the brittish
history. (*Gildas l. de excid. & conquest. Brit.*
Bed. histor. Eccl. l. 1. Galfrid. Monument. hist.
Reg. Brit. l 10. & 11.

7. And if wee discend vnto the particular differences, which then were betweene
S. Augustine, and the Britans, there is not
any one to bee found in any antiquitie, that
concerned the questions I haue in hand, but
in them there was an vniforme consent by
all writers, onely I finde that they differed
in some ceremonies about the consecration

of

of Bishops, but in no materiall thinge . (*S. Asaph. in vit. S. Kentegerni. M. S. in vit. eius & Capgrau. in Catal. in Kenteg.*) and our protestants differ from them both therein. *For the Britans did then confecrate Bishops with anointing their heads with holy Chrisme, Inuocation of the holy Ghost, Benediction, and Imposition of handes: Mos in Britannia inoleuerat in consecratione Pontificum tantummodo capita eorum sacri Chrismatis infusione perungere, cum inuocatione Sancti Spiritus, & Benediction, & manus Impositione .* And the Romans besides these necessarie things , in that consecration , kept and obserued the decrees of the holy Canons, in this busines; Which the Britans did not omit for any dislike they had of those sacred ceremonies, but by distance of place, and infested with Pagans inuasions, were ignorant of the canons, as our Authors say: *Infulam enim quasi extra orbem positi , emergentibus Paganorum infestationibus, canonum erant ignari. (M. S. de vita S. Kenteger antiq. & Capgrau. supr. in eod.)* and yet our protestants both knowinge the canonicall institutions, and what both the Romans and Britans, with all the Christian worlde at that time , thought

to bee essentiall, and necessary in this holy
Sacrament, neither follow the one, or other,
and so by al iudgement, haue depriued them
selues of lawfull and true Bishops, and con-
sequentlie of all true cleargie men, which
cannot be without true and lawful Bishops,
such as they want, to consecrate them.

8. The other differences betwene S. Augustine, and the Britans, may appeare out
of the words of S. Augustine vnto them, related by S. Bede, and others, and thus sett
downe by our protestant historians. *Augustines oration breifly was thus.* (*Bed. histor.
Eccles. l. 2. cap. 2. Stowe and Howes histor. in
Kentish. Saxons. K. Ethelbert.*) *although
deare bretheren, in many other points yee doe
contrary to our custome, or rather contrary to
the custome of the vniuersall church of Christ:
yet notwithstandinge if yee will in these three
things consent vnto mee, that is, to celebrate
the easter in due time, to accomplish the mi-
nisterie of Baptisme accordinge to the Roman,
and Apostolick church, and last of all to preach
with vs to this English nation, the vvord of
our Lord, all your other ceremonies, rites, and
customes, though they bee contrary to ours, yet
vvee vvill vvillinglie suffer, and bee content*
to

to beare vvith them. But they ansvvered they vvoulde doe none of these thinges requested. Where wee see, that S. Augustine and the Britans did differ principally, in these three things, and by our protestants themselues, S. Augustine held the truth in them, and the Britans were in error. And so likewise in all other ceremonies rites and customes then cōtrouersed: for S. Augustine iustifieth that the Britans in them all were, *contrary to the custome of the vniuersall church of Christ. In multis quidem nostræ consuetudini, immo vniuersalis Ecclesiæ contraria geritis* . And their learned contriman Gyraldus Cambrensis diuers hundreds of yeares since, beeing as a protestant, Bishop stileth him, *vetustæ cognitionis verè helluo*, an vnsatiable seeker forth of antiquities, with protestants allow-ance thus setteth downe the ceremonies of the Britans, wherein they differed from all other churches, in this order. *Bal. l. de scriptor. Britan. in Gyrald. Cambren. cent. 2. Gyrald. Cambren. descript. Cambr. cap. 18. Dauid Powell ib.*

9. *De quolibet pane apposito primum fractionis angulum pauperibus donant* . Of euerie loafe of breade sett before them, they giue the
first

first corner they breake to the poore . They sitt three and three together, at dinner in memorie of the Trinitie . They cast away theire armour, and bare headed aske the benediction of euery Monke or preist, or any wearinge the habit of Religion: The people doth greatly, and more then other nations, desire confirmation by a Bishop, and Inunction of Chrisme, by which the grace of the holy Ghost is giuen. They giue tythes of all things they possesse, cattell, sheepe sometimes whē either they marry wiues, or go on pilgrimage, or correct their life by the counsaile of the church . Aboue all forreine labour, moste willingly going on pilgrimage to Rome, they more readily vvith deuout mindes adore the Tombes of the Apostles. Wee see they yeeld deuout reuerence to churches and ecclesiastical men, and relicks of Saints, and portable bells, vvoaen books, and the crosse, & giue farr more honor to all these then any other nation . The immunities of theire churches, farr exceedeth the Indulgence of the canons. You shall not see any vvhere the Eremites and Anachorites of greater abstinence, or more spirituall . And speakinge of the Britans in the time of S. Germanus, and Lupus, when they were troubled with Pelagianisme, and first irruptions

ruptions of the Pagan Saxōs, thefe Authors
fay. Thefe cuftomes and ceremonies of the
Britans continued from them, to the time
of Gyraldus Cambrenfis , that died in the
yeare of Chrift 1190. *ab eorundem doctrina
hæc, vt fertur , vfqe in hodiernum documenta
tenuerunt.*

10. Thus wee haue learned all the differences, that were betweene S. Auguftine,
and the Britans: and finde , that S. Auguftine was the innocent partie in them all.
For amonge all thefe lafte recited , where
any thinge is remembred as fingular , and
differing from other churches, it is the cafe
of the Britans, and the Romans agreed with
the common and receued cuftomes of the
church of Chrift : And concerninge thofe
doctrines and cuftomes which our proteftants doe mofte diflike in S. Gregory , and
S. Auguftine, with his affociates , and the
now prefent Roman church, which are pil-
grimages, and efpecially to Rome, with the
honor of that holy Apoftolicke fee , reuerence of holy relicks , Indulgences, honor
to facrificinge maffinge preifts , and Religious men, and more Sacraments then proteftants admit, as namely the Sacrament of
con-

An historie of the holy priesthood, and confirmation, giuinge of the grace of the holy Ghost , by anointinge with sacred Chrisme, reuerencing of the crosse, and holie images , wee see by the testimony both of the Britans , and protestants themselues, that these were more zeloussly obserued of the Christian Britans at that time , whose faith and Religion is so much commended by our protestant writers , then they were by S. Gregory, or S. Augustine then, or be at this time by the present church of Rome, and the members therof.

11. Therfore it being the common and generally receued opinion, both of our English Protestant Bishops , as Parker, Bale, Godwin , with others , and their Doctors and antiquaries as Powel, Foxe, Fulke, Middleton, Gosceline, Stowe, Howes, Holinshed, and too many to be recited, that at the cominge of S. Augustine hither , the faith and Religion of the Christian Britans here, was in all materiall points sounde, and perfect , and the same which they receued in the time of the Apostles , much more and rather must they needes yeeld , and allowe that honor, to the Religion and doctrine of S. Augustine , and the other disciples of S. Gre-

Gregory, which they preached and planted here, being by so many and all humane testimonies before acknowledged in all matters controuersed betweene them, to be the vndoubted true, and perfect Religion of Christ. *Parker. antiquit. Britan. pag. 6. 45. 46. Balæus l. 2 de Act. Pontific. in Gregorio Magno & l. de scriptor. Brit. centur. 1. in Augustin. Dionotho. Godvvin. conuers. of Brit. Povvell annotat. in l. 2. Giraldi Cambr. de Itinerar. Cambr. cap. 1. Foxe Act. and Mon. pag. 463. edit. an. 1576. Fulke ansvv. to counterf. Cathol. pag. 40. Middlet. Papistom. pag 202.) Io. Goscelin. hist. Eccl. de vit. Arch. Cantuar. Stovve and Howes hist. in K. Ethelbert. Holinsh. histor. of Engl. cap. 21. pag. 102.*

12. And to make all sure, and vnquestionable; except with athests, and infidels, enemies to Christ himselfe, wee haue both the present and propheticall witnesse of God himselfe, that by no possibilitie can deceiue vn in this case, and this confessed, and receiued euen by our protestant writers, who first assure vs, that in the controuersie betweene the Britans and S. Augustine, God gaue so miraculous testimony, for S. Augustine & his Roman companions to teach
the

the truth in all thinges controuersed then
betweene them and the Britans, that the
Britans were therby so extraordinarily con-
uicted, and confounded (to speake in protestant wordes) *that they confissed in deede,*
that to bee the true way of righteousnes which
Augustine had preached, and shewed them.
(*Stowe and Howes histor. in K. Ethelbert.*)
and God could not possibly giue other testimony by these protestants, and all learninge, except hee would or could (blasphe-
mie to affirme) contradict himselfe, for by
all professors of Christian Religion he had
promised, that Catholicke church vniuersall should neuer err, and yet protestants
with others thus confesse: *all other churches*
throughout the world agreed with Augustine
in Christ. Of Gods propheticall testimonie
hereof wee haue many witnesses, Catholicks and Protestants, S. Asaph in the life
of S. Kentegern, many Manuscripts, the
Brittish history, Matthew of Westminster,
with others for Catholicks; and amonge
protestants, their first Protestant Archbishop of Canterbury, their protestant Bishop
Bale, with others. (*S. Asaph. in vit. S. Ken-*
tegern. M. S. antiq. in eod. Galfr. Monum. l.
7.

7. *cap.* 3. *Matth. Weſtm. an.* 465. *Matth. Parker. antiquit. Britan. pag.* 49. *Io. Bal.l. de ſcript. Britan. cent.* 1. *in Kentegern.*) this laſt ſpeakinge of the Pagan Saxons inuadinge this kingdome, and ouerthrowinge Chriſtian Religion, bringeth S. Kentegern thus to propheſie lōge before, how S. Auguſtine and his aſſociats ſhould reſtore it againe, *not onely vnto the auncient ſtate of Religion, but a better then it enioyed in the time of the Britans. Chriſtianæ legis Religio vſque ad præſinitum tempus diſsipabitur. Sed in priſtinum ſtatim immo meliorem miſerante Deo in fine reparabitur.*

13. The auncient Manuſcript hiſtory of S. Kentegerns life, S. Aſaph, Capgraue and others ſay, S. Kentegern propheſied this, and publickly told it, to his diſciples at the time of the death of S. Dauid, which as our proteſtants write, was aboue 50. yeares before the cominge of S. Auguſtine hither. (*M. S. antiq. de vita S. Kentegerni. Io. Copgrau. in S. Kentegerno Epiſcopo & Confeſſore.*) who beeing at that time as often, very earneſt at his prayers, *and much lamentinge, after being demaūded by his diſciples the cauſe of his great ſorrowe, after a ſhort ſilence, thus anſwered:*

E e   *Knovve*

Knovve you my dearest children that S. Dauid the ornament of Britanie, Father of his
contry, is euen novv loosed from the prison of
his flesh, and gone to the heauenly kingdome.
Vnderstand you that Britanie depriued of so
great a light, shall lamēt the absence of so great
a patrone, who opposed him selfe against the
sword of God, halfe drawne against it, for the
wickednes of the inhabitants thercof, that it
should not be fully drawne and bringe it to de-
struction. Our Lord will giue Britanie ouer to
forreine nations, that know him not. And the
Isle shall bee emptied of the inhabitants, by Pagans. The Religion of the lawe of Christ shall
bee destroyed, vntill a certaine time in it. But
by the mercy of God, it shall be againe repayred
vnto the former, and vnto a better state then
it was before. *Seruo Dei quodam die prolixius*
orationi intento, facies eius quasi ignea appa-
rens stupore & extasi circumstantes repleuit.
Intuebantur enim faciem eius tanquam vul-
tum Angeli stantis inter illos. Completa oratio-
ne, grauissimis lamentis se dedit. Et cum disci-
puli causam tristitiæ humiliter ab eo peterent,
paulisper in silentio residens, tandem ait. No-
ueritis filij charissimi, Sanctum Dauid decus
Britanniæ, patrem patriæ, carnis carcerem modo
egres-

egressum, regna cælestia penetrasse. Credite mi-
hi, quod non solum Angelorum multitudo in
gaudium Domini sui illum introduxit, sed &
Dominus noster Iesus Christus ei obuiam pro-
cedens, ad portas paradisi gloria & honore co-
ronauit eum, me vidente. Scitote etiam quod
Britannia tanto lumine orbata, tanti patroni
lugebit absentiam: qui gladio Domini propter
malitiam inhabitantium (emi euaginato super
illam, ne penitus ad internitionem extractus
percuteret semetipsum opponebat. Tradens tra-
det Dominus Britanniam exteris nationibus
Deum ignorantibus: sed & à Paganis ab indi-
genis euacuabitur insula, Christianæ legis Re-
ligio vsque ad præfinitum tempus dissipabitur
in ea: sed in pristinum statim, immo meliorem
miserante Deo iterum reparabitur.

14. Our proteſtant hiſtorians doe likewiſe relate the actuall chaunge of Religion
here then for the better, and for better preachers in theſe wordes. (*Edvv. Hovves* and
Stovve hiſtor. in K. Ethelbert. Gild. l. de ex-
cid.) *Amonge many the Britans doings which*
their ovvne hiſtoriographer Gildas doth la-
mentably sett forth in vvritinge, hee saith of
them thus, that they neuer tooke care to preach
the ghoſpell of Chriſt vnto the Angles, and

Saxons , vvhich inhabited the land amonge
them. But yet the goodnes of God prouided for
the said nation of the said Angles , much more
vvorthie preachers by vvhome they might be
brought to the faith. And then immediatly
they set downe S. Augustine, Mellitus, Iustus, and Iohn, with others sent hither by S.
Gregory , *to bee these much more vvorthie*
preachers, by vvhom this nation was brought
to the faith . And this might suffice in this
matter, but for the ful clearing of al doubts,
I will further & fully proue, how al preists
and Bishops in Britanie in this age, were sacrificing massing preists: and the best learned and most holy amonge them, did in all
things ioyne with the Popes, and church of
Rome ; and they which opposed moste against S. Augustine, and his associates sent
from thence in some ceremoniall customes,
did in these points & all others which protestants most dislike in Catholick Romane
Religion, vtterly disagree from these protestants, and hold the same doctrine & practise generally, as S. Augustine did, and the
members of the present Romane Apostolick church doe at this day.

THE

THE XXIII. CHAPTER.

Wherein demonstration is made both by pro-
testants, and other testimonies, that during
all this age and hundred of yeares vntill and
after the coming of S. Augustine, this king-
dome had many holy massinge preists and
Bishops, agreeinge in these, and all other
articles of Religiō with the church of Rome.

IN the later end of the fift hundred of yeares, of Christ, I made relation, how a-
monge many others, those two renowned
massinge preists, S. Dubritius the great
Archbishop of Caerlegion, and the Popes
Legate, made Bishop by the massing Bishop
and Legate of the see Apostolicke, and S.
Iltutus disciple of the same massing Bishop
and Legate S. Germanus were Tutors, and
Masters in Religion and diuinitie, not only
to the cleargie of this Iland but many o-
thers, and neither did, nor could teach them
any other doctrine in these points, then they
had receued from others, and practised by
themselues, about holy preisthood, and sacrifice of Masse; And as both protestants &
other antiquaries tell vs, both these liued
20. yeares at the leaste, in the beginninge

E e 3 of

of this sixt age , S. Iltutus beeing aliue and florishinge in the yeare 520. *claruit anno à Christi natiuitate* 520. and S. Dubritius liuinge two yeares after, *obijt anno gratiæ* 522. (*Bal. l. de scriptor. Britan. cent. 1. in Ilchtuto. & in Dubritio. Godw. Catal. in S. Dauids. in Dubritius.*) therefore wee may boldly say, that among so great numbers of their massing schollers , many of them liued a great part, if not all this age. The auncient Manuscript of the Saints of Wales, the Apologist of the antiquitie of Cambridge , and others thus testifie of S. Dubritius . (*M. S. antiq. de vit. Sanctorum Wall. in S. Dubritio. Io. Caius l. 1. de antiquit. Cantabr. Academ. pag. 145. 146.*) *Creuit illius fama cum vtriusque legis, nouæ & veteris peritia per totā Britanniam, ita quod ex omni parte totius Britanniæ scholares veniebant , non tantum rudes, sed etiam viri sapientes & Doctores ad eum studendi causa confluebant . Imprimis Sanctus Helianus, Sampson discipulus suus, Vbelnius, Merchiguinus, Elguoredus, Gunuinus, Longual, Artbodu, Longur, Arguistil, Iunabin, Conbram, Goruan, Guernabin, Iouan, Elheharn, Iudnon, Curdocui, Aidan, Cinuarch, & cum his mille clericos per septem annos conti-*

nuo in podo seu pago Hentlan super ripam Guy,
in studio literarum diuinæ sapientiæ & huma-
næ retinuit. Where we see he had a thousand
schollers at one time, and place, seuen yeares together that were clergy men students
in diuinitie, and in an other place, called
in the Brittish languadge Mocros, miracu-
loussy assigned vnto him, hee had as these
antiquities say, innumerable schollers many
yeares together, *cum suis innumerabilibus dis-*
cipulis mansit per plures annos regendo stu-
dium.l.de vit.Sanct.Wall. Caius sup. pag. 147.
148. *M.S. antiq. & Capgrau. in S.Iltuto &*
Tatheo.

2. The like they write of the scholes of
S. Iltutus, and S, Tatheus, or as some call
him Thatheus. The antiquaries of Cambridge alleage for the immunities and priuiledges of their vniuersitie, the auncient
Charter dated at London in the yeare of
Christ 531 of Kinge Arthur, that knowne
reuerencer of sacrificing preists, and Masse.
Charta priuileg. Arthuri an. 531. *apud Caium*
antiq. Cantabrig.l. 1.) and both Catholicks
and protestants testifie, that the auncient
vniuersitie of Standford continued in this
time, *and vntill S.Gregory interdicted it for*
heresies

(*Harding histor. in King Ethelbert. Stowe and Howes historie in Bladud.*) therefore wee may assure our selues, that notwithstandinge so many troubles, & alterations, as chaunced here in those daies, they continued the holy doctrine and custome of Masse, and sacrificinge preists; For S. Gregory so knowne and confessed a Patron and practiser of these thinges, neither would, nor could haue interdicted that vniuersitie, for any thinge which hee himselfe so embraced and honored. So that it is euident, that the whole kingdome of Britanie in this time followinge the doctrine which their scholes and vniuersities taught them, must needs then allowe these holy misteries of which I write. The same is euident, both by the Kings which then reigned here, as also by the Archbishops who ruled in Religious affaires. The Kings in the beginning of this age were Vther pendragon, who died about the yeare of Christ 515. beeinge for Religion of the same with the massinge Archbishops S. Dubritius and S. Sampson, with the sacrificinge Bishops, and preists, by whose generall consent he was crowned Kinge.

Kinge. *Vther conuocato regni clero, cœpit diadema Insula: annuëtibusque cunctis sublimatus est in Regem.* (*Galfr. Mon. l.8 cap.17. Math. Westm. ad an. 498*) and when his death was knowne they as solemly assembled to giue him Princely Christian buriall. *Cum obitus Regis diuulgatus fuisset aduenerunt Pontifices cum clero regni: tuleruntque corpus eius ad cœnobium Ambrij, & iuxta Aurelium Ambrosium more regio humauerunt.*

2. Next was Kinge Arthur, how he was engaged in this holy doctrines it is sufficiét Argument, that being but 15. yeares of age, and his birth by many not without exception, hee was with the generall applacse both of the sacrificinge cleargie, and their ghostly children, crowned Kinge by S. Dubritius the Popes Legate, and renowned massinge Archbishop, and primate of Britanie with the other massing Bishops therof. *Defuncto Vtherpendragon conuenerunt ex diuersis Prouincijs proceres Britonum, Dubritio Vrbis Legionum suggerentes, vt Arthurum filium Regis in Regem consecraret. Dubritius associatis sibi Episcopis Arthurum regni diademate insignuit.* (*Galfrid. Mon l. 9. cap. 1. Matth. Westm. ad an. gratiæ 516. Stowe histor.*

histor. Britans and Saxons in Arthur. Io. Bal.
l. de script. Brit. cent. 1. in Dubritio. Godwin
Catalog. in S. Dauids.) to this his whole life
in fighting against the enemies of that holy
Religion, the sacred churches, and altars
which he reedified for that heauenly sacrifice, and charters of immunities which he
graunted to the most knowne massing places of Britanie, as Glastenbury and others,
and the great reuerence he vsed to all mafsinge preists and Prelates, are sufficient testimony of this, and to bee seene allmost in
all histories, Manuscripts and others of that
time, and hee liued vnto the yeare of Christ
542. Now if wee come to the Archbishops
& Bishops vnder them, Matthew of Westminster and others tell vs, that for Yorke,
that renowned massinge man S. Sampson
was Archbishop there, 7. *yeares after the beginning of this age, anno gratiæ* 507. *Florue-
runt in Britānia Sanctus Sampson Eboracensis
Archiepiscopus, & S. Dubritius Vrbis Regio-
num Archiepiscopus.* (*Matth. Westm. an.* 542.
& alij. Matth. Westm. an. gratiæ 507.) what
a miraculous massing preist, and Prelate he
was, I haue spoken in the former age.

   3. That S. Dubritius ruled all in the Ar-
chiepis-

chiepiſcopal ſee of Caerlegion, where moſt
both Biſhops & preiſts were in theſe daies,
at the leaſt vntill the 16. yeare of this age I
haue ſhewed before, whē S.Dubritius with
the reſt of the Biſhops of Britanie crowned
King Arthur in that yeare. Who was Archbiſhop of London at this time, it is not ſo
certainly remembred in particular. But the
Author of the Brittiſh hiſtory tranſlated by
Galfridus aſſureth vs, that there was an
Archbiſhop of London at this time, & that
hee together with S. Dubritius Archbiſhop
of Caerlegion, & the Archbiſhop of Yorke
did crowne Kinge Arthur. *Trium Metro-*
politanarum ſedium Archi Præſules, Londo-
nienſis videlicet, Eboracenſis, nec non ex vrbe
Legionum Dubritius hic Britanniæ primas, &
Apoſtolicæ ſedis Legatus. (*Galfr. Mon.hiſtor.*
Reg. Brit. l. 9.cap. 12. 13.) and by the cir-
cumſtances of the hiſtory, theſe three Archbiſhops performed that great ſolemne coronation at the ſolēnitie of Maſſe, at which
both the Kinge, theſe three Archbiſhops
with the other Biſhops of theire diuiſions,
and the nobilitie of Britanie were preſent.
And this coronation is cheifely attributed
to S. Dubritius, becauſe it was in his dioceſſe.

ceſſe . *Dubritius quoniam in ſua dioceſi caria tenebatur, paratus ad celebrandum obſequium, huius rei curam ſuſcepit,* and he was the Popes Legate . And all hiſtories agree, that when the Biſhops, and cleargie, either of London, or Yorke diuiſion, were perſecuted by the Pagans, they fledd for ſuccour, to the knowne maſſinge preiſtes, and Prelates of Caerlegion dioceſſe, communicatinge with them in Religion.

4. S. Dubritius waxinge old, and deſirous to liue a ſolitary and contemplatiue life, the holy Saint Dauid was miraculouſlie choſen to ſucceed him. (*Capgrau. in S. Danid. Gyrald. Cambr. Itiner. Cambr. l. 2. cap. 1. Godwin in S. Dauids.*) I haue ſhewed before, that he was the ſcholler of the maſſing preiſt, S. Iltutus, ſcholler of the maſſinge Prelate & Popes Legate S. Germanus. This holy Archbiſhop was ſo renowned a maſſinge preiſt, and Prelate, that as wee reade both in auncient Manuſcripts, and other hiſtories, hee brought with from Hieruſalem, beeinge a pilgrime there, an holy and miracalous Altar, *giuen him by the Patriake there, on which he conſecrated the body of our Lord . In quo Dominicum conſecrabat corpus .*
(*M.*

(*M. S. antiq. de vit. S. Dauidis. Capgrau. in Catalog. in eod.*) and to make euident vnto all, that S. Dauid did say ordinarily Masse in Britanie, aswell as at Hierusalem, and likewise so did all the Bishops here of Britanie then, and with great solemnitie, to omitt many other memorable testimonies hereof, we reade in the antiquities of Glastenbury, Capgrauius, and others, & a Proteſtant Bishop writeth, that the history is still preserued engraued in Brasse at Wells in Sommersetshire, though hee somewhat minceth it, how S. Dauid and seuen other Bishops goinge to Glastenbury to dedicate the holy church there, Christ appeared vnto him the night before the intended dedication, and bid him absteine from dedicatinge it, for it had beene dedicated before to the blessed Virgin Mary his Mother. (*M. S. antiq. & Io. Capgrau. Catalog. in S. Patricio. antiq. Glaston. Godwin conuerſ. of Brit. pag. 11.*) and to testifie the truth of this vision, & testimony, left a miraculous wound in the right hand of S. Dauid, tellinge him how it should bee as miraculously healed as it was hurt, in this maner: *craſtina die cum Pontificalibus inductus, cum per ipsum, & cum ipso,*

ipso, & in ipso, in Missa pronuntias, ipso qui tecum loquitur operante, per ipsum quem sacro conficies ore, vulnus quod nunc abhorres, nusquam esse videbis. Et cum sanctus iussa complesset, sicut praedixit Dominus, efficitur sanus. To morrow when thou art adorned with thy pontificall vestiments, and shalt pronounce in Masse the words by him, & with him, and in him, he that speaketh with thee workinge by him whome thou shalt make with thy sacred mouth, thou shalt see noe where the wound, which thou now abhorrest. And when the Saint had done as hee was commaunded, as our Lord foretold, he was made sound. And it followeth in the same antiquitie, preserued in Brasse by Thomas Highes of Wells esquier, as that protestant Bishop writeth heretofore, *fixed vppon a piller of S. Iosephs chappell, which hee himselfe had read. Godwin supr. cap. 2. pag. 11.*

5. *Postea idem Episcopus Domino reuelante quendam cancellum in orientali parte huic Ecclesiae adiecit, & in honore beatae Virginis consecrauit, cuius altare inestimabili sapphiro in perpetuam huius rei memoriam insigniuit.* Afterward the same Bishop (S. Dauid) by the reuelation of our Lord, did add a certaine chaun-

chauncell to this church, in the east parte, and consecrated it in the honor of the blessed Virgin, whose Altar for perpetuall memory of this thinge hee did adorne, with a sapphire of an inestimable price. Where we euidently see, the doctrine & practise, both of the Archbishop, and Bishops of Britanie, seuen of them beeing then present, to goe on pilgrimage, to holy places, and relicks, that they were sacrificing preists, said Masse, and with great reuerence, and solemnitie, and in that holy sacrifice consecrated by consecratinge wordes of their mouthes, and offered the blessed body and blood of Christ, vsed the same canon wee now doe, as the wordes, *per ipsum, & cum ipso, & in ipso*, with the other circumstances tell vs, and so honored the holy Altars, whereon this heauély sacrifice was offered, that they there offered inestimable guifts, and ornaments to honor them withall, which is as much as any preist of the present Roman church teacheth, or contédeth at this time, or Catholicke Religion alloweth them to doe.

6. This renowned Archbishop so miraculous for his birth prophetically foretold,

his

his life, and death and so holy and pleasing
vnto God, that as I haue shewed in him al-
readie, God spared to take vengeance on
the sinnes of the Britans, for his sake, during his life, died in the yeare of Christ 546.
but 50. yeares before S.Augustines coming
hither, as our protestants themselues with
others witnesse. (*Bal. l. de scriptor. Britan.
cent .I .in David Meneuiensi.*)and by an other
protestant which saith,*he sate longe to witte,
65. yeares.* (*Godwin Catal. in S. Dauids I.S.
Dauid.*) hee liued within 16. yeares or nearer to S. Augustins arriuall in this kingedome, an 596. for as I proued before, his
predecessor S. Dubritius was Archbishop
there,in the yeare 516. and after, and died
not vntill the yeare 522. though in his old
age he had a little before resigned his charge to S. Dauid. (*Godwin sup.in S. Dauids.in
S. Dubritius. Bal. cent. I. in eod. Galfr. Mon.
l. 11. hist. Britan.cap. 3.*) there is some question in histories whether,as Giraldus Cambrensis and some others say, Cenauc was
immediate successor to S. Dauid, or S.The-
liaus, Telianus, Eliud, all one man, by o-
thers. (*Girald Cambr. Itiner. Cambr. l. 2. c.
2. Godw. M. S. Dauids antiquitat. Ecclef. S.
Daui-*

Dauidis apud Godwin *Catal. Epis. pag.* 506. *in*
S. Dauids.) but for this matter it mattereth
nothing: for this Cenauc was scholler, and
successor to S. Patern, that great knowne
massinge preist and Prelate, companion to
S. Dauid, in his holy pilgrimage: And so
could not differ from these holy Saints, in
so great questions in Religion. And for the
other S. Telian or Eliud, there is no doubt,
for hee was scholler to the renowned massinge Prelate S. Dubritius, and by him so
throughly instructed in diuinity, that being
indued with the holy Ghost, hee could perfectly expound all difficulties of holy scriptures. *A sancto Dubritio Episcopo in scripturis*
sanctis eruditus fuit, donec explicaret. (*M. S.*
de vita S. Theliai & Capgr. Catalog. in eod.)
and was so vndiuided a companion of S.
Dauid, his predecessor, not onely vnder
their Master Paulinus (not vnprobably hee
that liued to bee Archbishop of Yorke that
great massing Prelate in S. Augustines time)
but in his pilgrimage to Hierusalem, and so
by Rome from which hee could not differ
in Religion: and so intrely and nearely con-
ioyned in Religion, and affection, that as
wee reade in his life, they were both of one
minde,

minde, perfectly in all things; *Sanctum Dauid perfectæ hominem vitæ sui associauit: quos tanta coniunxit dilectio & sancti spiritus gratia , quod idem velle , & nolle ambobus esset.* Therefore hee could not possibly , nor the Bishops and preists vnder him, differ from S. Dauid , in so great matters , but were wholly of the same mind, and practise with him in those thinges . And the church of Rome in all Catalogues receueth and acknowledgeth him for an holy Saint, which it neuer did, will, or can doe, to any an enemie and apposite vnto it, in those misteries. And this sacrificinge massinge Prelate, probably was Archbishop of Caerlegion amonge the Britans , at the cominge of S. Augustine hither , liuinge longe after that time, and as a late writer holdeth . (*Engl. Martyrolog. die* 25. *Nouembr.*) vntill the yeare of Christ 626. liuinge before diuers yeares amonge the massing preists and Bishops of Fraunce, and not vnprobably was there when S. Augustine first landed here, and neither present at , or consenting vnto that opposition, to S. Augustine.

7. And concerninge the two other Archiepiscopall sees, London, and Yorke, although

though

though there is little memory left of Ecclesiasticall affaires in them, beeing both with
their whole diocesses in those times moste
greeuously afflicted, and almoste wholly
eaten and deuoured vpp, by the Pagan persecutors in Religious things; yet for these
doctrines wee haue in hand, there is sufficient testimonie left in antiquities, that so
longe as the state of Christian Religion had
publick and open profession, there was also
there the like publicke vse, and exercise, of
these points of Catholicke Religion; And
after the external face of Christianitie was
ouerthrowne, yet at the leaste in many places, of those Prouinces, a priuate vse and
exercise was still cotinued of these articles,
euen to the coming of S. Augustine and after, vntill the general conuersion of the Saxons themselues. And for Yorke wee haue
the knowne massing Prelate Pyramus cha-
peline to Kinge Arthur, that great Patron
of sacrificinge preists & holy Masse, which
as his place required, was deputed to say
Masse, and ordinarily so did before that Religious Kinge. (*Galfrid. Monum. l. 9. histor.
Reg. Briton. cap.* 8. *Matth. Westm. an gratiæ*
5.22.) and as Thadiocus succeeded him in
F f 2   place

place and dignitie so likewise hee was his
successor in opinion , and practise in these
questions, as will euidently appeare, if wee
onely confider that they were both ordeyned by the authoritie & Legantine power,
either of S. Dubritius or S. Dauid those famous massinge preists, Prelats, primats and
Saints. But wee haue the generall warrants
of the renowned S. Gyldas Badonicus ,
which now liued and vntill within 16.yea-
res of S. Augustins cominge hither , florishinge in the yeare of Christ 580. as a protestant Bishop and antiquary with others
writeth. (*Bal. l. de scriptor. Britan. cent. 1.in
Gilda Badonico.*) & proueth that in this time
all the preists of Britanie were, *sacrificantes
sacrificinge massinge preists , inter altaria, as
the holy altars,the seates of the celestiall sacrifice, sedes cælestis sacrificij* , and Probus that
wrote the life of S. Patricke, in this age testifyinge as much. *Gildas l. de excid. & conquest. Britan. Probus in vita S. Patricij inter
opera S. Bedæ.*

8. And if we turne our eyes to looke into
the further, and more northren parts of the
diocesse of this Archiepiscopall see in Gol-
loway, and Albania, wee shall finde many
par-

particular testimonies of this veritie. There wee shall finde S. Kentegern, that most miraculous holy Saint, so far a massing preist, and Prelate, and after the Roman order, that hee had in his schole or monastery vnder him in the north of Britany, besides 600. that were not learned, 360. learned diuines, trayned vp to preach, and offer the holy sacrifice of Masse. (*M. S. antiq. de vit. S. Kentegerni. Io. Capgrau. Catal. in eod. Io. Bal. l. script. Britan. cent. 1. in Kentern. Godwin Catal. in Asaph. Hector Boeth. Scotor. histor. l. 9.*) and he had an other as great a schoole and companie of massinge men in Britany, which he left to S. Asaph, and sent of these into all parts both of this our Britanie, and into other nations, as Norwey, and Island, beeing warranted in all these things by the Popes of Rome, where hee was seuen times on pilgrimage, *Romam septies adijt*; and in all things conformed himselfe to that holy Apostolicke church, and at his death, *gaue strict commaund to all vnder his charge, to be in all thinges obedient to the church of Rome: de Sanctorum Patrum decretis, sanctæque Romanæ Ecclesiæ institutis firmiter custodiendis, fortia dedit, ac dereliquit præcepta.* And that

hee

hee liued either after, or vnto the cominge
of S. Auguſtine I will demonſtrate herafter.

9. And to come to London dioceſſe, now
afflicted with Pagan perſecutors, yet wee
find Theonus a maſſinge preiſt and Prelate
familiarly acquainted with S. Dauid, that
maſſing Archbiſhop, hauing beene Biſhop
of Gloceſter before, to haue beene Archbiſhop there in theſe times. A Proteſtant Biſhop writeth: *Theonus being firſt Biſhop of*
Gloceſter, forſooke it, and tooke the charge of
London vpon him the yeare 553. (*Godwin Ca-*
talog. in London. in Theonus.) but the Brittiſh hiſtorye, proueth him to haue beene
Archbiſhop of London, before the death
of S. Dauid: *Theonus Glouceſtrenſis Epiſco-*
pus, in Archiepiſcopatum Londoniarum eligi-
tur. Tũc obijt ſanctiſsimus Vrbis Legionum Ar-
chiepiſcopus Dauid in Mineuia ciuitate. (*Gal-*
frid. Monum. hiſtor. Reg. Brit. lib. 11. cap. 3.)
and ſo hee muſt needs hee ordeyned Archbiſhop, by the conſent, and allowance of
that maſſinge high Prelate, S. Dauid. And
hee continued Archbiſhop there, vntill the
yeare of Chriſt 586 when together with
Thadiocus, Archbiſhop of Yorke, and very
many of their cleargy they fled into Walles
and

and other places . (*Matth. Westm. an.* 586.
Stowe histor. Galfrid. Monum. hist. l. 11. *cap.*
10.) And to proue all then were sacrificinge
massinge preists here, S. Gildas then liuing
at that time hath so before affirmed; the sacrificinge massinge which protestants and
others confesse, to haue beene then in London, and other places of that diocesse, confirme it; their flying for succour only to the
places, where Masse and massinge preistes
continued, as in Wales, Cornewayle, and
little Britanie, manifestly conuince it to be
so. *Stowe histor. in Constantine* 2. *Galfr. Mo-*
num. l. 11. *histor. cap.* 4.

10. This is proued by those holy churches, and massinge altars, whigh the Pagans did reserue, and not destroye, by con-
uerting to them to the Idolatrous worship,
and sacrifices of theire Pagan Gods . *Si*
qua Ecclesia illæsa seruabitur, hoc magis ad
confusionem nominis Christiani quàm gloriam
faciebant . Nempe ex eis deorum suorum tem-
pla facientes , prophanis suis sacrificijs, sancta
Dei altaria polluerunt. (*Matth.* Westm. *ad an.*
gratiæ 586.) And when aboue al other thinges questioned , our protestants moste disallowe the reuerence of holy relicks , and

not

not contendinge that there was any Christian Religion in these Archbishops & their cleargie, but either the massinge Religion, or their protestant profession, doe plainely confesse, that these were massinge preistes, and not Protestant Ministers, for they with other ātiquities acknowledg, that the greatest care which these two Archbishops, their Bishops, and preists had, in those tempestuous times, was how to keepe with reuerence, and from irreuerence, the holy relicks of their Saints, & so notwithstanding so many daungers, and difficulties, carryed most of them vnto these places of their rest, and refuge, so farr off, Walles, Cornwaile, and Britanie in Fraunce. (*Holinsh. histor. of Engl. Galfrid. Monument. histor. Reg. Brittan. l. 11. cap. 10. Matth. Westm. an. gratiæ 586.*) *Tunc Archipræsulis Theonus Londoniensis & Thadiocus Eborascensis, cum omnes Ecclesias sibi subditas solo tenus destructas vidissent, cum pluribus ordinatis, cum reliquijs Sanctorum in Cambriam diffugerunt, timentes ne Barbarorum irruptione, tot & tantorum sacra ossa veterum, à memorijs hominum delerentur, si qua imminenti periculo minimè subtraxissent. Plures etiam Armoricanam Britanniam*

niam petentes. Therefore no proteſtant can, will, or by the grounds of their Religion may ſay, that theſe were Proteſtants, but vndoubtedly Catholicke Papiſts, reuerencers of holy Maſſe, relicks of Saints, & ſuch doctrines, as proteſtancy doth not allow, & thereuppon they plainely call them, *ſacriſiculos, maſſinge preiſts. H. Matius Germanorum lib.* 5. *pag.* 39.

11. Neither did theſe doctrines and the profeſſion of them ceaſe here with vs, betweene this publick deſolation in the 586. of Chriſt, and the yeare 596. when S. Auguſtine came hither, euen in thoſe parts which the Saxons poſeſſed, but there were diuers Biſhops, and ſacrificinge maſſinge preiſts ſtill continuinge in them, and the holy ſacrifice of Maſſe was ſtill, though not ſo generally and publickly as before, continued alſo in this time, and many of the Saxons themſelues, euen from the dayes of Kinge Arthur, when many of them receaued the Chriſtian faith, ſtill continued therein, and this teſtified by proteſtant writers. (*Holinſhed hiſtor. of Engl. pag.* 122. 123. *l.* 5.) teachinge how vppon a great victory of that renowned Kinge againſt them, hee pardoned

ned al that would and did receue the Christian faith, which were many. And Hardinge with others testifieth, that Stanford at this time was a Christian vniuersitie, though with some errors. (*Harding histor.*) and yet a great part of them must needs bee Saxons. And in those very places themselues where the Pagan Saxons moste & principally ruled, and reigned, the Christian massing sacrificing Religion was there permitted, and tolerated euen by the Kings allowance, as a protestant historian proueth in these words. (*Holinsh. histor. of Engl. l. 5. pag. 107.*) *At the same time that Constantine* (the next Kinge to Arthur) *was driuen into Wales, there reigned amonge the English men, one Iourmericke the fifth, as Bede saith, from Hengist. The same Iourmerick though hee were not christened himselfe, yet hee permitted the Christian faith to bee preached amongst his people, and concludinge a league with the Scottish men and Picts, kept the same inuiolate duringe his life time.* So likewise it was in the kingdome of the Kentish Kings, extendinge to Humber, for Kinge Ethelbert had marryed a Christian, & gaue peace to Christians in his dominions, as wee

may

may also gather the like of the kingdome
of the east Angles, whose Kinge Scebert,
was a baptised Christian, except a protestant historian is deceued, in the yeare of
Christ 569. or before, then beginninge his
Reigne, and beeing christened in Fraunce
in the Regiment of his Brother and predecessor Kinge Carpewalde. (*Stowe histor. in
east Angles in K. Scebert anno. 569.*) and in
many other places of Loegria, this Englad,
the like instances may be giuen: for the eni-
mitie between the Saxons and Britans was
not principally for Religio, but who should
rule here, and possesse this kingdome: *asper-
nebantur vt plurimum Saxones Britonum Sacerdotum tum Gualiam incoletium doctrinam:
tametsi veram profiterentur, inuisæ gentis magis quam disciplinæ, de qua multa atque præ-
clara frequentius audiuerant, odio permoti.*
(*Hect. Boeth. l. 9. Scot. histor. fol. 177.*) and
they had peaceable commerce, amitie, and
correspondence with all other Christians,
round about them, French, Scots, and Picts,
as is declared before.

12. And to putt all out of doubt in this
matter, wee are taught by many credible,
and vncontroleable antiquities, that euen

at

at the coming of S. Auguftine hither, there
were diuers renowned maſſing, facrificing
Biſhops, here with their maſſinge preiſts,
that preached euen to the Saxons, and conuerted many, and that theſe holy Biſhops,
and preiſts did in all things agree, with the
Apoſtolicke Romane church, and receued
miſſion, power, and iuriſdiction from thence. Amonge theſe was S. Kentegern for the
Northren and other parts of this kingdome,
who preached to the Saxons & proued their
Pagan Gods (namly woden) whom principally they worſhipped as cheife God, to
haue beene onely a man, a Kinge amonge
them, and a damned creature. (*S. Aſaph.in
vita S. Kentegerni. M.S. antiquit. in vita
eius & Capgrau. in eodem.*) *Quem principa-
lem Deum crediderunt, & præcipue Angli, de
quo originem duxerant, cui & quartam feriam
conſecrauerant, hominem fuiſſe mortalem aſſeruit, & Regem Saxonum, à quo plures na-
tiones genus duxerant, huius inquit corpore
in puluerem reſoluto, anima in inferno ſepulta
æternum ſuſtinet ignem.* And that this holy
Biſhop liued vnto this time of S. Gregory,
ioyned in Religion with him, and by him
was warranted to preach to the Saxons, as
to

to other nations, we haue the greateſt warrant, wee can deſire in ſuch thinges, both
Catholicke and Proteſtant antiquaries, ioy-
ninge in this, that hee was a Biſhop 260.
yeares. (*M. S. antiq. & Capgrau. ſupr. Bal. l.
de ſcript. Britan. cent. 1. in Kenterno. Godwin
Catalog. of Biſhops in Aſaph.*) whereby it e-
uidently followeth, that beinge made Biſhop after the beeing of S. German, and Lupus here, as appeareth before, he muſt needes bee liuinge at this time, and it is particularly teſtified by the auncient writers of
his life, S. Aſaph his holy ſcholler and ſucceſſor, Iohn Capgraue, and many auncient
Manuſcripts, that hauinge beene ſeuen times at Rome, hee was there in the time of
S. Gregory, who approuinge his ſacred callinge ſent him with his Apoſtolicke warrant into theſe parts. *Vir Dei ſepties Romam
adiens Sancto Gregorio ſpeciali Anglorum A-
poſtolo totam vitam ſuam, electionem, & con-
ſecrationem, & omnes caſus qui ei acciderunt,
ſeriatim enodauit. Sanctus vero Papa illum
virum Dei & Spiritus Sancti gratia plenum
intelligens, in opus miniſterij à Spiritu Sancto
illi iniuncti deſtinauit.*

13. In the weſterne parts wee had then
besides

besides the Bishops which opposed themselues to S. Augustine, commonly recompted seuen in number, yet agreeing with him
in these misteries, the renowned holy Bishop S. Asaph, disciple, and successor to S.
Kentegern, in that see, when hee forsooke
it; This holy massinge Bishop ruler of the
colledge of so many massinge preists, as I
haue before related, did in all things ioyne
himselfe with the disciples of S. Gregory the
Pope, in so much as a Protestãt Bishop writeth of him: *A Gregorij Pontificis Romani dis-*
cipulis Angliam aduentantibus, authoritatem
accepit, (o. Bal. l. de script. Britan. cent. 1. in
Asapho.) he receued authority from the disciples of Gregorie Pope of Rome, which
came into England. And this is hee, who
as the same Protestãt Bishop writeth, wrote
the life of S. Kentegern his Master. Therfore this holy Prelate must needs bee a massinge preist, as all the other vnder him were
at that time. If we go further to other parts
of this nation, wee shall finde in the kingdome of the Mercians, or by some the easte
Angles, the renowned & miraculous Archbishop S. Iue, a noble Persian by birth, who
beeing sent thither by the Pope of Rome S.
Gre-

Gregory or Pelagius the seconde his predecessor both massinge preists and Popes, was
also a massing preist and Prelate, and dying
at the towne, now of his name called S.
Iues, in Hontington shire, gaue that name
vnto it. (*Annal. Monaster. Ramseiæ. M. S.
antiq. de vita S. Iuonis. Io. Capgrau. in Catalog. in S. Iuone Episcop. Florent. Wigorn.
in Chronic. ad an. 600.*) And to testifie that
hee exercised both his massing preistly, and
episcopall function there in preachinge to
the Saxons, his body was found, *buried in
episcopall manner, sepulchro aperto Episcopum
Pontificalibus indutum cõspiciunt.* This Apostolicke doctor of this nation as Florentius
Wigorniensis, Capgraue, and the old Manuscripts of his life call him, *Doctor Aposto-
licus & vere cæli nuntius Iuo, dyed* here as
Wigorniensis writeth in the yeare 600. foure
yeares after the cominge of S. Augustine hither: and hither also came with him, and
preached here, sent from Rome, besides o-
thers not named, S. Sithius, and S. Inthius
his associats, massinge preists. *Qui cum Romam peruenissēt consilio Papæ dispositione Dei,
Sanctus Iuo cum Sithio nepote, & Inthio cog-
nato suo alijsque quibusdam, in Britanniam in-
trauit.*

And to shew that hee was a true Apostle of this nation, sent by the see Apostolicke of Rome, coming through Fraunce hither, beeinge honorably entertayned by the Kinge and people of Fraunce, to stay there, would by no entreaty consent, but came as hee was, *à Domino destinatus*, ordeyned for vs by God, into England. *Cum Galliam cum suis intrasset, à Rege & populo honorificè susceptus, nec vlla gratia terrena quamuis assiduis precibus rogatus, ab ipsis retineri poterat, sed Britanniam ingrediens.*

14. And to passe into the kingedome of Kent it selfe, where S. Augustine landed, & settled himselfe, his successors, and see at Canterbury, there, we had at his cominge, and twenty yeares before, and before the time, that Theonus Archbishop of London, and Thadiocus Archbishop of Yorke with their massinge preists, forsooke their sees, in that kingedome and city itselfe of Canterburie, a renowned massing Bishop, S. Luithardus, and his massing preists, vsuallie sayinge Masse, the Queene S. Bertha being present in their thē cathedral church, dedicated to S. Martine, as all antiquaries agree, and as I finde in an old Manuscript history,

history , builded in the time of Kinge Lucius . (*Bed. hist. gent. Angl. l. 1. cap. 27. Io.*
Capgrau. in Catalog. in S. Lethardo Episcopo
& Confessore. M. S. antiq. in eod.) And by
the persuasion of this holy massinge Bishop
S. Luithard, the Kinge and Saint afterward
Ethelbert, entertayned S. Augustine with
all humanitie, and was by him after actual-
lie conuerted to the faith of Christ , in so
much that this holy Bishop is called , *Iani-*
tor venturi Augustini, opener of the dore to
S. *Augustine.* (*Capgrau. supr. in S. Lethard.*
Gulielm. Malm. l. 1. de gest. Reg. Anglorum)
And was before S. Augustines cominge
when he still liued a Pagan, fauourable and
gentle vnto Christias: *Benignus erga Chri-*
stianos in natiua gentilitate fuit. By occasion
whereof, his kingdome extending to Humber , and his sister beeing marryed to Slede
Kinge of the east Angles, and her sonne Se-
bert, or as Henry of Huntington calleth him
Sibrictus, or Siberctus, beeing a Christian
Kinge , so great parts of this nation were
free from persecution , and some of the Saxons , that were conuerted , became massing preists, longe before S. Augustine came
hither. (*Henric. Hunting. histor. l. 2.*) For such

G g   is

is numbred Godelbertus as a Protestant Bishop writeth , *ex quorundam coniecturis ge-*
nere Anglosaxo, aboue an hūdred yeares before this time an. 498. (*Pitseus historic. Rel.*
Tom. 1. *atate* 5. *Bal.* l. *de script. Britan· cent·*
1.*in Godelberto Presbytero.*) And as Sebastiā
Munster & the first Protestant Archbishop
of Canterbury witnes , S. Offo an English
Kings sonne in this our Englād, went hence and preached in Germany in the yeare
601 . (*Munster. in Cosmograph . in German.*
Matth. Parker antiq. Brit. pag. 8.) not without other associats of this nation, except we
will make , his case singular from all other
Apostolick men, & conuerters of contries.
And except wee will make a very bold ex-
positiō of the English Author of the booke,
de Virginitate, or *laude Virginum, of the praise*
of Virgins , commonly ascribed to our holy
learned Bishop, S. Aldelmus , callinge, *S.*
Gregory the Pope his Master, and Tutor, Pre-
ceptor & Pedagogus noster Gregorius . (*l. de*
laude Virginum. Bal. cent. 1. *in Adel. Pitseu*
To. 1. *in eod.*) wee must needs as the rule of
correlatiues, Master and scholler requireth,
make him scholler to S. Gregorie the great,
which liued but few yeares after S. Augustines

tines cominge hither, and being Pope then,
likely he was Tutor & Master to this aūciēt
English writer, before the time of his papa-
cie, as he was to many others, and not after.

15. So I might instance of others, but
these aboundantly suffice, to proue, that after the first plantinge of the faith of Christ
in this our Britanie, there neuer wanted in
it, either in the time of the Britans, Saxons
or whom els soeuer, Masse, massing preists,
and Bishops. For euen those Brittish preists
and Bishops, which moste opposed against
S. Augustine in some other things, were as
farr engaged in these articles, to bee sound
and Orthodoxe as S. Augustine was, and so
both practised here in Britanie, as I haue related before, & their most learned S. Kelian,
Columban, and Gallus, with others going
hence into other nations did wholly submit
themselues to the Popes of Rome; and their
cheifest S. Keliā was made Bishop of Mitz-
burgh by the Pope, receuinge power from
him to preach. *Romam profectus est, & offi-*
cio prædicandi à Papa receptus Episcopus, ordi-
tus. (*Manuscript antiq. de vita S. Keliani. Io.*
Capgrau. Catalog. in eodem. Sur. die 8. Iulij.)
And that S. Columbanus the man whose

autho-

authority was most obiected against S. Augustine, about the diuers keeping of Easter,
was a notorious massinge preist, as also S.
Gallus in as high degree, as any Catholicke
now is, it is testified in their liues, where
we find, S. Columban did dedicat a church,
and altar, with the relicks of S. Aurelia, &
adorninge the altar said Masse vpon it. *Bea-*
tus Columbanus iussit aquam afferri, & bene-
dicens illam, adspersit ea templum: & dum cir-
cuirent psallentes, dedicauit Ecclesiam, deinde
inuocato nomine Domini, vnxit altare, & bea-
tæ Aureliæ reliquias in eo collocauit, vestito-
que altari, missas legittimè compleuerunt And
in the same Authors wee reade, that S. Gallus did ordinarily vse, *Missam celebrare*, to
say Masse, and beeing vrged both by the
Prince, Bishops, and Cleargie, to accept of
the Bishoprick of Constance, hee refused it
and preferred Iohn his deacon, whome S.
Gallus had conuerted vnto the faith of
Christ. Who in his consecration was ledd
by the Bishops to the Altar, and solemnely
consecrated, and said Masse: in which after
the ghospell, as the maner was, S. Gallus
preached. *Episcopi duxerunt eum ad altare, &*
solemni benedictionis officio ordinauerunt An-
tistitem,

tistitem, consumatoque sacræ promotionis mi-
nisterio, rogauerunt eum sacrificij salutaris ce-
lebrare mysteria. Præmissis ergo ex more di-
uinæ oblationis initijs, post lectionem Euange-
lij rogauerunt venerabilem Gallum, vt multi-
tudini quæ aderat, verbi officio sacræ instruc-
tionis pabulum ministraret. Where wee fee as
much deuotion, and reuerence, vfed by the
greatefts oppofites to S. Auguftine, to the
holy facrifice of Maffe, facrificinge preifthood, holy water, holy oyle, to confecrate
altares, dedication of churches, and fuch
like matters mofte diffiked by proteftants,
as S. Auguftine vfed, or any learned Catholicke now profeffeth or defendeth.

16. And to remember *Maffes of requiem*
for the deade, fo foone as S. Gallus heard of
the death of Saint Columban, this S. Gallus fo renowned a man, *called his bretheren*
together, and they prayed and faid *Maffes for*
his foule. Audiens mortem S. Columbani col-
legit fratres, caufas meroris aperuit. Deinde
tanti patris memoriam precibus facris, & facri-
ficijs falutaribus frequentarunt. What forme
of Maffe both thefe, and they which then
continued in Britanie, vfed, I haue proued
before, from the Brittish antiquities, as alfo

G g 3   how

how al which here were contrary to S. Auguſtine in ſome ceremonials, I haue demō-
ſtrated by all kinde of teſtimonies, that in
theſe and al other eſſentiall and fundamen-
tall things, and not ceremoniall, or altera-
ble in Religion, they wholly agreed, and
without the leaſte difference, conſented
with S. Auguſtine, & the church of Rome,
and differed in all now controuerſed queſtions, from the preſent proteſtants of this
nation, and all others. And ſo Catholicke
Romane, or (as proteſtants call it) the papiſts church, as it hath euer ſince to theſe
dayes of innouation from then, beene the
onely knowne and viſible church, as theſe
men freely confeſſe, and acknowledge, all
antiquities, writers, and monuments ſo teſtifying; ſo it was in the ſame maner the onlie true, viſible church, in euery age, or hundred yeares from Chriſt, and his Apoſtles
vnto that time, no other in any thing reſē-
bling the preſent proteſtants congregation,
beeinge knowne, or heard of, at home, or a-
brode, by their owne confeſſions, and all
Arguments, in any one of thoſe ages, of the
primatiue church of Chriſt, And ſo I end
this hiſtorie.

F I N I S.   A TA-

A TABLE OF THE
CHAPTERS.

THE I. CHAPTER.

WHERIN facrificinge and Maſſinge Preiſthood, Preiſts, and
the ſacrifice of Maſſe, are proued by learned Proteſtants, &
other teſtimonies, from the hiſtory of Melchiſedech. *Gen.* 14. pag. 8.

Gg 4 phes

Chap.

ftian Religion, in this kingdome of Britanie, in this third hundred yeares, yet the holie facrifice of Maffe, facrificinge and maffinge preifts and Bifhops, ftill here continued, without any totall difcontinuance.
pag. 323.

Chap. 18. How the holy facrifice of
Maffe, facrificing and maffing preifthood,
preifts and Bifhops continued in this kingdome of great Britanie in all this age, without any interruption or difcontinuance.
pag. 338.

Chap. 19. Wherin is manifeftly proued,
that all this fift age, the facrifice of Maffe,
maffinge preifts and Bifhops, did continue
in honor in this our Britanie.   pag. 366.

Chap. 20. Wherein is proued by proteftants and others, that the church of Britanie & Rome, accorded in this age in thefe
mifteries: and how all the Popes being maffinge preifts and Popes, yet no one of them
made any materiall alteration in this facrifice.   pag. 388.

Chap. 21. Wherein being confeffed by
our proteftant writers, that all the Popes of
Rome vnto S. Gregory were maffing preiftes, and Popes, yet not any one of them by
thefe

these protestants confession, made any the least materiall chaunge, or alteratiō in these misteries.   pag. 403.

The

The Errata.

Pag. 38. line 1. members, Numbers.
Pag. 197. line 23. Martianus, Martinus.
There are two cyphers X. (Pag. 130. & 174.)
in the chapters, in steed of X. and XI. and so
consequenter, which should haue made the 23.
chapters, to haue bene 24.